For Solo Violin

The Zargani family in 1935.

For Solo Violin

A Jewish Childhood in Fascist Italy

A Memoir by Aldo Zargani

Translated by Marina Harss

PAUL DRY BOOKS
Philadelphia 2002

First Paul Dry Books Edition, 2002

Paul Dry Books, Inc.
Philadelphia, Pennsylvania
www.pauldrybooks.com

Text type: Granjon
Display type: Mona Lisa Solid, Shelley Allegro Script, and Sonata
Composed by P. M. Gordon Associates, Inc.
Designed by Adrianne Onderdonk Dudden

The publishers wish to thank Gilad Gevaryahu for his editorial assistance.

1 3 5 7 9 8 6 4 2
Printed in the United States of America

Library of Congress Cataloging-in-Publication Data

Zargani, Aldo, 1933–
[Per violino solo. English]
For solo violin : a Jewish childhood in fascist Italy : a memoir / by Aldo Zargani ; translated by Marina Harss.
p. cm.
ISBN 0-9679675-3-8 (pbk. : alk. paper)
1. Zargani, Aldo, 1933– —Childhood and youth. 2. Zargani, Aldo, 1933– —Homes and haunts—Italy—Turin. 3. Authors, Italian—20th century—Childhood and youth. 4. Jews—Italy—Turin—Childhood and youth. 5. Fascism—Italy—Turin—History. 6. Holocaust, Jewish (1939–1945)—Italy—Turin. I. Title.

PQ4886.A75 Z4713 2002
858′.91403–dc21
[B]

2001055735

ISBN 0-9679675-3-8

Contents

Preface to the English Edition

Inside of us—almost certainly in our brains, but modern science has not yet deciphered in what manner exactly—several distinct souls take shape over time, coexisting side by side. This is a theory of Plato's which was refuted by Aristotle; the controversy continued to fill the philosophical gossip pages into the Middle Ages until the appearance of *The Divine Comedy,* in which Dante Alighieri defends Aristotle's thesis (Purgatory, IV, 5–6):

> And thus the error is disproved, which holds
> The soul not singly lighted in the breast.

Still, I am with Plato because in the undecipherable confusion of my identity I hear discordant, dissonant voices which do not originate from only one person. I often wonder whether these voices emerge from my multiple souls, or from those of my mother and father or even, at times, whether they are voices in real time or emerge instead from the "virtual" mouths of characters in novels.

In this dissonant polyphony, there is one particular voice that I hear; at times it cries or yells out in pain, but just as often it makes me laugh. It is the silvery voice of a child from sixty years ago who could be me—I'm not sure—crying out his unquestionably justified lament. A lament which is the book that is now in your hands.

As you will discover, that child saw it all, both good and bad. But what this book doesn't tell you is that, in that terrible winter of 1944, in the snowy mountains of Piedmont, at the age of eleven, he encountered America and fell in love. As the result of a series of fortuitous circumstances, he was able to read *The Grapes of Wrath* (ed. Bompiani, 1941). This small and singular literary encounter occurred thanks to the Fascists, who, with their customary strange logic, had allowed the works of John Steinbeck to be published in Italy in order to demonstrate to the Italian populace the sorry state of America. Steinbeck had an altogether different effect on that boy, and instead of disdaining or hating America, he began to dream of it in the night of the Second World War.

Among the many things his immature brain could not fully grasp: "How could people who were so poor travel around the United States . . . in an automobile?" And so it was that *The Grapes of Wrath* became the first science fiction novel he ever read, at a time that—God help us—was more like a horror movie.

Welcome, my American friends, welcome to the enchanted, infernal cavern of the circles of this boy's childhood, improbable but true. Come, come see the monsters of the ego, the id, and the superego. Come, come tremble with these little child-monsters at the specters born of the final agony of the Third Reich . . . You'll see with your own eyes a war of specters, an armistice of ghosts. It's dark inside, but there's room for everyone.

Aldo Zargani

Rome, 2002

For Solo Violin

1 ⁂ The Glockenspiel

Last month I was in Basel, *papà,* and I saw you from a distance. You were standing with *mamma* on the Wettsteinbrücke, the bridge in the center of the city.* I was coming from the Freiestrasse, which is no longer the magical place it once seemed to us, travelers from an isolated Italy, in 1939. It is just a typical commercial street.

As I walked toward the river, I recognized the diagonal stripes of the sentry box in the middle of the bridge, the art

* A friend of mine who lives in Basel tells me that the bridge at the Spillman Restaurant is the Mittlerebrücke, not the Wettsteinbrücke. This is but the first example of the "approximate" geography of my memories: I will indicate them to the reader as they appear. [Asterisked notes are the author's; numbered notes by the translator are at the end of the book.]

deco statues, and the Spillman Restaurant, with its terraces overlooking the Rhine and the granite slabs of its façade. Near the water's edge, they merge with the stone slabs to form the first arch of the bridge. I recognized the university bookshop, all glass, black marble, and chromium plating, modern for all time, and the hills of Germany across the river, shrouded by the funereal fir trees of the Black Forest. And then, between two streetcars, I caught a glimpse of you, from behind. You seemed to be inspecting the prices on the restaurant menu.

When I called out to you, you disappeared, swept away by the breeze, which was heavy with the fragrance of the wet snow and soil of the Alps. But for just one moment, I glimpsed alongside you two small children, comically alike in two identical tweed coats with half-belts over short pants and low socks sucked down into the heels of their shoes.

The Old Town in Basel is a curious place, with its spires and bell towers built out of blood-red stone: it is like a Nuremberg toy, a make-believe world of houses and objects, all interconnected like the restaurant and the bridge. Basel is all of a piece with its cathedral: the houses, the churches, the gargoyles spitting out rainwater, the bronze dogs growling at the colorful statues, the frescoes on the façades of the merchants' houses, the wrought iron everywhere. The city comes alive for the visitor, parades before him, and then, with an almost ironic air, disappears into the past. Things materialize and then vanish, just as you have, almost without a trace.

Those old mechanical toys fall apart if one touches them, but from a safe distance one can watch their movements over and over again, just as we now watch images on a videocassette. Trembling and clicking, the mechanical figures file past the upturned faces of the small crowd which has formed in the square; as the clocks strike in bell towers all across Germany, the King, the Queen, the Soldier, and the Moor form a buzzing parade of tarot figures. The precious, useless glockenspiels are urban ornaments, merely toys, but even so, the parade of automatons always closes with the same figure: Death carrying her scythe for reaping the wheat in the fields. This figure embodies Time, which, like the Rhine, flows inexorably—or perhaps not so inexorably—in one direction. But on this occasion, Death frightens no one; in her robes, she is a threat only to the clock puppets, or at least so it would appear.

In the city, within the close, inlaid maze of its streets, if you ask for Swiss wine at a restaurant, the waiters assure you that they have "local" Rhine and Alsatian wines, and they sketch on their little pads a place just beyond the windowpanes, no further than Lorrach or Colmar, but already in France or Germany.

The river here is wider and stronger than the Po in Turin; it is crisscrossed by motorless ferries that bob across the current, hooked onto steel cables pulled from one shore to the other. The boats go back and forth; *papà,* I remember how you explained the mechanism to me then. The boats, connected thus to the hidden mechanism of the city, are, like the glockenspiels, another charming amusement for the traveler. They reveal to us once again that life is not only an inextricable knot of mysteries, but that it can also be easy, like the tricks performed by grownups for children after joyful holiday meals: two forks balanced on the mouth of a bottle, a coin stuck to the forehead which then drops into a glass, the crystal wineglass that sings when its brim is traced with a finger dipped in wine.

Back in September of 1939, everything was just as it is now, except that the bridges were blocked by barbed-wire barriers, and Swiss soldiers stood behind sandbags, rifles in hand, staring out from the shadows of their helmets at the darkness of the German forests across the river. Once again, they were defending their city-state, so threatening and desirable to the unseen inhabitants of the region beyond the Rhine who lurked behind the trees.

Papà had heard that there was an opening for a viola instructor and had decided to try his luck with the attitude that "if it works, it works, and if it doesn't, too bad." He applied for the position. *Mamma* was enthusiastic about the idea. She loved and respected him; he was not cultured and pessimistic, as she was. In Turin, we packed all of our winter clothes into three suitcases and a hatbox, and, happy fugitives, hopped onto the first train. You wanted to save us, *papà,* before the forces of Evil joined together to bring on the Second World War; you wanted to take us with you into this Toyland and disappear, swallowed up by the trapdoor hidden behind the dolls of the Glockenspiel. To slip through after the hour had struck, when Death and her scythe had disappeared with a pirouette . . .

The plan was too ambitious to succeed.

And, in fact, when I returned with my mother and my brother, Roberto, to the little room of the pension where we were staying, *papà* was lying down on the bed fully dressed, and the yellow comforter had fallen to the floor, as comforters do, according to Jerome K. Jerome's *Three Men on the Bummel* (ed. Corbaccio, 1930).[1]

Despondently, without even glancing in our direction, he explained to us in a subdued voice that seemed to drift from an ongoing conversation that he had been turned down. There was a German on the commission of the Basel Conservatory who had inexplicably asked him to play "The Ride of the Valkyries." On the viola! For many years after that, this Nazi-musician, born of the black forests and bearing the mortal weapon of Wagner—the enemy—inhabited the darkest recesses of our family's imagination. And to *mamma* that small, unhappy event became a major episode of the European Resistance. But *papà,* after the bitter confession at the hotel ("Yes, but, my dearest Eugenia, I did not play well at all . . ."), never returned to the subject, conscious as he was, as a professional, of his own limits.

On that day, when *papà* had finished scowling—and perhaps even crying—and lifted his large, delicate hands from his eyes and arose from the bed, on that day we began to search for other possible means of escape. Or rather, the two of you did, because we were still young, only five and six years old, and followed you blindly and trustingly. Things became more difficult after that.

We discovered that the city park, despite its impeccable appearance—as neat as any private garden—had been turned into a refugee camp for fugitives from the East; they lived under the trees in cabins built out of pine logs. It was there, in those humid and fragrant woods, that I saw Jews for the first time, non-Turinese Jews, as if in a zoo. Large, fleshy, smiling girls cheerfully plopped my cap on my head as I hesitatingly ate the single dish, a sweet concoction made of rice, apples, and cocoa—a strange meal for a boy from Turin, Via Berthollet, 39. I could not understand why I was forced to eat it with my cap on. Eventually I broke into tears, for, mindful of my manners, I kept removing the cap, but each time I did, the girls put it back on my head, laughing.

They had never seen Jews like us either, that's for sure.

After intense discussions in a strange language which sounded like German but wasn't, these brothers in faith from the East explained to us that we didn't qualify for refuge in one of the little fir huts with hearts carved into the shutters and the doors. I think that our meager Jewishness, combined with the fact that, to them, we appeared to be simply Italian, led them to believe that it was not necessary to welcome us into their crowded garden. And, in my memory, they were not especially nice about it.

Our final attempt to stay in that city took the form of a meeting with the head rabbi, who lived in his Austro-Babylonian synagogue. He was an elegant man dressed in black, with a rosy complexion and a white beard in the manner of Freud, who gave my brother and me each a piece of candy. As he spoke, he looked compassionately into all of our eyes, including my brother's and mine. He realized, of course, that even though we were children, we understood the rejection we had experienced and would remember it, as we have in fact remembered it. The rabbi explained to the four of us in his halting but gentle Italian that the people in the refugee camp who had not accepted us were not hostile as they had seemed, but rather that, given the chance, they themselves would have gladly fled to Italy, which, despite its Fascist government, seemed to them a far, far safer place than this toy city wedged into Valhalla.

This was not the belief of my parents, and they were right, but faced with such gentle firmness, and in the absence of money or employment, they were forced to come to the conclusion that there was no hope for us in that place; we took the next express train from Basel back to Hell.

The trapdoor of the Glockenspiel had snapped shut again; the figures had disappeared with a final click, leaving us behind, with seven years of troubles ahead of us. Seven years that come back to me and are multiplied in a tangle of cogwheels from which, when the hour strikes, my mind can sometimes emerge with the figures on the Glockenspiel for a gasp of air.

My dear *mamma* and *papà,* I am retelling here some of the events that whirled together during those days. I glimpsed you on the bridge more than once during this trip; I saw you looking at the river, the hills on the other side, and you seemed to be enjoying that strange, funereal, joyful city. You seemed so trusting: you, *mammina,* with the fox wrapped around your neck, its eyes open wide as it bites its tail, and you, *papà,* with your handsome gutta-percha raincoat, so much nicer than those one finds today. And I saw, as I trailed behind you, in the shiny glass of the university bookstore, the reflection of two young boys, ridiculously and misleadingly dressed as twins.

In your serenity, do you remember the German enclave near the train station and how we stared with fear and a mouse-like curiosity at the first SS officers we had ever seen?

There is a first time for everything, even for the lead-colored uniforms and eyes. But now, as our paths cross, you seem not to have lived through that first time. You wander about peacefully, always in the vicinity of the bridge, followed by your two children with the sole purpose of being observed by me, along with the fountains, the sculptures, and the figures on the clock. Perhaps it is that failed escape from the reality of Hell that condemns you to the Limbo of this interminable and, God willing, tranquil stroll.

You are images, shadows from that remote September, and I watch you, but I have given up trying to catch your attention. Mechanical toys have a limited ability to communicate, even if sometimes they inspire an almost intolerable sadness.

We, your ridiculously dressed children, are now in our sixties, and you, *mamma* and *papà,* are still forty in that cold autumn. I remember your youth, and I can smell its fragrance, and each day I retell myself the events that followed in your brief lives, played out so long ago. I wish you did not have to remain there in the cold next to the Rhine, guarding the past.

"No, no!" I cried out under the frigid rain, turning away from the shimmering shop windows full of toys. "I won't buy a toy here in Basel for my grandson Mario Davide's birthday!"

In the shop windows, a miniature world buzzes with lifelike activity: passenger and freight trains whistling at railroad crossings and in train stations with slate roofs, slick with fake rain; mine carts pushed along by tin miners bending their mechanical joints; motorcycles with sidecars; soldiers presenting arms in sentry boxes; white-and-pink-colored merry-go-rounds; a proud, cruel-faced couple dancing the tango, straightening up with a click after performing a *casqué;* little houses with real smoke billowing out of the chimneys; convertibles with entire miniature families consisting of mother, father, and two children, faces expressionless, putt-putting along on a miniature highway, tiny fluttering flags frozen solid in tin, and above the pretend border the inscription *Wilkommen in Deutschland.* Welcome to Germany.

2 ✻ April

Mamma is the first to hear a bell tolling in the distance as we descend toward Bioglio sometime around April 30, 1945. Then from the west, other bells in other valleys join in, and all of a sudden the festive dinging and donging of bells fills the entire sky. We run to find out what good news the bells are tolling, tolling, tolling.

"No, Madam, the war isn't over, not completely over, anyhow, but it will be over soon, you can be sure of it. Ha ha!" The parish priest is forced to pause for a moment by the roaring of a silver-colored Lancia Aprilia—menacing from the front but with its tail between its rear wheels—running on a mixture of gas and alcohol. "Hitler has committed suicide, my dear woman, shot himself, and that is good news indeed!" he cries out from the churchyard, as happy as if it were Easter (and, in fact, Easter had just passed), yelling loudly, not just in order to make himself heard over the roar of the Aprilia as it rushed down the valley, headed perhaps towards Ossola, with one last joyful, noisy blast. At the good news of the Chancellor's suicide—a commonplace end, pistol shot to the head—the bells of Europe ring out to the glory of God and of the Saints, and I listened to their ringing.

𝄋

Childhood is like a telescope attached to a microscope; in my case, when I peer through it I see the dark night of the Shoah, Hitler's killing spree, the catastrophe that filled my childhood, a distant period in which the existence of so many people we loved disappeared into nothingness, for no reason at all.

In the course of this agonizing search, this digging deep into the past and into the depths of my mind for the reasons behind events whose causes were hidden away in the diseased minds of their authors, I have experienced a curious phenomenon. I am now more than sixty years old, and my life is divided into two unequal parts; those seven years of persecution have expanded out of all proportion and become an excrescence of my soul, pushing aside half a century filled with the normal stages of life, confining them and all of the various ordinary trials of a life into a tiny space. The injustice which befell me as a child has unbalanced my personality and left me with this not uncommon, invisible wound which I have perceived in others, like my brother, Roberto, for example, who is one year younger than I and whose character is so different from mine. Anyone, gentile or Jew, who knows the facts can understand the gravity of the massacre perpetrated in Europe; but only those who were children, Jewish children, during those years are affected by this incurable, debilitating illness.

In order to be able to recreate again and again within itself the distant memories of a past that never recedes, my mind has altered the usual way in which we perceive time —which in reality flows away from us, along with childhood—allowing events from the past to become moral, fable-like constellations shining brightly, a constant and never-ending present.

I am like the soldiers from Napoleon's army who, having made it across the Berezina in one piece, inflicted willing and non-willing listeners for generations with the retelling of the story of the rout of the French army: of how Kutuzov's artillery drilled holes in the ice of the frozen river and entire regiments were swallowed up whole, of how the flags froze solid, and of how a few men survived to describe the carnage in nineteenth-century novels, only to end up as one of my mother's nightly readings. Brrr!

%

The spring was slow in coming in 1945, but the sun, feeble as it was, was enough to melt the snow and the chilblains on our feet, hands, and ears. Will anyone who endured the Second World War ever forget that intolerable itching?

And if spring took its time coming that year, it was partly my fault. In a flurry of careless lyricism, had I not begun an essay my mother had assigned on the subject of "The End of Winter" with the words: "Finally, after the frost, comes the refrigerating spring," meaning of course to say "refreshing"? Everyone laughed; even the snapdragons split their sides laughing when they finally bloomed. As they laugh even now when I come across them in a field.

In the first days of April, the valleys surrounding the few mountain huts of the Urì changed. Suddenly, as the snow melted, a forgotten silence returned. But in the sky the thundering of Flying Fortresses went on as they flew over continuously by the hundreds, on their way to Germany to blow its cities to bits; the pale blue of the Piedmontese sky was streaked with trails of condensation. I thought, or rather believed—*Ani ma'amin be'emunat ha'Mashiach . . .*[*]—that those strands, resembling the white fingers of a hand, were the embodiment of justice, of victory against our enemies, of vengeance.

Silence had returned to the fields and the woods, which flowered despite the fact that the earth and the air were still cold. The sound of gunfire had ceased completely; not even the partisans were shooting their obligatory few rounds, just for the record, in the eventless afternoons. The last

* "I believe with complete faith in the coming of the Messiah; and though he may tarry, I shall wait for him every day." Maimonides, "Principles of the Faith," No. 12.

noisy raid had occurred over a month earlier, in the first days of March. Everything seemed suspended in silence, minute after minute. The familiar and futuristic *gra gra gra* of the Beretta machine guns and the *ta pum*s of the German-made repeating rifles had ceased.

One morning, we heard cowbells announcing that Giuseppe, a shepherd we had befriended, was about to pass by the town with his herd, as he had for years. From indoors, we listened to the sounds of the cows as they slowly ambled, stopping here and there for grassy replenishment on their way to the high pastures. Giusèp wasn't from the area, but he came through twice a year, once on the way up and once on the way down. Every year he added new chapters to his tale, and after he came through, for a few weeks, it was carefully analyzed and taken apart.

Mamma was standing near our largest pot—it was made of aluminum and no longer had handles—and, looking over at Roberto and me, waited for Giusèp's timid knock on the door. She went to open it, leaving the pot in its place. Outside, standing apart from the herd, was Steila, a small, auburn-colored cow with long, fluttering eyelashes and horns which were so small that they were almost invisible; she belonged to a Piedmontese mountain breed which I haven't seen in many years and which, who knows, may no longer exist. "I was passing by," said Giusèp in Piedmontese dialect, "and just wanted to say hello; I'll be staying here a few days with my herd." *Mamma,* trying to disguise her impatient anticipation, greeted the shepherd, gave him a brief summary of our health, and, in Piedmontese dialect, asked him how he, himself, was doing. Giusèp, a young man with curly blond or perhaps reddish hair, shook his head, uttered a sound similar to that of his cows, and looked into my mother's eyes with the flippant smile of a man who is calm, serene, and unpreoccupied: "No news from Walter. His band has gone to another valley and, that *disgrasià* (rascal), he's got his Sten, his submachine gun, and hasn't bothered to send a word, not a word. Please pass the pot." *Mamma* handed it to him, feebly protesting, "But why do you trouble yourself?" The shepherd plopped himself down under the good-natured Steila and began to milk her, and we heard the sweet sound of milk against aluminum, gradually less and less metallic and more and more foamy. Roberto and I went over to take the heavy, warm pot which he handed us, no longer smiling, as he murmured quickly with his head down to hide his feelings: "Say a prayer to your God for my Walter. *Arvdse* (goodbye), *arrivederci*."

At that point, we should have said a *berakhah,* one of the many benedictions which the Jewish religion dictates as a sign of gratitude to God for bread, wine, the first fruit of the year, thunder, lightning, babies, the birth of a boy, the birth of a girl, sunrise, sunset, rivers, the sea, the Earth, the wind . . . But we did not know the benediction a hungry Jewish family should recite when a shepherd—in order to protect his fearless son through an act of Christian charity—gives them milk.

19
April

Papà hadn't played the violin in almost two years, since September of 1943. His last concerts, which are a part of the small history of the Jewish community of Turin, had been held at the Jewish Colonna e Finzi School.[1] They were wonderful concerts, or so I've been told; mainly, I remember dreading that my father, standing there in his concert attire, would embarrass us with the melancholy sound of his viola, in front of all of those people who were listening so closely, practically at attention.

Up in the mountains in 1944, *mamma* begged him to start playing again, hinting at a time in the not-too-distant future in which he would otherwise find himself "rusty." He had hidden his "good" viola and violin—made by eighteenth-century luthiers in Cremona—with a *salumiere*[2] and a pharmacist in Turin and had brought with him the "bad" violin, with its varnish so garish it looked almost pink. But he had never played it. He claimed this was so as not to call attention to us; in reality it was because he had lost all hope.

It was an extraordinary event in those silent first days of April when *papà,* without saying a word, brought out his violin and began to play. He started with the *note tenute,* the "long notes"; this is a tedious exercise that is done to develop, through endless repetition, complete control over the right hand. One moves the bow in a slow, controlled gesture, and the note—a single, randomly selected note, a C, a D, or a B-flat—must be absolutely clean, without the slightest hint of tremolo, as one maintains a constant volume for as long as possible.

Papà played long notes, and only long notes, for hours and hours and days and days. The first notes he played were trembling and unsure, and then gradually they became longer and more solid and more tedious.

I thought back to afternoons in Turin, when Roberto and I sat bent over our schoolbooks as *papà* played for hours, shuffling from room to room, from hallway to hallway in his slippers and pajamas—elegant, but pajamas nonetheless—varying the volume of the long notes with such control that we could not tell how far away he was or where the sound was coming from. He had invented a game to make the tiresome long notes more difficult for himself and also in order to use us as mice in his experiment, laying traps for us like a cat, crouching in wait for us to fall into an idle stupor in front of ink-stained schoolbooks, our empty gazes wandering off into the distance. Every so often the long note would be interrupted by a jab of the bow on our sleepy shoulders: "Hey there!" He didn't hurt us; he was just announcing that he had scored a point on one of those endless boring Turin afternoons.

But now in April of 1945, our neighbors—farmers and passing shepherds—were not the least bit bored. They strained their reddened ears to hear what to me seemed like a medieval form of torture. "You never told us your papa was an artist," they said to me. With the patience of people from the mountains, combined with enthusiasm for something completely new, it was clear they expected great things from that monotonous, endless performance.

The news of the presence of a genuine violinist, who actually played music, spread around the valley, and after a few days neighbors and partisans were asking, almost in unison and with a confidence that bordered on impatience: "Now play something nice for us, professor." He turned around and, without being asked twice, went into the house, picked up the pink violin, and came out with it in his hand. He tuned the instrument and played a piece that he called "the Bach aria,"* which, since his youth, he had used as a daily exercise at the end of his practice sessions. Standing in the courtyard, he drew his shoulders back, making himself look thinner and taller in the midst of the crowd of listeners sitting or crouching in expectation of the much-anticipated concert. In order to play the dictatorial Bach, the violinist must stand at attention like a Prussian soldier.

Any reader who has no interest in music may skip the following paragraphs and begin again with the line: "Before the concert in the courtyard . . ."

%

Bach, in his sonatas for solo violin, accomplished something which seems impossible: he made the violin perform counterpoint, that great achievement of German choral music, the abstract capstone of the Lutheran Reformation. There are those who argue that no violinist in Bach's time was capable of playing this experimental music; violin tech-

* It was the Adagio and Fugue of the Sonata no. 1 in G Minor for solo violin, BWV 1001, by J. S. Bach.

nique has advanced, like almost everything else, in the last centuries. The notes, which are played consecutively (given the sequential character of the instrument), seem, in the mind of the listener—in the mind, not in the ear—to be sounding out separate but simultaneous motifs, written *punctum contra punctum.* The experiment conducted by the composer, violinist, and listener evokes a music which, after it has been played, does not appear to have been notated, performed, and heard but only conceived in the mind. It is a challenge to time, and through these musical abstractions which sink individually like space probes into the vastness of the human mind, each listener, bewildered, deciphers his own emotions, which were unknown to him until that very moment.

I trembled in anticipation of a false note, but none came.

The violin is a difficult, even hostile, instrument, like the seventeenth century from which it emerged. It is prone to conspiracies and betrayals. The left hand, which appears to support the instrument—while, in fact, it is clutched by the lower mandible in a sonorous vice against the aching shoulder—is actually responsible for the intonation of the instrument, from the first to the almost unattainable fifth position. The right hand can press down with more or less force as it moves the horsehair bow across the strings, or can move the bow with more or less speed, or can modify its point of contact with the strings, but the bow must always remain parallel with the bridge of the instrument, under penalty of death. And out of this to-ing and fro-ing emerges a disembodied voice, a music which is syntax without words, and which multiplies *ad infinitum* the arcane meanings emitted by the simple vibrations of four strings made out of catgut.

The violinist is an acrobat who walks without a net or a counterweight across a tense cable above an abyss; if he falls, he will be crushed to death by his carelessness or impale himself on the sharp end of a wrong note.

But *papà* was as calm and composed as if he had never stopped playing; the bitter medicine of the long notes and the silence of those days of waiting had produced their algebraic, expressive effect.

As he played, the people listening experienced successive and simultaneous feelings of pride, security, and triumph, but also of anxiety and frightening uncertainty. For a moment, we heard a solitary invocation to some inconceivable transcendence. Other voices then intermingled with this unanswered invocation, transforming its singing voice, no longer solitary, into a kind of prayer, which gradually became a protest; then the voices together became the previously longed-for transcendent response. And suddenly the violin intoned a kind of choral hymn of gratitude, which again became a prayer, and finally again the solitary song returned.

As soon as the Bach aria was finished—this aria which declared that all of us, All of Us, would one day return to the valley and that the days of wrath and justice would arrive—*papà,* handkerchief still tucked into his collar, bowed in silence to the applause and acclaim from his peculiar audience. They had clearly understood this solitary hymn of triumph and sorrow. He turned and went into the house, dripping with sweat from the hard labor which is playing the violin.

※

Before the concert in the courtyard, around the middle of March of 1945, I had learned to pronounce my first three words of French: *"Je suis juif."* A new terror had spread through the valleys, which in January had shuddered at the news of ferocious Mongolian mercenaries climbing up the mountainsides alongside their Nazi masters. In March we were expecting the French, who were sweeping through the Alps to avenge the betrayal of June 1940. *Mamma* taught us the three words which were supposed to protect us: *"Je suis juif."* History's wheels turn quickly, and at that moment the Dreyfus Affair belonged to the distant past; "I am a Jew" seemed like the magic phrase to save Jewish children from the blow of the French sword.

But the French didn't come, and there were no vendettas in the mountains; rather, after the silence of the first days of April, everything became a tumult of fear and joy. As soon as the roar—half alcohol, half gas—of the car and the trucks had gone by, as soon as the reptilian tail of the silver Aprilia had disappeared, *papà* began to listen to the radio continuously, intent on deciphering the voices emerging from the liberated cities: "You are listening to radio free Vercelli . . ."

"You are listening to radio free Novara . . ." ". . . free Turin . . ." "Aldo says 26 to 1 . . . Aldo says 26 to 1 . . ."*

Mamma wanted us to understand everything that was happening, even though we were only children. She would say to us, or rather proclaim: "You must remember these days for the rest of your lives." On one occasion, after the hymns of the radio free broadcasts from the plain, she looked at us, her eyes swollen with tears that refused to flow, and clapped her hands together in wonder: "It has returned, we are living it, and this time we will not suffer the defeats of the last century. This is the spring of Reason; the old world is dead! Germinal has returned . . . this is the new Germinal!" (*Germinal,* Émile Zola, ed. Sonzogno).

"It's over," exclaimed our father, "yes, it's really over, Aldino, but the last days are the most dangerous, keep that in mind, we mustn't be the last to die." The same idea that had filled the thoughts of every mud-covered soldier in 1918 was ever present in the minds of the victors and the vanquished all the way from Berlin to Milan: "I will not be the last to die!" And meanwhile, columns of German soldiers staggered toward the almost unattainable borders, thrashing about like frantic, cornered serpents.

* The coded order for the General Insurrection bore my name; was this a coincidence or a magical sign?

3 ※ Bombardment

In 1942, after one last quiet summer, came the sleepless period of the wails and thundering of air strikes. We became accustomed to the nightly raids; every morning life began again, more and more ragged than the day before. The intensity of the attacks could be measured two days later by reading the newspaper; the names of the people killed in the raids were printed in boldface. These columns of names, which were later banned by the Fascists—they determined that the reports "affected the morale of the population"—put in black and white what had happened during the terrible sleepless nights. We trembled as we read the names of friends; on streetcars and in their homes people would set the paper down and close their eyes, murmuring,

"Them too, my God, them too..." Entire families perished, and there were no funerals; they had been banned by the regime at the start of the raids.

The absence of an anti-aircraft defense was barely masked by a few batteries of Flak guns—German artillery with long, vertical cannons—and a shabby emergency unit was thrown together, made up of "militarized" civilians. The UNPA, as it was called, obstructed the work of the real firemen, who were always present, brave, and effective, as they put out fires from their ladders: black shadows in the midst of the air raids.

At our house, a phosphorous incendiary bomb—an octagonal, red-hot prism—sliced through the roof, the ceiling, and the nice table in the parlor, and came to dazed, sizzling repose on the three-by-two-meter Heriz rug. The firemen arrived and threw the table out of the window, wrapped the rug around the bomb (why they did this I never understood), and then threw the bundle out as well. In its descent through the brisk night air, the smoldering ember reignited before fizzling out once and for all. With the help of the burning rug, it completely destroyed a Guzzi motorcycle with sidecar parked on the street below, the pride and joy of the husband of the hairdresser from Via Ormea. Satisfied with a job well done, the firemen left their axes, belts, and helmets in the hallway and retired to the bathroom to move their bowels with the tranquility of the just, wiping themselves with pages torn out of *I pugni di*

Meo by Giovanni Bertinetti with illustrations by Attilio Mussino (ed. Lattes, 1927).[1] My favorite book.

On the night of November 18th, there was a cruel and dramatic crescendo in the nightly dance: alarm after alarm went off, there were three waves of bomb attacks, and no one slept at all. Still, the sleepy, pale-faced, and worried people who emerged on that cold and smoky November 19th did not yet comprehend the significance of the new, growling force of the four-engine Lancasters. Incredulously, they read the coarse, yellowish leaflets on which was printed the following message, in Italian riddled with errors: "People of Turin, this raid is just a warning. Leave the city at once. On the 20th of November the city will be heavily bombed." How could anything be worse than what had just taken place?

On the night of the 20th, we all realized that our world was coming to an end, that Italy, the cradle of Latin civilization, heart of the Christian world, beacon for all peoples, was doomed to perish as the result of one simple and incredible mistake: it had taken the wrong side and, in so doing, had become the enemy of the entire planet. (Later, after the frenetic illusions of the 1950s—the decade of reconstruction—we were forced to accept that our world had disappeared in just one night, to return only once in a great while in the dreams of the oldest Turinese.)

The flames, intensified by the wind, became one giant tongue licking at the red-hued vault of the sky, in which one could almost see, like torches lost in the smoke, the onion-shaped domes of the synagogue burning along with everything else. We watched from our balcony, and *mamma* wept, holding us close to her with her left hand and crying out as she made a sweeping gesture across the burning horizon with her right arm: "Look, children, look at what Mussolini has done to your city, to our Italy!" *mamma* cried out, and the crackling of the fires was also a cry, the death rattle of the city. Turin, that martial, geometric, baroque capital, with its refined eighteenth-century *palazzi* and its delicate simulations of Parisian luxury, was being consumed alive on the funeral pyre of a night in the Fascist war.

On the morning of November 21st, a significant portion of the population of Turin—practically everyone—decided to leave town. On our way to the train station, the crowd became denser, and I caught a glimpse of the hopeless rescue attempt going on at the Politeama Chiarella Variety Theater on the Via Principe Tommaso. There, spectators, comedians, musicians, and dancers were buried alive under the walls and roof because they had been too caught up in the performance to notice the danger. Much later, I heard a story about a dancer who was pulled out of the rubble three days after the fire. Her hair had turned completely white. Wearing only a gold lamé brassiere, she made a mad dash down the street, screaming in horror, and died on the spot.

It was impossible to reach the Porta Nuova Station because the crowd, not quite panicked but absolutely determined to leave the city immediately, had completely and systematically filled the Corso Vittorio, the Sambuy Gardens, Via Sacchi, and Via Nizza. *Papà, mamma,* Roberto, and I stole into a freight yard away from the crowds, followed the tracks until we came across a train, and climbed aboard. We had no idea where it was headed, and we didn't care. After I-don't-know-how-many hours of waiting and another six hours of travelling to cover about fifty kilometers, we got off in the middle of the night at Asti. We were welcomed by the Black Shirts, the *Avanguardisti,* and the *Giovani Italiane,* who sheltered us in the gymnasium run by the *Gioventù Italiana del Littorio.*[2]

That night, as people peed on the ground between the cots, I had trouble falling asleep and overheard a worrisome conversation between a *Giovane Italiana* and a Black Shirt. The girl suspected, but fortunately was not certain, that we were Jewish; she quivered with indignation at the idea. She vibrated like a tense string with her moral imperatives and wanted to wake us and throw us out. "That will teach them a lesson." The Black Shirt, perhaps simply out of a desire for peace and quiet, tried to placate her, arguing that there was no way to be sure that we were actually Jewish and that we didn't seem the type: "What makes you think they're Jewish anyway, the stench of sulfur? Well, their city is on fire," he whispered to her, chuckling calmly. "You can't just throw people out in this cold. Think of the children . . ."

I finally managed to fall asleep, almost at daybreak, by singing a lullaby to myself:

Dreams, dreams,
Strange things they hold,
So strange in fact
They can't be told,
But tonight I'll tell you all,
Things I dream of big and small . . .

On the morning of November 22nd, or perhaps in the afternoon, we began our brief but lively stay with the Mortara sisters and their elderly mother. They lived in an apartment facing an ancient, crumbling square.

Before it changed our lives, or rather turned them upside down, the war offered us the rare opportunity to inhabit worlds which were destined to disappear soon after and allowed us to observe their last moments. In those days Turin was a metropolis, abuzz with ideas and cultural activity. Asti, on the other hand, was a provincial place, sleepy in its actions and its thoughts. Everything there seemed old, worn, disheartening, and devoid of hope. Everything, including the people.

The Mortara sisters rented us a room in their apartment. It was dark and filled with nineteenth-century furniture, not quite sumptuous nor utterly humble but broken-down and dusty, with torn and faded upholstery and heavy curtains—everything a bit grimy but not excessively so, smelling of cabbage like an old concierge. The art nouveau polished briarwood radio didn't really change the overall effect of the place: this was the dry shell of a once-prosperous family which had many, many years earlier, succumbed to moral starvation rather than to material hardship. From the hallway, one entered directly into a large sitting room, in a corner of which a kitchen had been created with the help of a partition of frosted glass panes which did not even reach all the way to the caisson ceiling. This was where the old mother slept, as her room had been rented out. On the walls were a great number of photographs with gold-hued wooden frames enclosing the pale, nineteenth-century faces of the family's forgotten forbears. In addition to these icons, there was one anomalous photograph in a chromed-metal frame on the radio: a young Air Force officer stood laughing with one hand resting affectionately on the wing of his ultimately not-so-dependable Savoia-Marchetti.

The two sisters, half-Jewish and over thirty, were so different from each other that they did not even seem related. The older one had an olive-colored complexion and protruding eyes. Tall and dark-haired, she dressed in a slovenly fashion; she ran a button shop, once a fabric store, on the Corso Alfieri. She did not spend much time in the house, and when she did, she usually left her coat on and hardly acknowledged us. She was the mistress of that dingy household. The younger sister, Elisa, on the other hand, was slight and pretty, bleach-blonde with eyebrows reduced to fine lines, as was the fashion of the time. She was excitable, always perfumed and fashionably dressed, and she wore shiny silk stockings, with the seam in back, of course, and very tall platform shoes made out of snakeskin with cork soles.

The two sisters did, in fact, have one thing in common: together, they brutalized their mother almost every day. I have no idea what the cause of their cruelty was; the mother was old and confused and could hardly obey their requests, but I'm sure their real reasons lay in their own anger and frustration, for which the little old woman was not the least bit responsible. They would lock themselves in a room and hit her, and we could hear her whimpering pitifully, "Ouuch! Ouuuch! Please stop, pleeeeease." The daughters would yell, "Quiet! Quiet!" and slap her some more. What can I say?

The two sisters also had in common certain sordid "services" which they performed for soldiers eager to evade death, albeit temporarily. They concocted deadly compresses out of buttercups and cigars, which they would apply, for a price, under the arms of young men who were in no hurry to visit the Russian steppes, at least not right away, and who opted instead for a fever and hallucinations.

Elisa, the pretty, high-strung sister, had been widowed at the beginning of the conflict; her husband was the carefree officer in the photograph, who had "fallen heroically from the skies above Malta." She was a Fascist and a teacher of "fine literature." As Asti had no Jewish school—the only kind of school we would have been allowed to attend in accordance with the racial laws—we took our lessons with her. Roberto was an unwilling student, but Elisa was taken with my docility, born of frustration. She doggedly insisted on my learning Giosuè Carducci's *Song of Legnano* by heart, and I still shudder as I remember the task, which at the time seemed impossibly difficult: "And here a messenger arrives in Milan / From the Porta Nova, with reins flying . . . Do you remember, says Alberto da Giussano . . . Oh, golden haired, oh beautiful, faithful Empress / Oh pious one, have mercy, have mercy on our women." And on and on, up to "The sun / Shone, sinking beneath the Resegone."[3]

And that would have been the extent of it if my beautiful instructor, in her intense desire to teach, had remained quietly seated behind the walnut table. Instead, as I sat there making a concerted effort to memorize the poem, I would become fascinated by the spectacle of her beautiful, veiled legs. In these times of scarcity, where did she find silk stockings, dark and sheer, almost gray? And why should I limit myself to admiring the ankles when I could easily glance at the knees, which in the first half of this century were still a source of great excitement, especially for a sensitive boy like me? She would caress her legs, cross and recross them, allowing her skirt to rise far above the limits of common decency and engraving on my mind forever the rustling of sin and desire. I could see and hear her slender thighs rubbing against each other, amazed at the solemn warnings symbolized by the gradations in the shading of the stockings, which became darker as the skirt slid higher and higher, toward a place which I could not quite picture but where I suspected the velvety presence and warmth of pale bare skin . . . It wasn't so hard to imagine! I have no doubt that she was aware of the direction of my glances: first of all, because the too-frequent vacillations of my memory betrayed the confusion produced by this gradual uncovering; and second, because every so often she brusquely pulled her skirt down to her knees with a vexed air. Only when I had learned one or two more verses would she reward me with another slow ascent, which I hoped would go even further than the previous one.

The full enigma of sex was not revealed to me on Piazza Catena—that happened later on, in the Salesian boarding school—but those legs and those small, snakeskin shoes led me down a stretch of the path of no return toward the mysterious empire of Eros. It is funny that *mamma,* always on the lookout for mischief, did not catch wind of the initiation to fetishism which was taking place in that gloomy parlor in Asti. The only explanation I can think of is that her Jewish-Turinese moralism numbed her to this kind of provocation and to its collateral effects: an astonishing, unexpected, and delicious tightening of the perineal region underneath my short trousers.

Cohabitation was leading us toward deeper and deeper revelations, and would perhaps have created unexpected relationships. Elisa was more desperate than immoral: her husband had died, and, deprived so young of the object of her dearest affections and desires, she could not sleep at night and was tormented by the memories and impulses of her lost love. She was forced to take increasing doses of the sleeping pill Lepetit, a depressive barbiturate, which she called "my only salvation."

One night, my teacher suddenly and tensely declared that she was going to bed early, and as she walked off—rustling, tip-tapping, and swaying her hips—she was probably already under the influence of the Barbera wine which, during the privations of the war, was promoted as a "valuable and complete source of nutrition for all ages." As we sat in the dining room chatting with the elderly mother, in Elisa's room the combination of Lepetit and wine was quickly dissolving the aviator's widow's last remaining scraps of modesty.

Without warning, Elisa threw open both sides of the French doors to the dining room. And there she stood, not completely in the nude, which might have seemed more decent, but decked out—my God!—in microscopic black panties and a lace shelf brassiere. I saw her nipples! She exhibited herself in this way, holding her hands out beseechingly, so as best to display her lovely, "fetching" body, as people said back then: dazzling and white as the moon, exposing a vertiginous distance from her navel down to the tiny panties. She implored my father in a mawkish, stammering tone, "Mario, I'm not feeling well, come to me . . ." Then slid down, gracefully, slipping one straight, tapered leg against the other (perhaps in a simulation of modesty or perhaps in real pain) with her hand resting on the doorjamb, displaying her radiant nudity. As we all watched the magnificent performance in awe-struck silence, I, and perhaps Roberto, relishing every second of the scene, *papà* instinctively rose up to supply the help that had been so gracefully implored. But *mamma* shot up and, exclaiming "The children! The children!" swept Elisa away. *Mamma,* and not *papà,* took Elisa back to her room and closed the door behind her forever.

The following morning my mother rushed to the office of Asti's superintendent of schools and asked him *ex abrupto* if two Jewish evacuee children should be deprived of school and forced to learn life "from the streets" simply because of who they were. Through the bureaucratic maneuvering of the antiracist superintendent, I entered the fourth grade at the Vittorio Alfieri School in Asti as an "auditor, 1942–43 school year."

In that class, there was only one platform shoe; it was a black orthopedic boot, and it belonged to the schoolmistress, who had one leg that was shorter than the other.

4 ✻ December First

Eight A.M., December first, 1943. As she had every morning since our return to Turin, the maid brought in our breakfast: *Frank* blend, a coffee-like concoction made out of roasted chicory with a few drops of condensed milk, and *papà*'s newspaper, *La Stampa.* According to his daily ritual, *papà* unfolded the paper, and immediately began to say and do things that we later realized were completely justified by the circumstances but which, at the time, shocked the maid into a statue-like silence, tray in hand, pale, paler than pale.

"Oh God, oh God, oh God, ooooooh Gooooood!" my father exclaimed, kicking the covers and pulling the tasseled nightcap off of his head; he got out of bed and took off his pajama trousers, making no attempt to hide his dangling parts—extremely uncharacteristic for a man as modest as he was—and pulled his trousers on while still wearing his pajama top. He had forgotten to pull on the long woolen underwear which he always wore in winter and which, along with his nightcap, his Military Cross, and his chronic bronchitis, were the last vestiges of his service in the Great War: Assault Engineers, eighteen months on the Kras.[1]

"For God's sake!" he repeated, removing his trousers in order to put on his long underwear. From his tone one could suppose that this last, less dramatic invocation of that personal and transcendent God of the Jews was induced more by the difficulties encountered in his hasty dressing than by the tragedy of what he had just read on the front page of the newspaper. As he removed the pajama top, standing there for several moments in his undershirt and long underwear—both of the highest quality, from before the war, with only a slight but indelible halo around the crotch and a few moth holes—he commanded us in a choked voice: "Read the newspaper." He had a strange tone of voice and the look which he often adopted when he encountered bad news; it seemed to imply that the terrible news in the paper was somehow the work of his own family. It must be a hereditary trait, because I am the same.

We passed the newspaper around, from me to my brother, Roberto, and from him to *mamma* and finally to the maid. We read it quickly and in silence because there wasn't much to read or to say. All eight columns were filled with huge black letters proclaiming: "All Jews to be sent to concentration camps!" Though we had been gripped by a sense of panic since September, at that moment our state of mind took a dramatic turn for the worse. In reality, the announcement simply signaled the falling away of our last illusions;[2] ever since the armistice, there was nothing preventing the complete annihilation of the Italian Jews.*

Not long before, perhaps on the 15th of October, in the course of our flight from Asti, across Piedmont, we had stopped briefly in the thermal spa town of Acqui and were surprised to find Field Marshal Rommel's entire general staff quartered there, their shoes still full of sand from the

* The newspaper was announcing the November 30, 1943, order by the Interior Minister Guido Buffarini Guidi, specialist in Jewish matters since 1938, to all the police precincts. See Renzo di Felice's *Storia degli ebrei italiani sotto il fascismo (History of the Italian Jews under Fascism)* (1961). In May of 1993, at the Central National Library in Rome, I was able to read the article more calmly. The headline does not fill the entire page, and it is not written in large black letters as it is imprinted in my memory. On the bottom right of the first page, it spans only the seventh and eight columns. It reads, without any emphasis: "All Jews to be sent to concentration camps." Buffarini Guidi's order, a few lines long, is followed by a short comment in italics explaining the moral necessity of this precaution in response to the Allied air raids. A return to the original mission of the Regime is called for, by which "all" the Jews will be sent to concentration camps, even those who had been given "discriminated" status in 1938. It is not explained why they had been "discriminated," thereby suggesting that they were filthy war profiteers. In actuality, the 1938 racial laws had protected (or so they claimed) those who had been baptized prior to that date, the veterans of the war in Libya, of the Great War, and of the Spanish Civil War, as well as, naturally, those who joined the Fascist party early on.

Deutschland über Afrika campaign. They were an unwelcome sight to people like us, who wished to see as little of the Germans as possible.

Panic-stricken, we desperately sought help, notably from *papà*'s wealthy, aristocratic friends from the days when he had been a brilliant concert performer, long before he resigned himself to the humble yoke of the EIAR[3] orchestra "in order to be secure and comfortable, and support a family."

Until a few decades before my birth, Turin had been a European capital, and the advent of the automobile had helped to free the city from the trap of provincialism. In the twenties, the remnants of its glorious past and the cultural reality of the time formed an impressive arc which reached from the Savoyard and papal aristocracy to the Napoleonic aristocracy and on to the wealthy professionals and businessmen of modern times, who were devoted to the arts and the cultivation of their artistic sensibilities. Turin was a vastly more cosmopolitan city than the provincial and vulgar Milan. It accepted the anomalous and aspired to the cultivation of the exceptional. Not surprisingly then, it resisted the rise of Fascism and its grim, provincial populism; there was real loathing for the "people's trains" and the "afterwork clubs."[4] In 1938, the Jews who were young, wealthy, adventurous, or specialized enough began fleeing to the United States. Others submitted to their social exclusion within that beautiful city, undergoing a gradual transformation from outcasts to victims—in the Empire of Indifference—and in some cases, ultimately, from victims to combatants in the Resistance.

On October 15, 1943, in a villa outside of Acqui—far from the field marshal's shiny green Mercedes Torpedo parked in front of the Grand Hotel Terme—we sank into the deep armchairs of an elegant cream-colored parlor with windows overlooking a lawn dotted with trees and a tennis court where a young man and woman were playing, dressed in whites. As we conversed, we could hear the rhythmic *toc, toc, toc* of the ball hitting the racquet. Nearby on a small table stood carafes of juice with little ice cubes floating on top. But the drinks were not for us; they were for the tennis players, who every so often broke off their game and came indoors, overheated and smiling, for a drink. *Papà* was talking to an aristocratic lady with bluish hair, describing our condition to her anxiously: ". . . the *Jeestapo* is after us . . . the *Jeestapo* has all of our names and addresses . . ." The lady could not contain herself for long and, articulating clearly, said to him: "Geh-sta-po, it's Geh-sta-po." I think this was the only help she gave him that afternoon, because as we exited the gates of the villa, *papà* cursed angrily, muttering: "Well, children, now you know: It's the Geh-sta-po that's after us."

That may have been the last episode of indifference we encountered that day: in the afternoon, when we returned to the boarding house where we had been staying, the owner "invited" us to leave, immediately, as soon as our bags were packed. He had figured out that we were Jews, or perhaps someone had tipped him off, and he was terrified.

Since November 20th or thereabouts, after crisscrossing Piedmont, horrified by news of the capture and disappearance of friends and relatives, we had been living at number 36, Via Berthollet. Our hideout was located directly across from the entrance to our old building, number 39, which we had abandoned during the raids that destroyed half of Turin the year before. The building had been left standing along with a few others on that street, but we were careful not to set foot there. Now we were all in one room, in the apartment of our old *havertà,* Antonietta.[5] We had been forced to let her go after the passing of the racial laws of 1938, and she had since married a worker from the Fiat factory who was a passionate hunter and, during those turbulent weeks, a heroic striker. He was always slightly inebriated, never very agreeable.

On the morning of December first, the scene with father and the newspaper occurred in this apartment. We had been hiding there for ten interminable days, imprisoned in a bottomless pit of boredom, unable ever to leave the house. *Mamma* wouldn't even let us go out of the room for fear of our "being a nuisance"; nor would she let us get too close to the window "because someone might see us." Our hostess, out of affection and perhaps nostalgia for our old working relationship, served us our meals, tidied up the room, and took significant risks on our behalf. Her husband, on the other hand, did not hide his discomfort with our presence and displayed a clear desire to get rid of us. He went on frequent patrols around the neighborhood, and on one occasion he saw two agents of the Gestapo go in and out of the doorway to number 39, pause on the sidewalk, peer up at our windows, and look carefully all around. They had our precise and up-to-date address, just as they had the address of every Jew, a gift from the "mild" Italian racial laws to the German allies. These men could not accept the fact that we weren't simply sitting at home waiting for them, patient and resigned, suitcases packed. For those readers who are fortunate enough never to have seen a Gestapo agent, I think that it is worth explaining just how one recognized them: first of all, they were German; second, they wore long black leather coats; and above all, they were convinced of their invisibility.

Our only comfort in that small room were two large, docile, and bored Spinoni dogs that stank of wet fur and of whatever other odors they picked up on their peregrinations through the swamps on the outskirts of the city. They left piles of shit proportional to their size; fortunately, Antonietta cleaned up when she saw them.

After the first panic produced by the newspaper headline had subsided, all four of us got dressed and finally went outside.

%

Nine A.M., December first, 1943. We rang the bell of the archbishop's palace, at number 700 on the street named after it, which had suffered serious damage in the air raids.

The person who came to the door was one of those strange beings who only inhabit parish churches and priest jokes. His beret was pulled down to his eyebrows, and his face was bloodless and of indeterminate age, unevenly shaved, with prickly hairs sticking out here and there. His gray scarf was tucked into a gray jacket over a gray shirt, all of them wrinkled, over shoes which lacked any shape but which were highly polished.

We followed him up the grand staircase and found ourselves in a room with dark red couches all along the walls, which were covered in light purple damask silk. On the walls hung the oval-shaped oil portraits of the archbishops of Turin. A few of these portraits, maybe half a dozen, had been graced by the addition of a halo, indicating the promotion of their subjects to the upper echelons of that deceased fraternity.

The disheveled man mumbled something, bowing slightly, and closed the door behind him, leaving us alone for several minutes in religious semidarkness.

As *mamma* implored us to "please hold still!" and stop making squeaking sounds with our shoes against the parquet, His Eminence Cardinal Maurilio Fossati and his secretary, Monsignor Barale, entered the room wearing worried, inquiring expressions as if they were preparing to tend to the sick. They knew us already from my father's previous visits, and they had of course read the newspaper. The small, rotund, aging cardinal and his extremely tall secretary received us in that manner peculiar to priests—and to shepherds with their flocks: with their arms open wide but without touching us, and with a dignified air of sadness, their heads slightly bent toward one shoulder. They invited us to sit in a corner of the room under one of the huge windows. This became the theater of their whispers and of my father's exclamations.

"You," he began, vehemently, "disciples of Christ, cannot accept this ignominy!" Despite the desperate circumstances, *papà* could not keep himself from uttering such inopportune and imprecise theological remarks, hinting polemically at the eternal quarrel between the two religions of the Good Book. Worse yet, his arguments were interspersed with ideas he had picked up from his beloved theosophical readings—not exactly the finest publications to come from the Laterza Publishing House.

The two good men were able to calm my father down; at first he had refused to leave the palace "with the children," insisting, "They'll kill them, Your Eminence, they'll kill them. You know it's true." We were told to return that afternoon with our suitcases; my brother and I would be taken to one of their boarding schools. *Mamma* and *papà* were relieved to hear the creaking door of Christian charity—unofficial and powerful—as it slowly opened to admit my brother and me. Not a moment too soon!

%

Nine forty-five A.M., December first, 1943. As soon as we stepped outside the Archbishop's palace, we were welcomed by the screaming of the sirens announcing the first daytime air raids of the war. The dread and anguish of our imminent separation was mitigated by the alarms: the hunt for Jews was suspended during the aerial attacks. The implementation of our slow execution required calm, organization, and bureaucratic formalities which the chaos of the real war made unworkable. For a few moments we again became normal people running the same risks as everyone else around us. We must have been truly agitated, and our guard must have been dangerously low, because, as we looked up at the sky and heard the first explosions, *mamma* and *papà* began to cry out in the street, which looked blue in the cold shadows of the frozen buildings under the calm sky: "They're coming! They're coming! Show them! Kill everyone! Destroy everything!" Our minds clouded by grief, we had mistaken a modest air raid for the Final Judgment.

A monk rushed out of the baroque Church of the Visitation—which belonged to the Capuchin order—with its small, curving façade. Panting, he descended the steps, his sandals clacking against his bare feet. "For the love of God, what are you doing outside? Come in, my good people, take shelter!" "We are Jews, condemned, and the bombs don't frighten us; they're the least of our fears," answered my mother, staring straight into the watery eyes of the monk with a look of accusation and protest which admitted no response, a fulminating gaze which my daughter Lina has inherited, employing it in far milder situations. And the monk did not respond, except for his rapid flight and the violent banging shut of the church door.

As the intermittent hiccupping of the alarms sounded the all clear, we rushed toward the San Giovanni Vecchio Hospital to pick up the results of a stool test which my father had insisted on because he'd noticed I continually scratched my bottom.

⅋

Ten fifteen A.M., December first, 1943. The hospital is an imposing baroque structure of dark brick; there is nothing Mediterranean about it. The majestic interior is Christian in the gloomiest sense of the word: the wards are built in the shape of a huge cross, and at the point of conjunction of the arms, above a large, bare altar, hangs a giant cross of dark wood which reaches up almost to the dreary skylights. The building was conceived as a temple of pain meant to aid in the slow, melancholy dissolution of body and mind. Giant windows fill the cathedral of disease with white light.

A young doctor with gold-rimmed glasses brought us over to sit in a passageway empty of beds. "Wait here, and I'll go get the results and come right back." The frost in our hearts, the white light, and the black cross acted on our fragile emotional state. The four of us embraced, more and more tightly, and began to sob, and then to weep disconsolately. When the doctor returned, we turned toward him with our reddened eyes full of tears. "What's wrong? Why are you crying? It's only worms!" And brusquely, *mamma,* who for some reason on that dangerous day felt impelled to announce our identity left and right, answered, "Forget the worms! We're Jewish, they're after us; they're going to kill us! That's why we're crying!" The doctor said nothing, staring, and then he approached us and became the fifth member of our group. His name was Alfredo Pagani, and for the rest of the war that young doctor had only one purpose in life outside of his work: us.

%

Two P.M., December first, 1943. I don't remember where we had lunch—there's a gap in my memory, and suddenly I find myself in the middle of another air raid. This time it's a big one, with huge explosions, and I have taken shelter under a doorway on the Via Madama from the debris falling like a red-hot hailstorm on the basalt slabs of the street. The people, standing halfway under and halfway out of the doorway, cried out, "They've hit the *Snia.* They got the *Snia Viscosa,*"[6] and as they watched, a column of dark smoke rose up, forming a black cloud at the end of the long, rectilinear street.

After the intermittent sirens announced the all clear, *mamma* ran home to pack our suitcases; they were to drop us off at the Archbishop's palace at five o'clock that evening. *Papà,* Roberto, and I walked toward the smoke, which by now obscured the icy white light of the sun. As we approached the epicenter of the disaster, fire trucks and ambulances passed by us, the wails and hiccups of their sirens mimicking those of the alarms which were coming to an end.

The afternoon raid was the real thing; the planes which that morning we mistook for the Final Judgment were scouts sent on a reconnaissance mission to locate the exact spot to destroy: an industrial area of the city which housed engineering and chemical facilities. The metal shutters of the stores had been sucked out toward the street, and iron fragments hung from buildings as immobile as Napoleon's flags frozen over the Berezina, revealing the incredible power of the tons of explosives and the infernal force of their exhalations. The street was littered with roofing tiles, glass, clothes, mattresses, and shattered furniture that had been sucked out of the windows; the streetcars were on fire, and we had to step carefully to avoid the sparks of the electric cable which had been cut by the blasts and hung down onto the street.

It turned out that the black cloud was rising not from the *Snia* but from the *Riv,*[7] and the bodies of the workers, who had suffocated by the hundreds inside, were being carried out in piles and taken away in trucks, on *motocarrozzini,*[8] and on handcarts. Arms and legs, blackened with greasy soot, stuck out from under the tarpaulins and bounced as if they belonged not to human beings but to rubber dolls. To prevent the workers from running off during the raids and wasting an entire day of work, the *repubblichini*[9]—probably out of stupidity rather than Fascist cruelty—had ordered that the factories be locked as soon as the first alarm went off, thereby dooming those inside.

A policeman—a Turin *civic,* as opposed to the hated Fascist police—walked toward us holding his bicycle. He could barely breathe, having snatched several bodies from the fire. As he inhaled, his lungs produced a whistling sound, and his mouth was completely blackened by the poisonous smoke. He turned his colorless face upward toward the sky in search of clean air and then bent over and coughed even as he continued to walk, clutching the bicycle. When he was close to us, we heard him muttering in Piedmontese, not to us but to himself, between the gasps and coughs: "Fascist murderers, they killed them all."

%

Five P.M., December first, 1943. I can still see two faces, a woman's (long hair) and a man's (big ears), bending down toward me. From below, I can see that they are smiling, loving, smiling, smiling, and asking: "What would you like us to give you?" I look up at those two beloved faces before me, outlined against the sky, and thoughtlessly ask for black, calf-high boots and knickerbockers. These were two articles that I had long dreamed of wearing and to which *papà* was opposed. He claimed that "children dressed that way look like old dwarves." Instead, he made us wear short trousers, even in winter, with low shoes and short socks without elastic which were inevitably sucked into our shoes. Once the parenthesis of the war, with its inevitable loosening of rules, was closed, *papà* returned to his old obsession, so much so that in 1946, when I proudly entered the Tempio Piccolo for my bar mitzvah* decked out in a black jacket and short gray trousers, my friends, relatives, and schoolmates whispered to one another, "Aldo looks like a referee!"

But in this moment of farewell, everything was allowed, and my parents ran blindly through the bombed-out city in search of the objects of my desire. Poor Roberto, who hadn't even been asked, seconded my requests.

At around seven o'clock, as the wintry darkness gathered around us, I began to cry, convinced that *mamma* and *papà* had been picked up by the police. At first, the cardinal thought he would be able to manage the situation easily: he found a spinning top in one of the drawers of the huge eighteenth-century desk and handed it to me. But the toy was useless. This was not the crying of a child; at ten one doesn't cry in this way. This was the somber lament of a person whose life has been torn apart by the realization that he has lost the people he loves most in the world. I experienced the same pain when first *papà* and then *mamma* left me for the last time and forever, after the war. But that day at the archbishop's palace, the pain was a million times more wrenching, because children do not listen to reason, and because this was my parents' first death.

* The public ceremony upon which, at the age of thirteen, a Jewish boy becomes an adult from the religious point of view and is obligated to observe precepts and laws.

The hapless cardinal and his faithful secretary did what they could to console me, but they did not seem to realize that my heart had been pierced by a crown of thorns, like the one that Christ reveals under his tunic, his hands dripping with blood, as he accepts the world's torments unto himself.

※

Nine P.M., December first, 1943. By the time *mamma* and *papà* finally appeared, the cardinal was dressed up as a *Befana,*[10] and Monsignor Barale was singing nursery songs, hopping on one long leg under his cassock. I had been crying disconsolately for two hours. Not even the sight of my mother and father, back from the dead, calmed me down. As they helped me put on the knickerbockers, they too began to cry, and *papà* kept saying to me, "You look like a little man . . . a little man." In the end I quieted down, and they left Roberto and me in the large, white nuns' dormitory, fragrant with the smell of candle wax, in large beds hung with snow-white curtains. I tried to sing myself to sleep:

> The elephant, the elephant in breeches,
> Arm in arm with the mosquito,
> Up and up, through the air, he reaches,
> To digest his heavy meal, *bon, bon* . . .

In the priests' boarding school, I would have time to sing all the verses of this song, my mother's lullaby, night after night.

§

Nine-thirty P.M., December first, 1943. "It was awful," the cardinal whispered to my father, his hand clutching his forehead as they left the dormitory together, "just awful."

Only then, as I fell asleep, did I realize that the good man had understood my terrible distress, that he had felt it himself, and that he simply had not been able to find the way into my soul, because he was a Catholic cardinal and I was a Jewish child.

5 ※ Bruegel

ESTOTE PARATI.[1] It was written in black, in capital letters, on the walls of the refectory, the dormitories, the hallways; *estote parati* were the words written on the doorway to the Middle Ages. Even children must be prepared for a good, Christian death. "Prepare yourself!" the walls cried out to me. They cried out, even though I had come to the school in order to escape the carnage raging outside.

In the Canavese,[2] I found out what a "good end" was—a good, simple, Christian death, as described by the priests. On December 2, 1943, I realized that I was in exile when I heard them explain that a good end is a slow death, in full consciousness, where physical pain is conjoined with repentance for the sins of an entire miserable, difficult lifetime. It is achieved, amid wheezing and gasping, only after the performance of the Sacraments: Confession, the Eucharist, Extreme Unction, and off you go, down, down, into oblivion. Here I was fleeing from the Empire of Panic outside and taking refuge in the past, in the rural world of Cavaglià,[3] medieval and real, not like the healthy country life I had read about in my "Books for Young People."

In this day and age, we have forgotten the stench and horror of human toil when it is employed as an energy source from birth until death. We can no longer imagine the infections that killed people slowly—or suddenly—at every age, the gangrene and the carbuncle, the babies whose mouths and eyes were covered with flies in the arid summer, the scabs hiding festering wounds full of pus which never healed, men deformed by hard labor at fifty, women withered at the age of twenty-five, the promiscuity, incest, and brutality that exist behind the dark resignation, the mute rage, the constant and endless waiting for a liberation which never arrives, best manifested in Millenarianism and the songs about the Land of Plenty, the cunning, and the humility.

"Prepare yourself": The Middle Ages are a place of transit and refuge for Barbarians, Romans, and Jews, an unwelcoming haven for those who are fleeing from something or someone. He who has been there keeps it hidden away in his heart. My middle ages took place in the year 1943, and all around me was the harsh winter of northern Italy: the

Alps and Apennines closed in over the Po River Valley, creating a furrow filled with mist, frost, and ice.

In order to get through the winter, the children of the medieval countryside are bundled in layers of clothes and wear something called a *mefisto* on their heads. The *mefisto,* for those of you who have never encountered one, is a kind of stocking knit out of scratchy wool which is wound tightly around the children's shaved heads, from the forehead to the nape of the neck, to protect the brain from meningitis and the ears from otitis. It is then tied under the chin to protect from diphtheria. In the front it descends to a point between the eyebrows. It is Mephistopheles' head covering and derives its name from that medieval demon who, rightly, feared sinusitis.

The *contadini*[4] wear their shirts against the skin, even in the dead of winter, when they add woolen undershirts worn over them, a kind of predsecessor to the sweater. They do not wear pajamas or distinguish between their nightshirts and the shirts they wear during the day. In the morning they jump up from their beds and stuff the long shirttails of their nightshirts into their trousers; for belts, they use pieces of rope. The children, even the boys—with grotesque femininity—wear long, scratchy, woolen stockings up to their thighs and fasten them with bits of elastic. They are constantly sniffling, but are not acquainted with the use of the handkerchief; instead, they blow their noses by pressing one nostril and then the other with their bare fingers. And there is worse.

The constant torments of the medieval countryside, which happily no longer exists, have now been forgotten and substituted by the myths of the horrors of urban life. Amnesia has won again, and no story or description can succeed against this inexorable force.

In the countryside, pandemic dementia was the legacy of a horrifying past; and in the present of 1943 it was apparent in generation after generation, brought on by widespread avitaminosis and the lack of iodine. At the time, this was an inevitable circumstance; the distance between Cavaglià and the sea, now less than an hour by car, then seemed insurmountable. The *contadini* were horrified by their mentally and physically deficient children. They loved them but were ashamed of them and of the nonexistent sin which they represented, and so they hid them under the stairs or in cellars, or tied them to the bedposts. You can find these beings to this day, peering out of Bruegel's paintings or from the cornices of Romanesque cathedrals, crouching on the flying buttresses of gothic cathedrals, on doorways, and in stained-glass windows. These poor souls look out at a world which they do not understand, and which they could never have understood, even if they had not been sent off to stand guard in paintings or on gutters, the rainwater pouring like fake spittle down their receding chins.

The Collegiate Church of San Quirico d'Orcia School is held up by one of these miserable souls, placed there by his mother and father in 1100. And in all this time, he has never tired of staring at the passersby, as if seeking to understand something which is beyond his comprehension; luckily for all of us, he has not yet figured out the puzzle. Whoever sees him there, holding up a high gray stone wall all by himself, shudders in amazement. The day that the stone boy completes the puzzle and shudders—and I believe the day will come—the church will crumble.

Sometimes, when they are very young and can still be integrated into a group, these deficient children are mixed in with the others in the care of the priests. In fact, about ten of my classmates were "slow," and the priests never lost the opportunity to use them as warnings to the other, "normal" students: you see, we are all the same, we are born incurably ill, and it is only death that heals us. "Blessed are the poor in spirit: for theirs is the kingdom of heaven."

One of them, skinny, tall, and dark-skinned, with a long nose and a fierce look in his eyes and a receding forehead, was a sweet kid who only uttered one word: "goat." He used it at all times and for everything, animate or inanimate; naturally, his nickname was "Goat." And then there was "Kita-kita karamba," whose name was derived from the strange sounds he made when he was angry. Mostly, what made him angry was when people called him Kita-kita karamba. And the boy who refused to pee: he would dance around all day long, jumping up and down and squeezing his legs together to distract himself. We called him "the Ballerina." He always looked terribly surprised when he saw the pee running down his bony legs in their long, droopy stockings.

The children of the *contadini* brought rough hemp sheets from home to the harsh, "modern" Salesian boarding school; they could not stand sleeping on exotic and slippery cotton sheets and would never have permitted themselves the luxury of linen sheets, which were only for wealthy landowners. At night, the dormitory rustled like a burning haystack with the sound of these hemp sheets, as the children tossed and turned in their monotonous dreams.

Practically every night of the winter of '43–'44 in Cavaglià, as soon as we had crawled into bed after the evening prayers, and the lights were extinguished, a fart would ring out, and Don Prunotto, the supervisor, would call from his bed where he lay motionless, without even opening the curtains: "Ferreri!" And the whole dormitory would sing out, in unison, like a Gregorian choir, "Wroo-ong!" and wait for the next resounding fart. "Quazzo!" "Wroo-ong!" Fart after fart, the supervisor had to guess whose posterior had produced it, and the game ended only when Don Prunotto had demonstrated his skill as a musical critic. Only after the farting Olympiad was over, did our spirits drift off to sleep, watched over by the future prelate, and only then could I quietly sing my little lullaby to myself:

The ants, the ants in their new suits,
Took a bath, took a bath in ruby red wine,
As they studied their Latin roots,
And went over their lesson, *bon, bon* . . .

I was not one of the stars of these nightly concerts. In reality, the farting game was dominated by three or four of the fifty boys in the dormitory; they were virtuosos who were capable of modulating the voice emanating from their sphincters in order to imitate those of the other boys. But I was held in high esteem for a different ability: during the showers—which took place once every three weeks—I could hide my little testicles and penis between my legs, pushing them back toward my buttocks, and become a girl. From the front, the pure, white skin of my pubis lacked any sexual attributes. In the wafting mist of the showers, the children would squeal "Belly dance! Belly dance!" and clap their hands in time as they hummed an exotic tune. I entertained them by swaying my hips and making "Oriental" motions with my arms. This was the only part of my body I could move, because if I moved my legs, my childish anatomy would be revealed.

Sex was our main spiritual preoccupation, an ardor which filled our minds, aggravated by malnutrition. Women were our spiritual torment, and the priests trembled.

One of us, whose nickname was *"Pincoscia"* but whose real last name was Inguscio, carefully kept a postcard which had been sent from Somalia at some unknown time by some unknown person and had landed in our Middle Ages. On it appeared a lithograph from the not-too-distant nineteenth century: an Italian soldier wearing a sun helmet and a handkerchief posing sternly, his mustache curled up at both ends, eyes looking straight into the lens, almost at attention, with his arm wrapped around the shoulders of a black woman. We of course were not interested in his gesture of casual—and none-too-friendly—possession, nor did we linger over the sad face of the black girl, with her head leaning over to one side; we ignored her large, callused, and dirt-covered feet. But we never tired of staring at the naked body of that poor young woman: those perky breasts which were infinitely more cheerful than her face, and the pubic hair which had been blotted out but was—perhaps intentionally—still visible.

The priests, not all of whom were saints, shared a common terror, not so much of what we might actually do—which was not much, given the circumstances—but of our evil thoughts. My father brought me *Signal* regularly, every Thursday: it was my favorite magazine, a German—Nazi, though not overly so—version of *Life* magazine. In it, I would carefully scrutinize the war photographs: photos must be read slowly and, in order to be understood completely, must be meticulously studied, because the best photographs not only reveal what occurs in the moment in which the light acts on the silver salts but also allow the viewer to deduce an infinite past and future beyond what is caught in the frame. As I was carefully considering a German Tiger tank which was rolling over a small house, crushing it with absolute ease and indifference, the monitor asked to see the magazine, walked away with it, and then returned it with the following page missing. On that page there had been a photo of the prima ballerina of the Opera of Berlin doing a split as she agonized in the Dance of the Swan, a photo which I had completely ignored. Accustomed to the naked Somali woman and still filled with the memory of the veiled, shimmering legs of my teacher in Asti, I was completely anesthetized to ballerinas in white tights. But this the monitor could not have imagined.

At the school, we never had enough to eat, and hunger was an infinitely greater problem than the cold or the filth: at breakfast, they gave us an aluminum bowl filled with ersatz coffee along with half a piece of dark bread made of bran and straw. In the evenings, they sent us to bed with the other half a piece of bread and an anchovy in our stomachs. At lunch, when they saw us grumble at our main meal—which consisted of a hot soup—the priests spouted out their moral ideology: idleness is the father of all vice, and in order to stay in good health, we should always get up from the table hungry.

Luckily, the *contadini* children received packages of food from home. Filippo, who slept two or three rows from me, kept lard sandwiches, wrapped individually in wax paper, in his iron nightstand. When I could no longer bear the gnawing in my stomach, I would feign illness at the five o'clock wake-up call and stay in bed, and just as soon as everyone was gone, I would trot over warily to the nightstand and gulp down as many sandwiches as I could at once, without leaving a single crumb. Few today can imagine the redemptive value—as compared to a 6:00 A.M. Mass—of a lard sandwich in the winter of '43. When night fell, and poor Filippo decided to enjoy one of his own sandwiches in the darkened dormitory, he would discover that they were gone, and, unwilling to believe the evidence he was feeling with his fingers, he would blindly open and close the pieces of empty, greasy paper, mumbling meekly about his cruel destiny, which lay wide-eyed in the darkness a few beds away. As soon as a new bundle of sandwiches arrived, I would prepare to strike again. It was stealing, but I did it without regrets, and to this day I feel no remorse at all.

Only a few days had gone by since that sad December 2nd when I arrived at the Salesian school, and I was beginning to get used to life there: the chilblains, the scabs with pus underneath, the shaved heads. I soon discovered a theme that returned again and again in the freezing 6:00 A.M. sermons and the improvised harangues that we were forced to submit to throughout the day: "Do not renounce eternal bliss for the sake of a moment of pleasure!" I knew that eternal bliss meant Heaven; I had learned it on a day in 1938, in the Parco Valentino in Turin. A group of children had noticed the Star of David which I still imprudently wore on my collar and had informed me, without rancor or condemnation, that those future delights were forbidden to me: "At the most, you'll be in purgatory." I knew all about Hell and Purgatory from the Doré engravings in our edition of *The Divine Comedy;* the tangles of bodies and naked torsos of women in chains had already attracted the morbid attention of this young Piedmontese sadist.

But I did not know what "moment of pleasure" they were referring to. *Mamma* and *papà* visited only once a week, on Thursdays, when they could, and I had already mourned their deaths on the night of December first. The bitter cold increased daily with the approach of the winter solstice, which submerged everything in darkness. Food was scarce and could hardly be called a pleasure. My first encounter with Christianity, with its dark, agonized crucifixes, *Christus Patiens,*[5] had profoundly unsettled me, as if I needed unsettling; we were not treated with overt cruelty, but neither did we feel loved, nor were we any longer really children. Groups of German soldiers wearing black helmets, accompanied by the rhythmic and threatening clanging of their ammunition pouches, marched by the school. Even the skeletal trees seemed to hold their branches up in a terrified gesture of surrender under the leaden sky. They woke us at five in the morning, and by eight o'clock in the evening we were in bed. So what was this "moment of pleasure"? What could it be?

I began to ask my schoolmates how it was possible to find a moment of pleasure in that place, but they did not know, or else their answers were heavy with elusive double meanings, neither of which I could understand. The only exception was Inguscio, *il Pincoscia.* Not long before he invited me to join the fraternity of worshippers of the Somali woman, he asked me, without double meanings or obfuscations, if I had ever "touched" myself. Then, with an air of medical know-how, he asked me what I had felt. I answered that yes, I had touched myself and had felt something, but that I couldn't really describe the feeling. "You're on the right path," *Pincoscia* informed me hurriedly, relieved to have reached the end of a conversation of such an intimate nature. "Keep trying, and you'll see." With an allusive, devilish air, he raised his dark, southern, conjoined eyebrows and turned to go back to his bed from the frigid latrine which had been the theater of our brief encounter.

Back in my own bed, after the initial shivering had passed, I began to amateurishly maneuver my tiny member. The final pleasure, which took me by surprise, was ruined because when I felt something wet, I was convinced that it was blood and that I was menstruating or hemorrhaging. As my classmate Professor Umberto Chapperon—who later became a philosopher and the director of Olivetti—explained scientifically to my class in the last year of middle school, it was simply the marrow of the spine which was flowing and gushing forth, producing this pleasant sensation; its undesired collateral effects, according to Chapperon, included tuberculosis of all types and the incapacity to comprehend the conditional tense when translating from Latin into Italian: in other words, feeble-mindedness.

But in the freezing Vercellese,[6] under the ice and the snow and the faded, reddish sunsets visible between the black trees, with the *contadini*, their whiskers speckled with ice and wearing clogs, headstockings, and rope belts, in that colorless, forsaken place of misery and frozen ponds where people skated as they do in the Flemish winter of Bruegel paintings, I bade farewell to eternal bliss; I had created my own pleasure for the first time, and now I could sleep, in a state of mortal sin, in the clear, starry, arctic night, singing to myself, content and oblivious to the world:

> In the heart, the heart of the artichoke,
> A tiny flea plays tricks and jokes,
> My little Aldo ate it whole,
> Gulped it down, and it was gone,
> *bon, bon . . .*

6 ⚜ Lina

I have very few memories of the house on Corso Francia, on the western limits of Turin, where I was born in 1933. I remember the kitchen, a huge storm, the Alps—white and looming above us—Aunt Lina* (*papà*'s sister), and her hus-

* Zargani, Lina. See Liliana Picciotto Fargion, *Il libro della memoria* (Milan: Mursia, 1991), p. 629. Liliana Piccioto Fargion, in a research project funded by the *Centro di Documentazione Ebraica Contemporanea* (Center for Documentation of Contemporary Jewish Life), gathered and set out, in 945 pages, personal data and information regarding the deportation of 8,869 victims of the anti-Semitic persecution in Italy and in the Dodecanese—at the time, known as the Italian Aegean Islands and now part of Greece—between the years 1943 and 1945. This figure represents twenty-seven percent of the nearly 33,000 Jews residing in Italy in 1943 and ninety-six percent of the nearly 1,900 Jews residing in the Italian

band, Rino. They had money, and they used to come over to pick up their favorite nephew—me—in their Lancia Augusta.[1] This was around 1936 or 1937; *mamma* and *papà* were still young. They stood and waved at us from the balcony of the huge tenement block where we lived. This building, along with several others in the Fascist—but not yet Piacentinian[2]—style, formed part of an immense arrow of buildings, swarming with people, which pointed toward nearby France.

It is a tribute to the mysteries of the human psyche that my brother, Roberto, after fifty years, is still poisoned with envy at the memory of the roar of the engine and the screeching of tires which called for me, not him. He was just a baby in my mother's arms—he was born in 1934—and was left behind on the balcony to wave with the others.

The aroma of gas fumes and of the famous Lancia fabric of the seats always made me queasy. Nothing, not sitting in the front seat or opening the windows, could save me from the inevitable outcome of the first turns on the road up to La Morra.[3]

These fondly remembered but actually quite trying outings were also envied and obstructed by my grandmother

Aegean Islands. The total number of victims listed in the book, which does not include those killed in acts of resistance, is about 1,100 people short of the number of Italians registered at Auschwitz, due to the authors' decision not to include the names of people for whom no other confirmation was found. Our friends, acquaintances, and relatives who were deported are all listed in the book. None of them was ever seen again.

Ottavia, née Ventura, born in 1872 in Livorno. She was jealous of her unpleasant son-in-law Rino, a steely native of Turin, and of his nice car; she thought she, more than I, deserved to be invited along on these Sunday drives. And she had reason to be jealous: in Piedmont in 1937, a spin in a luxury car produced sensations and emotions which could be described over and over again to one's friends and neighbors. As we sped through fields, forests, vineyards, and ancient villages, goats, cows, birds, horses, farmers, and farmers' wives stared admiringly at this image of modernity speeding through an Arcadia similar to that found in the paintings of Massimo d'Azeglio.[4] When we arrived home again, I was still nauseated, despite the beautiful landscapes which had flown past my window, and humiliated by my vomiting, which seemed like the ultimate lack of gratitude for my aunt and uncle's generosity. As we approached our destination, the brainwashing began: "Don't say anything to Grandmother! Don't tell her we took you out for a drive!"

My aunt Lina was killed at Auschwitz more than half a century ago. In 1970, I went to visit the factory of death in Upper Silesia, a dark, gloomy place, perfectly adapted to the function the Germans put it to: a region of coal mines, mud, and black firs on the European plain which reaches all the way to the foot of the Urals, coated by a thick mass of clouds, a gray shroud reaching to the horizon.

⁂

For months in 1945, Jewish families gleaned every shred of information about the last moments of freedom and life of those who had been killed in the camps from witnesses and from the few people who had returned. My father—by moral choice—and my mother—for didactic reasons—hid nothing from me in the twenty terrible months after 1943, and, after the end of the war, *mamma* and *papà* insisted that I hear these stories of survival and death. We Jews, before taking refuge in the ephemeral Kingdom of Memory, did all we could to remain on the flowered path of disbelief: for months we waited in vain for the return of the survivors, unable to accept the reality, which was already obscured by the Empire of Indifference which had returned only weeks after the end of the war to the world of the non-Jews. At first, when we spoke of the horrors we had seen, we encountered sympathetic reactions, but soon the responses changed in tone: "Well, you know, my son broke his foot in '44, and we had to set it with a piece of wood from the carpenter's shop, imagine!" We were seen as petulant whiners in a world of courageous, stoic folk full of Christian forgiveness.

In those days of waiting, my distraught *mamma* imagined a Jules Verne-like scenario, à la *Michael Strogoff* (ed. Bietti, 1920), in which one of our beloved relatives, having forgotten his identity, was wandering the Asian steppes among the birches and the firs; he was happy but could not remember the past, and in fact it was his amnesia that had saved him, and the kind-hearted farmers loved him as they had loved us. But one day, perhaps in the distant future, he would remember everything and would return on a steam locomotive decorated with the cast-iron hammer and sickle from the Putilov Works and the red flag, his memory full of the waving of handkerchiefs and the tears of his new friends he had left behind . . . But late in 1945, as the winter approached, even she began to accept the fact that these people were all gone, and then she would tell the story of how, in the frigid November of 1918, grandfather Attilio had yelled out to the crowds on the old Via Roma as they celebrated victory: "Five sons—they all went to the front, and they all survived!" In fact, one of them had died. Grandfather imagined that his son was alive but suffering from amnesia and wandering around on the Asian steppes. He gave orders that the gate to his house should never be closed, nor the one to his family's factory. "That way, when he returns, even if it's dark, he'll know we're waiting for him . . ."

To his last day in this world, November 4, 1951, my father never gave up prophesying the future or handing down the law. In fact, astutely taking advantage of the pathos of his final hours, after forcing us to listen to the fluttering of his expiring heart, he made us promise that if one of us ever had a daughter, we would name her Lina. I obeyed, of course, at the first opportunity, and Lina finally returned.

❦

Before the war, my aunt and uncle used to invite me—and sometimes my brother—over to their beautiful, delicious-smelling house; Aunt Lina would let me listen to records on their mahogany electric gramophone and show me exquisite color reproductions of paintings as we waited for Uncle Rino to come home from his job buying and selling nonferrous metals. I remember that in Francesco Hayez's[5] painting *The Kiss,* a young girl leans back, her eyes closed, awaiting a final kiss from a soldier who holds her with one arm wrapped around her extremely fine waist, his right hand touching her cheek. This painting expresses perfectly the final moment before absence, an absence which might be made eternal by Death, as only it knows how.

My aunt also let me look at the *Novissimo Melzi,* an illustrated encyclopedia which wasn't as new as its title suggested, with detailed engraved diagrams of machines and illustrations of trees and tables of peoples and races, some of which were falling out of the book. She was impressed by my precocious intellectual curiosity and never noticed that what interested me most was a plate entitled "Forms of Torture." They were all there, from flogging to quartering, which was represented by a naked woman who was being carried by the knees and armpits to a special table with all sorts of constraints, chains, and levers by two medieval guards wearing helmets, armor, and iron gloves.

When Uncle Rino came home, the long but always interesting lunch began. A fragrant meat stew, substantial in and of itself, took second place to our careful observation of our uncle's behavior. Before lunch, he would read to us from

Ciondolino, by Vamba[6] (ed. Bemporad, 1896), in his elegant, phlegmatic Piedmontese accent; the book was about a boy who had been turned into an ant. He demanded our absolute attention and would ask us, out of the blue, to comment on the moralistic passages describing what happened to children who misbehaved. Once he was through reading, he would take a mechanical pencil out of the pocket of his jacket—as sculptural as his Piedmontese accent—and, rotating it between his index finger and his thumb, place a microscopic dot in the margin next to the last thing he'd read. This is just one example of his odd behavior. My father hardly drank in those days when he was still a joyful man, and at our house wine was a rare treat, but Uncle Rino used to tell the maid to pour a few drops of wine into our crystal goblets, which were filled with soda water made with *Idrolitina* powder. The maid—pretty, blonde, and silent—wore a white apron and velvet Friulian slippers,[7] and she served us as if we were little princes. For some unknown and deeply moral reason, our steely Turinese uncle insisted that after every single bite, we eat a little piece of bread, no matter how small, and he was not amused when Roberto and I, chuckling to ourselves, ate big pieces of bread followed by little pieces; in our childish game, the bread itself became an accompaniment to the bread, in an infinite circle. Leaning over his plate, he would watch us with his serious but benevolent eyes peering over his glasses, making sure we followed his Judeo-Turinese dietary prescriptions to the letter. In this way, he tried to correct the unacceptable tropical, Sephardic disorderliness we had inherited from our ancestors from Livorno and North Africa, a characteristic we shared with his lovely Moorish wife and also his terrible, avid mother-in-law, whom he hated, our grandmother Ottavia, who had been a midwife, an artist, and an adventurer.

The Sephardic Jews are the Jews from Spain, many of whom were Arabicized by their long, secular sojourn in North Africa after being expelled from Spain. In fact, the Turinese Jews are also Sephardic, but they have the "advantage" of having escaped in time from northern Africa and more "chic" places like Provence and Paris, after the Saint Bartholomew Day Massacre. With their rigid, moralistic ways, they were part Huguenot, though they didn't know it, and they did not suffer gladly the Jews from the "East" or the "South."

In April of 1939, when *papà* was still playing the violin, and the EIAR was in its last days—as was Uncle Rino, who died shortly thereafter of a stroke—my aunt and uncle celebrated their silver wedding anniversary with a lavish party, and on that night Roberto and I were left home alone for the first time in our lives, after being warned repeatedly to "behave, for goodness' sake!"

Mamma and *papà* were decked out in their finest, and they paraded before us, arm in arm, with pretended nonchalance. *Mamma*'s appearance bordered on the unbelievable; to me, it seemed like an insult to her identity as a Jewish mother:

she was wearing makeup, and her shimmering eyes revealed to us her true female nature through her maternal exterior. Suddenly she had turned into a woman, no longer endowed with reassuring homeliness. She was wearing a long black dress which was not low-cut but had long sleeves of voile which clung to her short, plump arms; at the time, I thought they were stockings. She was wearing practically all of the family jewels, which made her sparkle like a strange, threatening idol. But even that would have been endurable had it not been for the embroidery of colored beads which adorned the front of the evening dress. This embroidery depicted—and my unconscious still recoils at the thought—a giant, multicolored parrot, red, green, white, yellow, and blue, with its beak over her right breast, its little curled feet at the level of her pubis, and its huge, colored tail reaching down to the very edge of the skirt. With a final wave, they closed the door behind them, just in time for me to realize in horror that not only was *mamma* tottering on high heels, which I had never seen her wear before, but she was actually *swinging her hips.*

As soon as they left, Roberto and I climbed into our beds and stared open-eyed at the ceiling, contemplating our fears in silence. After a few minutes, Roberto rolled over, propped himself up on one elbow, and said in a sleepy voice: "Hey . . . I bet thieves are going to break into the house." He insisted on going into the kitchen and dragging out a chair and a butcher knife; he climbed onto the chair, knife in hand, and stared at the Yale lock as it glimmered creepily like an eye in the darkened hallway.

Mamma and *papà* came back at ten-thirty, out of breath and feeling guilty; they had left the party before dessert was even served. Every single light was on in our apartment, even in the bathroom and the storeroom. Roberto had opened every door, creating a single, reassuring space in which to combat the constant threat represented by the gleaming of the Yale lock. In the end, he had sat down on the chair and fallen fast asleep, his head resting on his little chest like a sparrow; but still, he grasped the butcher knife and sat only a few feet from the door.

A few months earlier, in 1938, Uncle Rino and Aunt Lina had sent their only son, Eugenio, to London to complete a professional course. Eugenio was very tall and terribly handsome, a member of the honorary Savoy Cavalry Guard with their silver helmets and golden crests, but not very intelligent. The idea was that he would stay there "until the end of the racial campaign," as my Aunt said to everyone, pointing at Eugenio's picture. "He'll be back before the winter fog sets in." Perhaps they hoped that the anti-Semitic laws were just a propaganda ploy, like the use of "voi" rather than "lei,"[8] and national self-sufficiency, and *Lanital*—a wool substitute made from milk, which, absurdly, was even scarcer than wool—and the Fascist salute. Perhaps they thought that all of it would soon be over and forgotten?

I think Eugenio lived out his days in Vancouver, on the Pacific coast, without ever again setting eyes on his father, his mother, or his best friend, Felicino Ottolenghi,* who was also very tall and handsome and a member of the honorary Nice Cavalry Guard—golden helmets, silver crests—and not very intelligent. Perhaps he remembered the Turin of his childhood as a far-off dream, obscured by the fog of memory. We came across Eugenio's friend, who was also his cousin—as well as ours—in more desperate times, in 1943. He was sitting nonchalantly with his legs crossed at a table next to the window in the Caffè degli Specchi[9] under the arcade of the Piazza Carlo Felice, at the corner of Via Roma.[10] The jet of the fountain in the Sambuy Gardens was reflected in the window, and this reflection was in turn reflected ad infinitum in the mirrors of the café. The autumn light penetrated the arcades, half of which were from the seventeenth century and the other half of which had been designed by Piacentini.

Everyone knew that the handsome, friendly, spoiled young man had never accomplished anything in his life, good or bad. His father, Silvio, was the owner of the most important camera shop in Turin, which was called Nothing Escapes . . . When he had begun his career in 1912, he had decided to go into the unusual profession of photojournalism; his motto was "nothing escapes my lens." He came from Livorno, as did all of my father's relatives. An artist and an autodidact, he wanted to make something out of his son but failed.

* See L. Picciotto Fargion, *Il libro della memoria,* p. 454.

Silvio Ottolenghi arrived in Turin at the end of the nineteenth century with my paternal grandfather, Eugenio, with whom he shared a single, rented bed; it was an excellent way to save money without great sacrifice, given that my grandfather worked during the day and Silvio worked at night. Before he was given the honor of working in the Fiat factory on Corso Dante as a watchman, Grandfather went around the arcades on the Via Po from morning to evening selling pencils, which he kept in a box that hung from his neck. He attracted the attention of passersby by twiddling eight pencils between the fingers of his two hands. Even though I did extensive research into the life of Grandfather Eugenio, every picture I found shows him exactly as I remember him in his last years: drooping shoulders, clothes sewn out of heavy material, full eyebrows knit as if trying to understand something, whiskers sloping at the same angle as his shoulders, knees slightly bowed. He appears never to have been young. He always looked like an elderly, dignified country gentleman.

When my grandfather came home for his turn in the bed, Silvio would go out to the Piazza Carlo Felice, across from the Caffè Mugna. He ran a *tombola*[11] stand with prizes, of which the only one of any value was a Malacca walking stick with an ivory handle. Silvio's trick was that when someone won the walking stick, he would follow the lucky winner down the street, pleading and whimpering until the person relented and returned it to him out of sheer pity. After wiping away his crocodile tears, he would return to his corner and begin to spin the *tombola* once again. By the time I saw the cane, it had become a family curio: the ivory handle was in the shape of a sphinx.

Felicino began his undistinguished career at the Umberto I Military School, where he was remembered for many years as having been "the worst student in the school's history." Then he became an officer in the prestigious Nice Cavalry Guard and took part in the Ethiopian venture, on the occasion of which his father immortalized him in a classic photograph in 1934 in which he appears wearing a sun helmet and a cocky, provocative smile. And then . . .

And then, one day in his thirty-second year, Felicino laughed in that Futurist manner of his from inside the café at my father's horrified look as he silently mouthed the words, "Come out here!" Since 1939, "no dogs or Jews" had been allowed to enter that café, which, by the will of the same god of armies who kill Jews, no longer exists. And yet Felicino continued to go there, out of indifference, but perhaps also out of a natural boldness, even in mid-1943. He was an indolent man but also an extremely brave one.

There is another photo of Felicino taken, as always, by his father; it is archived in my mind in black and white like the original, which was taken in 1942 when the Fascists decided to humiliate the young Jewish men of the city with a kind of light, senseless forced labor. They were made to carry railroad ties from one pile to another and then carry them back again. This spectacle took place to the great amusement of the entire city, Jews included, in a bleak part of Via Cernaia, near the Porta Susa Railway Station, where the RAI skyscraper now stands. In this photo from 1942, Felicino laughs scornfully—just as he did in 1934—as he holds a railroad tie over his head, bare-chested and Herculean. He seemed immune to the traumas of reality; and perhaps this state of mind is the indispensable prerequisite to heroism.

Felicino answered my father's call and came out of the café under the arcade, newspaper in hand, surprised, or feigning surprise, with his horselike sneer, at the terror his presence there had provoked. "I'm not in danger, Mario, I'm sleeping with the German consul's mistress, and no one can touch me." He was tortured for days in the cellar of the Albergo Nazionale to make him reveal the hiding place of his prosperous father. Not only did he not betray his father, he managed to work out a completely harebrained but miraculously successful scheme. He corrupted a Gestapo agent by revealing to him where a ring with a giant diamond was hidden. The German policeman, a thief and a tyrant but not, it turned out, an anti-Semite or a Nazi (but how could Felicino have known this?), took the ring for himself and went to the Ottolenghis' hideout to warn them that they should flee before their son broke down under torture.

The photos remained in beautiful silver frames on his father's chest of drawers until his father died in 1954.

At the beginning of the air raids in November of 1942, and ever since her husband's death, Aunt Lina was living alone in Turin with her housekeeper on the Corso Fratelli Cairoli, a tree-lined avenue that ran alongside the Po. On the other side of the river, the forest-covered hills cast their shadows on the single row of eighteenth-century houses of the Corso Moncalieri, a melancholy, silent avenue.

Before fleeing the bombed-out city, Lina put her lovely things away in trunks which she hid in a cellar. On top of her furs, silk dresses, and bric-a-brac, she placed terra-cotta pots full of salt, a clever hygroscopic technique which turned out not to be so clever after all. When we found my aunt's "things" at the end of the winter of 1946, we discovered that the salt, having absorbed large amounts of moisture, had corroded the terra-cotta and slowly seeped into everything: her furs and astrakhan fur muff, her silk blouse with the big pink flowers and pale lilac-colored stamens, her briarwood boxes, and her pretty porcelain fox terrier.

My aunt was an elegant woman, and, at the time of her murder, even though she was past fifty, she was still quite beautiful; her curly black hair was just beginning to turn attractively gray. She was slender and tall, even next to my father, who was a very big man. Like him, she had a strange nose, not particularly "Jewish" except in its dimensions. On an old identity card, my father's nose is classified, with a comical bureaucratic attention to detail typical of the time, as "Greek." Their noses seemed to emerge directly from their foreheads, and there was something rigid about them which did not fit with the dark flash of their eyes.

They had been born to a poor family of people who had left the ghetto with no money to their name. Like my father, and even more than him, Lina was proud of the social dignity she had acquired. Neither of them had any facility with the written word, but because of their Tuscan origins, they spoke a pure Italian which was free of dialect or regional inflections. In addition, a distant North African ancestor—by rape or adultery?—had conferred to the family a refined air, which must have been advantageous in the society of the early, optimistic days of the twentieth century, with its preoccupation with appearances.

The two were siblings not only in their appearance and in the elegance of their dress—which made them seem like the heirs of a long line of privilege—but above all in their manner. Both of them spoke in a language which now seems antiquated and which was perhaps already outmoded at the time: the language of gestures, which is incorrectly termed "theatrical" because it is often abused by actors.

When Nazi Field Marshal von Keitel brought Germany's unconditional surrender to the Allies in May of 1945, he clutched his marshal's stick in his left hand and held out his right hand to the American general, who not only did not accept it but ostentatiously put his hands behind his back, all the while staring directly at him and shaking his head in refusal, his face frozen in an expression of stony disgust. *That* was speaking in the language of gestures.

During a rehearsal on June 8, 1939, or perhaps on the 10th, my father was informed that he had been laid off from the orchestra of the EIAR, in accordance with the racial laws. When he returned home mid-morning I, who had not yet begun school, was skating around on the waxed floors in my slippers; I greeted him joyously, without noticing his gloomy state. I didn't understand that that very moment marked the beginning of everything that was to come. *Papà,* on the other hand, paid no attention to me and nervously changed out of his everyday clothes into his best black suit as he said to my mother: "I'm going to the union, and we'll see what they say. I don't know what will happen, but I need to go. If I don't go, it's worse, don't you think? If I don't protest at this very moment, it means that somehow I accept what has happened. Later, I'll write them a letter, but right now I'll go and file a complaint in person."

He was very nervous but not quite desperate. He started to put on his spats, and had placed the elastic in its position, near the heel of the shoe, but couldn't find the little hook which fit into the buttonhole, hooked each button, and pulled it back through the buttonhole. In those days, this gesture was accomplished in a flash, mechanically: this antiquated system, which in fact required a certain amount of skill, was the manual predecessor of the zipper and was almost as efficient. *Papà* searched for the little hook with the silver handle but couldn't find it on the dresser or in any of the places he usually left it; as he searched for it, his nerves were quickly giving way to anxiety. Because I was small, I could see that it had fallen under the bed, and I picked it up and silently held it out to him, expecting caresses and recognition. Instead, when he saw the object in my hand he assumed that I had been hiding it all along, and, in a flash, his anxiety turned to anger. He slapped me on the cheek. Then he laced his spats, the tip of his tongue in the corner of his mouth, with the same expression he used when he undertook delicate maneuvers like spooling strings on the pegs of his viola or peering through the bridge as he placed it in the correct position. Meanwhile, I sobbed in silence.

At that moment, the effect of his gesture—the slap—was revealed. *Papà* straightened and, peering down at me, realized suddenly and involuntarily that I was innocent, and did as he believed was just: he kneeled down before me, and, leaning toward me, took my hands in his, kissed them, and said: "I'm sorry, please forgive me. Please excuse what I've done." The next moment, he was running down the stairs, bowler in hand, jacket unbuttoned, skipping steps, ready and determined to present his useless protest.

After the war, when we went through my aunt's things, we found an envelope with "Mario," her brother's name, written on the outside. Inside, organized chronologically, were the reviews of my father's concerts, many by Andrea Della Corte, and one, a curiosity, in which he was described as a violist. The envelope also contained the announcement of the enactment of the anti-Jewish laws of 1937 and 1943, as if, with this gesture from the heart, her brother's successes and the melancholy sound of his instrument compensated for the humiliations which had been inflicted upon her.

My aunt suffered from the cold, and in winter her hands would become frigid, a condition which she attributed to a mysterious disease of the liver. She used a muff, in which she kept little tubes of paper filled with warm coal which emanated a glowing warmth. My hands also became cold in the winter, and sometimes she would let me put them in her muff and warm them with her own, and we would walk like that, her hands holding mine, through the beautiful streets of Turin.

When her husband died, she began to go around with *Commendatore* Angelo Treves, who I believe was also rich. Though I never met him, I, the wounded party, could describe my rival in great detail, in the most prejudiced and least reliable terms. This late love, as well as her taste for comfort—which she was not prepared to sacrifice—was the principal reason why she did not come to live with us. After our short but unforgettable stay with the colorful Mortara sisters on the *piazza,* we had moved and were now living cheek by jowl in a hole-in-the-wall in Asti. In the spring of 1943, as my aunt entered that dismal place, she exclaimed: "But Mario, I can't live here, it's impossible!"

My aunt had betrayed me for another, but still she should have come to live with us, not so much because of the uncertain future which lay ahead but because the spring and summer of 1943, after Stalingrad and the defeat in Africa, after the fall of Fascism, was a period of calm in quiet, impoverished, dusty Asti. Those months were filled with bike rides with *papà* and dips in the Tanaro River—but only before the hemp which grew alongside it began to rot, because afterward the river water was bad for you. In addition, there were celebrations, which proved to be unwarranted, of the fall of Fascism and the armistice. It was an intermission, a sweet respite, complete with measles, mumps, scarlet fever, and the ensuing convalescences.

By the time the September panic came, Roberto and I were strong enough to withstand the last, terrifying strikes of the dragon's tail. Thanks to Asti, we were healthy and serene, immune to childhood illnesses, ready to confront the plague which was filtering through the Brenner Pass and spreading throughout Italy, carried by the polluting armies of Keitel—who had cleared the Alps in April—Reder, Kesselring, Kappler, Wolff, the Adolf Hitler SS division, and, lastly, the Hermann Goering armored division, bristling with long-barreled, camouflaged canons.

On September 29th in the early evening, we went to the station to pick up my father, who was returning from Turin. He got off the train looking ashen, sweat pouring from his brow: something terrible had happened, but he could not or would not tell us what it was. Once we had left the crowds behind, he whispered to us—in a whisper which was like a scream—wild-eyed: "They've taken Lina, they've taken Lina, they've taken Lina."

She had been captured with her lover by the SS at a villa not far from Biella, in one of the first Nazi actions against the Italian Jews. There is no doubt that someone had informed on them. I am aware of several hypotheses as to who the informant was.

Her maid, Livia, a lovely blonde, who in the past had sewn slippers for us, told us that "Madam" was aware of the arrival of a truck which had driven up from Biella to round up Jews, but that she had wasted time trying to pack a few things and had come face to face with an SS agent at the back gate.

Livia too was taken to the Albergo Nazionale, the headquarters of the SS for Turin, Asti, Biella, Cuneo, and Ivrea, but had subsequently been released because she was an Aryan and, better yet, a native of Friuli. She had, however, been present at Lina's interrogation by Captain Schmid, and for that reason was called to testify at his trial in 1945, during which the defense was able to prove that the officer had, if perhaps with excessive alacrity, simply followed the orders of his superiors to the letter.

Livia cried as she spoke, staring directly into the eyes of the accused with her own, which were deep blue and filled with hatred and suffering: "Madam's hands were cold, as they always were, and she kept them in the pockets of her *tailleur* . . ." And then Livia pointed a trembling finger at the SS agent and said, "And that man there, he yelled at her, he screamed out in Madam's face, 'You Jew! Take your hands out of your pockets in the presence of a German officer!'"

7 ✻ The Colonna e Finzi School

Be astonished, O ye heavens, at this, and be horribly afraid, be ye very desolate! (Jer. 2:12.) When I was a child, the golden letters on the façade of the synagogue did not proclaim these words to the indifferent and unknowing passersby on the Via San Pio V in golden letters, as they have for the last fifty years, ever since the horrors of the Shoah.

The gigantic Russo-Arabian-Turinese structure, topped by four threatening onion-shaped domes, dominated my neighborhood, the eighteenth-century Borgo San Salvario, an area made up of dark streets leading from the Parco Valentino to the Porta Nuova Station. The domes were covered in black slate tiles laid like scales and topped with golden spires. The interior was also golden, at least until it was destroyed by the fire of 1942, which melted the gold leaf that covered the plaster. Sifting through the rubble of the building in 1945, several kilos of the precious metal were extracted, which were then used to pay for the reconstruction of the temple. Alas, it is no longer made of gold.

Next to it, at 7, Via Sant'Anselmo, stood the small eighteenth-century building of the Jewish Community. After the passing of the racial laws, it grew to include a nursery, an elementary school, a middle school, a high school, and professional training courses. It was filled with children who had been thrown out of the public schools, on top of the children who would never have set foot in the schools of the Kingdom of Italy in the first place. The middle school has since been named after Emanuele Artom, the leader of the *Brigate Giustizia e Liberta*.[1] Artom was captured by the Italian Fascists in 1944 and, after being "unmasked" as a Jew, dragged behind a truck, naked and hunchbacked, and then beaten and killed.

The area leading up to the last and most sumptuous section of the Corso Vittorio and onward toward the Parco Valentino was remarkable principally for its two cafés set across from each other. In the summers before the war, the *dehors*—which is how the Turinese referred to the tables set outside—filled the sidewalks, along with two *Damenorchestern*—orchestras made up entirely of women. The female musicians, dressed in black and wearing heavy makeup, dripped powder and eye shadow as they stood under the harsh sun with their string instruments. In 1939, at the Corso Cinema a few yards away, we saw Germanophilic matinées presented by the German Consulate. As I watched, I too was pierced by the lance of the grim traitor who with his dark helmet resembled a bird of prey; this, despite the constant shuffling of my father who, immune to the creepy sylvan aura—in black and white—impatiently counted the seconds till the end. To him, Fritz Lang was merely Niebelungen-like, silent, German, and free of charge.

In 1941, as a form of civil *mitzvah,* my father went to see *Jud Süß*[2] by Veit Harlan. He went by himself, expecting the worst. On his return to Via Berthollet, his ashen expression told us everything. He held his hands together, his large, feminine fingers intertwined, and said to mother, who tried in vain to calm him: "Eugenia, it is a terrible hatred, I've never seen anything like it, I can't even understand what they are thinking. What will this lead them to? To them, we're worse even than cockroaches!"

The family name of the custodians at school was Fernex. The husband was a Jew from Savoy, and his wife was a Friulian *goy*[*] who flipped the lights on and off on Saturday. They had a son, Bruno, whom I later came across on a plane to Rome; by then, he had become a melancholy trade union rep-

* Goy (plural: goyim) means "non-Jew" or "gentile" in Hebrew. It suggests the notion of "pagan." Not only man rests on Saturdays, but the entire universe; nothing and no one must work, not man, not animals, not machines (or so the observant Jews of Turin liked to imagine).

resentative. He died young of a drawn-out illness, watched over by the benevolent shadows of his mother and father, in the Rest Home of the Turinese Jewish Community. Just before his death, he began writing, and he did so continuously from morning to night, alone. His writing was undecipherable, and no one will ever know what he meant to say or to whom. Bruno's father, Aldo Fernex, the custodian, had been a partisan in one of Garibaldi's brigades in the Val di Lanzo; he died fighting the Nazis during the roundup which took place on January 14, 1945, in Ala di Stura.

The young Fernex couple greeted us happily every morning, smiling at each child as he entered. After the last one arrived, they would scrutinize the street and bolt the door shut, and then disappear into their quarters. Perhaps this private ritual was meant to keep out the cruel world of their enemies?

Beyond the heavy door lay the complex world of the reprobates. The youngest students formed a choir of treble voices; we sang concerts in the gymnasium as well as in the religious ceremonies held in the golden temple. The temple was no longer called the synagogue because anti-Semitism and the surrounding Christian culture had attributed sinister, evil undertones to that word, which comes from Ancient Greek and means "meeting place"; at best, it seemed like a ridiculously old-fashioned term. The origins of the term "temple," like the rabbi's cassocklike garb, lay in the recent decades of assimilation, between 1848 and 1938; this term seemed more reassuring. Thus, like "good Italians," we Jews went to temple on Saturdays just as Christians went to church on Sundays. A plaque by the entrance memorialized the visit of "His Highness, Prince Umberto of Savoy," who had honored the sacred gathering, et cetera . . .

The choir director was Vittore Veneziani, who had been forced to resign his post at La Scala in Milan. He was an elderly man with a hoarse, irascible voice, and he croaked at us like a toad (which he also resembled physically) and banged out the notes on the piano. I was completely tone-deaf but felt protected from his wrath by the crowd of terrified, stiff children around me; in any case, I only moved my lips, never uttering a sound. I could not imagine the impression which we gave as a group, especially as I didn't understand the words we were singing, and also because, immersed in the polyphony of my neighbors, I couldn't hear the group as a whole. But during our concerts, people were moved to tears as they applauded, and the beginning of the subsequent piece was always drowned out by a chorus of sniffles. I only recently found out that among the pieces we sang were: "Va' pensiero sull'ali dorate . . ." from *Nabucco,* "O Signore, dal tetto natio . . ." from *I Lombardi,* and "Dal tuo stellato soglio" from Rossini's *Mosé.* We were brave anti-Fascists without even knowing it.*

In the temple, it was worse: at the end of our choruses, the faithful, forgetting their holy prayers, would break into

* A. Cavaglion, *La scuola ebraica a Torino (The Jewish School in Turin)* (1993).

applause. The tall, gaunt silhouette of Disegni, the head rabbi, would appear, imposing silence in less than paternal terms. And then the *chazan,* Rabbi Peres, carried on with his fruitless but powerful lament: "Elijah, o Prophet Elijah, descend among us with the Messiah, son of David."

My teacher was the terrible Miss Amar, which appropriately means "bitter" in Hebrew. The classroom was oppressive, darkened by a huge blackboard and inadequately illuminated by two grimy panes of frosted glass against the dark Turinese winter sky.

Miss Amar was an armoire from the shoulders to the hips, an armoire in a black dress from which emerged two normal, feminine legs. Her face was handsome and cylindrical like her body, except for the cheeks, which were beginning to feel the pull of gravity. She kept her long, raven-black hair pulled back; like her dress, it was silky and threatening. She had large, black, kind eyes; but kind eyes are an ethnic trait of Jews, just as being tall is a trait of Scandinavians. Even the meanest of Jews has kind eyes. But when Miss Amar was angry, she would knit her brow, her alabaster skin became as pale as porcelain, and her coal-black eyes revealed her true nature: a Japanese warrior-god, sheathed in leather armor and carrying a flag, like the ones painted on vases in the parlors of respectable homes, staring threateningly at the portrait of Ludwig van Beethoven on the opposite wall as he stares arrogantly and symphonically out at the room. Yes, incredible as it may sound, Miss

Amar's handsome face was a cross between Beethoven and a samurai unsheathing his sword.

My mother and father tried in vain to convince me of my teacher's considerable, but invisible, goodness. Today, fifty-five years later, I confirm my judgment: she was heartless. Though I must admit that once, and only once, I glimpsed a flash of humanity in that harsh, unpleasant person.

I was tall for my age, and for that reason Miss Amar made me sit at the back of the class. But I was well behaved, so I didn't have to sit at the desk closest to the hallway, which was reserved for the victims of her torments—she enjoyed slapping people on the nape of the neck, forcing them to stand next to their desk, forcing them to leave the classroom—who typically sat at the back of the class. The few students who had repeated a year were mostly from the poorest families in the community, and they had now been joined by a few Polish children. They were dressed in typical gray orphanage uniforms—long pants and military cloaks—and had to repeat the lower grades because they spoke no Italian.*

I don't want to expostulate on the scant sympathy shown by the "advanced" Turinese Jews toward their cousins from

* I learned only recently, in 1994, that those children were actually Croats, probably saved by the occupying Italian army. But at the time everyone said they were Polish. Perhaps in the minds of the Jews of Turin, Poland began at the entrance to the Postumia caves?

the East. Many Turinese Jews considered them to be responsible for the persecutions the Turinese were now experiencing and feared that their insistent traditions, outlandish habits, poverty, and even their excessive numbers (a problem which, as we all know, was soon solved) would attract trouble to civil places like Italy, where the incredible horrors which occurred on those distant, gloomy plains "are just not possible! It just can't happen!" These are things from our past which today's Jews do not easily admit, but which they nevertheless cannot forget. Our collective memory as western Jews has been illuminated by the glare of the ovens, which swallowed up with equal efficiency the terrified Helot masses and the self-satisfied pillars of the middle class.

The boy who sat next to me was one of these Poles. His name was Jan, and he did not understand a word of what was going on around him; he felt humiliated and never spoke with anyone, but just sat there at his desk, dressed like a street sweeper. He suffered Miss Amar's scoldings without a hint of protest; the only visible reaction was the reddish blotches which would appear on his sweaty face as he stared down at the ground with his straight hair stuck to his forehead, patiently waiting for the outburst to end. Not only was he a martyr, but he was unlucky: one day, during the dictation, he finally recognized a word and dipped his pen in the inkwell to write it down, but he accidentally dipped a large piece of blotting paper in the inkwell, too—why blotting paper always falls into inkwells is a subject of discussion unto itself—which made a giant ink stain on his composition book. Panic-stricken, he slapped the composition book shut and then opened it again very slowly, only to reveal the mess he had made: the *dictée* had become a Rorschach test.

While he was surely thinking to himself in Polish that it was all over for him, the teacher came over to his desk and led him out of the classroom; as his hands were completely covered in ink, she had to take him by the ear. Alone in the hallway, the street sweeper did the only thing he knew, which was to run, in no direction in particular, toward his far-off home, and when the teacher decided it was time to allow him to come back in, he was nowhere to be found. I don't know what happened next, but the Fernex couple went into a state of red alert. In any case, he could not have gone far in that subalpine city, because after much panicked to-ing and fro-ing, the teacher finally came in and said, with tears running down her cheeks: "He's on his way. When he comes in, give him a round of applause." He returned, we clapped, and so did he. That was the only time Miss Amar acted kindly that I know of.

One of the poorest and most wicked children rang in the spring of 1940 by bringing a paper bag to school and—with the conspiratorial smile of a pornographer—letting us peek in to see a swallow he had killed with a Flobert air gun. He too was dragged out of class by the ear, along with his victim in the paper bag, and went home grinning to himself, thus unwittingly emulating the hero of De Amicis's *The*

Heart of a Boy[3] and vindicating Jan. This boy is now a retired diver who worked for many years in the Port of Haifa.

Each year, at Purim—the Jewish Carnival—the school held a solemn ceremony for the students, parents, and patronesses of the school, the latter in full regalia despite their advanced age. These philanthropists were relics of a lost time when the school had been a refuge for the impoverished and a breeding ground for budding rabbis who were respectful of their patrons. Purim is a celebration of one of the Jewish people's many escapes, during which the cruel Haman is hung in effigy and subjected to the taunting of children. Haman is the persecutor who, on the advice of the beautiful Esther, was condemned by the Persian Emperor Ahasuerus: "[T]his is Ahasuerus who reigned, from India even unto Ethiopia, over an hundred and seven and twenty provinces—that in those days, when the king Ahasuerus sat on the throne of his kingdom, which was in Shushan the castle . . ." (Esther 1:1–2.) This Ahasuerus saved the Jews because of his blind love for Esther. He is honored at Purim, which in Hebrew means "chance," or in other words, the probabilistic nature of the universe. While probabilistic events around us were taking a sinister turn, as is their wont, and explosives and flamethrowers were wreaking havoc from the Don River to Tripolitania, the school was holding an awards ceremony in the gymnasium to honor its exceptional students in which scant mention was made of Esther Scroll, which is like a tarot deck containing the Emperor, the Empress, the Lover, Justice, the Wheel of Fortune, the Hangman, the Moon, the Sun, the Stars, the Judgment, the World, the Fool, and Death. It is the only biblical text in which God is never named, and, in fact, there is no God in the tarot deck of cards. God plays his hand, and, some might dare to claim, He cheats.

In the gymnasium, each of us waited expectantly to be called upon to accept, before this assembled group of adults, patrons, and one or two baronesses, an award proclaiming our proven intellectual superiority. When a name was called, the lucky honoree stood up and, in a flurry of applause and approving nods, climbed to the coveted heights of the podium. When Elena Ottolenghi was called, she accepted the *Novissimo Melzi*[4] with the humble, properly embarrassed air of someone who does not feel worthy of the honor but bows to a sense of duty. Red-faced from embarrassment and freckled by nature, she turned toward the applause, communicating with her coquettish eyes and her adorable little face, as she pressed the large book to her as-yet-nonexistent chest, that it was not she but the class who deserved the prize, and that she was merely accepting it in its name. As I suffered an attack of envy, Miss Amar called my name, and two years in a row I was handed an envelope containing twenty-five lire. A blue business envelope.

I was disgusted by the fact that I received a cash prize rather than a book. As an adult, I have come to regret my reaction, but at the time, I folded and unfolded the envelope and returned to my spot, humiliated because the money, which was the fruit of our much-envied Jewish solidarity—“always amongst themselves, never for anyone else”—was the damning evidence that my father was unemployed. I also received applause but not with the same intensity, in large part because I was incapable of showing the slightest gratitude. For fifty years I have tried to explain my envy to Elena Ottolenghi, and she has graciously, tolerantly accepted it, explaining over and over that in reality, the *Novissimo Melzi* belonged to all of us, including me. The struggle which occurred inside my small, envious, and prematurely class-conscious brain was manifest to my mother and father, who praised me, kissed me, and generously brought me to the Fogola Bookstore to cheer me up. In 1940, they spent those twenty-five lire on *Grimm's Fairy Tales,* published by Hoepli, I believe, a book that helped prepare me for my life in the Salesian school a few years later. And in 1941, they bought me the *Novissimo Melzi,* in an edition from which, to my great regret, the illustrated table of “Methods of Torture” had been excluded.

Jan was moved to another class, and Massimo became my deskmate. He was a nice boy and had the peculiar characteristic that everything about him was square: his chin was square, as was his head, and the part in his hair, which was (and still is) at a right angle to his forehead. He wrote in square letters with a small square pen. During dictations, I couldn't help admiring the angular writing as it appeared mechanically on the page, as if created by an automaton. It flowed from a beautiful pen of colored glass, unlike mine, which was made of cheap wood painted to look like marble. My father, though his social standing remained intact, was out of a job, and so I "benefited" from *tzedakah*. In this manner, school supplies became my own personal misfortune.

In the language of the prophets, *tzedakah* means justice, as well as rectitude, honesty, salvation, victory, and good works: the Jews do not simply give to the poor but render justice to them. *Tzedakah* is written above the slots where people insert money for the needy. And it is the name for the subsidy which the community renders to the hungry. The abominable *tzedakah* provided for my school supplies, which were chosen by the rich patronesses, to whom I also attribute the depressing garbage-collector outfits worn by the children from the orphanage. The patronesses distributed shabby wooden pens decorated with marblelike patterns, pens which were made to be chewed on, pens which reeked of economic isolationism. They also gave us wooden pen holders with sliding lids and a little notch for your finger, and thin, drooping notebooks with horrible pictures on the cover, like the one with the Somali *Balilla,*[5] barefoot and smiling, proud of his uniform with its leg-bands: a futurist figure laughing boisterously. My supplies included objects which would be the pride of any present-day collector, but at the time they symbolized only our poverty. My well-to-do schoolmates pulled luxurious pen and pencil holders out of their satchels, made of imitation alligator skin, with three, four, or ten compartments; some of them could be folded into two sections. The *tzedakah* did not supply pen-wipers, so my mother made them for me by lovingly cutting my father's old trousers into little squares of exquisite, if prehistoric, cloth.

The *tzedakah* was humiliating because it put me on the same level with the bewildered Polish children and the murderers of swallows. I was mortified and bitter; perhaps these feelings prepared my unconscious for the larger concepts of revolution, social justice, communism, and class struggle. I must confess that my faith in socialism is inspired more by the pen-cleaners made for me by my mother than by my meager, sleepy readings of Karl Marx.

Massimo, my square friend, was the ideal deskmate: always generous with his blotting paper, a purveyor of silent snickers and hidden jabs of the elbow to punctuate the sillier moments of our lessons, which we suffered in silence. Today, his name is no longer Massimo but Yoram.

In 1978, I was struck with a bout of depression. I realized I needed to do something about it one morning when I could not get out of bed because I felt that my slippers were threatening me; I was afraid they would bite my toes. I decided that the best cure would be to leave my slippers behind and go on a long trip to the Land of our Fathers.

At the precise moment when my plane landed in the Lod airport, heavily—weighed down by my leaden thoughts—a rubber boat was silently gliding along just off of a beach north of Tel Aviv, carrying five or six fedayeen who were armed to the teeth. Along the paths between the dunes, they asked for directions to the Tel Aviv-Haifa highway. And each time their interlocutor helpfully pointed them in the right direction, he received as thanks a few bullets in the head. After having brought an early end to, among others, an American ornithologist who was doing research for the *Christian Science Monitor* on the sunbird, a small bird similar to a hummingbird, they got on a bus, aboard which their political action was interrupted by Israeli soldiers. In the battle that ensued, the bus caught fire, and thirty-seven people, including the crew, were burned alive.

Luckily, I was on a bus going south, toward the Negev Desert, which is warmed by the torrid *Hamsin* wind and is home to the Bedouins, who at the time were still nomadic, sardonic, and friendly. Yoram, my old deskmate, called me at the kibbutz Gvuloth and told me to "wait a few days, until the craziness is over." Israel had just released its Golem, *Tzahal,*[6] blind bearer of justice, its own version of *Frankenstein* (Cinema Nazionale, Turin, 1940).

When Yoram pronounced the craziness to be officially over, I took a bus north, and it was then that my heart was stung for the first time by the beauty of the *Galil,* Galilee, its mountains wet with rain, the emerald homeland of the Mishnah, of the Talmud, of Christ, the Kabbalah, and the Samaritans.*

* The Samaritans were non-Jews who inhabited Galilee and converted in biblical times, convinced that the Holy Name would protect them from wild beasts. Unlucky souls! The Mishnah and the Talmud are

The bus descended into wadi, ascended slopes, and navigated from crest to crest, revealing the gray-green-blue-white light of this enchanted place. The blue flashes of the small lakes at the bottom of valleys corresponded to blue patches in the serene, wet sky, marked by striking white Jewish and Arab villages, friendly but not overly so.

Yoram came to meet me at the barbed wire that defends Bar-Am, beaming his affectionate, rectangular smile. These fences were the mirror reflection of the ones at Auschwitz: in this case, rather than demarcating the area of death and suffering, the barbed wire keeps death and suffering from entering the kibbutz. Massimo, who was still square after all these years of erosion, had become an apple specialist. "You see," he said to me as we walked down a lane in the orchard, "the fundamental issue, the obstacle to the growth of productivity, is the mechanical harvesting of the apples; for it to work, the apples must grow on horizontal branches. We've managed to modify the structure of the trees with hormones." The orchards covered several valleys. It was winter, and the trees were bare; with a start, I realized that the apple trees were square.

It was the evening before Purim, and despite the dearth of young people—they had been carried away by Franken-

commentaries on the Torah and constitute the heart of Jewish thought. The Kabbalah consists of Jewish mysticism in contrast to rabbinical rationalism.

stein to Lebanon—people were preparing the children's speeches and prizes for the following day.

That night I was kept awake by a terrible storm. The lightning and thunder in the blue valleys seemed more the handiwork of the gods on Mount Olympus than of He Whose Name Goes Unspoken. But, along with the crashing water and thunder, I could hear the rumble of the tanks as they returned from the mountains of Lebanon. I dreamt I was hearing the silver Aprilia from 1944 sputtering along on its mix of alcohol and gas, this time climbing up and down the valleys of Galilee in 1978. At dawn, as I was boarding the bus headed back south, my schoolmate handed me a package: "They're 'Haman's ears'; you can celebrate Purim on the bus. It's too bad you won't see the awards ceremony. In any case, our young people from the kibbutz have all returned safely."

In an act of disfigurement unworthy of a civilized country like Persia in 450 B.C., Haman's ears—after he was already dead one hopes—were cut off, and for centuries this deed has been reenacted in the form of pastries which recall, in their sweetness, this casual salvation of the Jewish people. These pastries are neither strange nor exotic, and they have many different names: in Rome they are called *frappe,* in the Veneto *cròstoli,* in Tuscany they are *cenci,* in Piedmont *bugìe,* in Lombardy *chiachiere,* in Emilia *sfrappole.* They are eaten in all of Italy and during Carnival, by everyone, *goyim* or Jew.

%

To be honest, Miss Amar did have one redeeming quality: due to a millennial Jewish tradition which resurfaced as a political response to the racial persecutions, all students of the Colonna e Finzi School were required to be geniuses.

Miss Amar swore that by the New Year we would learn how to read and write: and learn we did. The few unfortunate souls who made it past the New Year without being fully alphabetized were looked upon with disapproval, and their parents, who were severely criticized by the teachers, sought out psychiatrists—unemployed Jews, of course—who could help them save their offspring from this profound source of shame.

One day I saw Signor and Signora Maroni,* who were old friends of my parents, bundled up in heavy, worn overcoats, walking through the corridors with dejected expressions because of their children's test results. They had a son, Umberto, who was a friend of mine, and several other children, among whom there was a girl whose name I can't remember. Perhaps Nilde? The Maronis were short and thickset, and Signor Maroni wore thick glasses with tortoiseshell frames that accentuated his innocent, surprised expression. His wife had a sweet, round, pale face which emerged, with a melancholy smile, from a rabbit-fur collar. Unlike us, they received no help from relatives. And Signor

* Maroni, Pace Augusto, and Scandiani, Bianca. See L. Picciotto Fargion, *Il libro della memoria,* pp. 407, 527.

Maroni was not an out-of-work violinist but a bookkeeper who had once worked for the city and who now had no pension or severance pay. He depended wholly on the bitter *tzedakah.*

The Maronis received not only notebooks but also food subsidies from the *tzedakah.* They did not survive the first period of panic at the very start of the deportations. One morning, in the middle of December 1943, the Fascists (or perhaps the Germans) cut off the Via Carlo Alberto and rounded them up with the others. They had no papers, real or false, and no ration cards. Who knows how long they had gone without food. They were never heard from again. Umberto and his siblings were saved by the priests and now live in Israel, where they have proven that not knowing how to read after barely two months of the first grade means nothing at all.

We young cosmopolitan Jews, contemptible figurines with fake Turinese accents meant to disguise our evident Middle Eastern origins, were able to learn the rules of written Italian through the brusque methods of our teacher, and by Easter of 1940 we could even read and write in Hebrew, though we couldn't understand a word of what we were writing, even with the addition of the vowels.* We learned the prayers. For the rest, not even Miss Amar—the great

* Hebrew is a kind of shorthand; it is written only with the consonants. The vowels are crutches for people, like me, who are still illiterate.

champion of blows to the neck for those who dared to pronounce the silent "e"—not even Miss Amar knew very much. Everyone knows that three diagonal dots are pronounced "u," like the dot placed in the middle of "waw." The two dots were Miss Amar's favorite trap as we sat bent over our books with skullcaps on our heads, index fingers pointing desperately at the undecipherable text, because the sacred language has determined that the "e" with two dots is not always as silent as it should be since on some occasions it must be pronounced in order to avoid terrifying collisions of consonants with dots inside of them. And there are other situations which are even more serious, which I will spare the reader. We learned that when our prayer books said YHWH—and I won't bore you here with the names of the Hebrew consonants—it must be read *Adonai,* which means "My Lord," with the special possessive "ai." For all intents and purposes, *Adonai* means "God," whose name however can never be pronounced. It can be written but not said out loud, but who could pronounce "Y" "H" "W" "H"? Martin Buber has said that one of the reasons that the Name cannot be pronounced is that it was originally accompanied by a gesture, which was an integral part of it, and which had already been forgotten in biblical times*—like the V for victory sign that Churchill used with an embarrassed smile to comfort the inhabitants of London

* Martin Buber, *Mosè (Moses)* (Genoa: Marietti, 1983)

as they dug out the remaining furnishings of their bombed-out homes.

Adonì, like *Adonai,* means "my Lord," but with the modest possessive "i," it comes closer to the Roman *a dottò.*[7] *Adonì* is used in Israel on a day-to-day basis, for example in parking lots.

Once we had conquered the rudiments of reading and writing, our small minds, already overheated, reached the boiling point. The contradictory school plan of study employed a single book which had been designed to create the perfect Fascist and was full of terrible claims about the Jews. Alongside the mandatory program imposed by the authorities of years XVIII, XIX, and XX of the F.E. (Fascist Era), we were taught sacred history. We learned about Abraham, Jacob, Moses, and all the rest, the creators of all sorts of moral laws meant to pacify the unpronounceable tetragram, coming and going, thirsty for justice, never satisfied with ritual or prayers, sometimes benevolent and other times ferocious. At the end of every morning, He would turn his back on His people when the teacher ordered us to stand at attention and "Salute *il Duce!* Salute the King!" We clicked our heels and raised our right arms stiffly in the Fascist salute and then put away our notebooks and were on our way out the door, confused and bewildered by the contradictions in our education and in ourselves: half warlike and menacing, the other half psalmodizing and retrograde, one half despising the other.

The conflict between Nazi-Fascism* and Judaism was painful in and of itself, but for children six, seven, and eight years old, its effect was devastating (move over, Sigmund Freud): I was ashamed of being Jewish because of the things that appeared in *Defense of the Race,* a racist and anti-Semitic newspaper edited by Telesio Interlandi and Giorgio Almirante,[8] but also because of *Marc'Aurelio* and *Bertoldo,* two humorous weekly magazines that featured many large noses in their pages. The "respectable" newspapers also made many unflattering references to us: one morning in 1941 on a bench in the Parco Valentino, I picked up a paper that my father had just finished reading and had to ask him what "Jewish hatred" meant. *Papà* got up from the bench, threw *La Stampa* into the trash, and stood before me trembling with emotion, pointing toward heaven with one hand and at my small chest with the other: "It means that even they in their infamy can read in our faces a sign of the merciless justice which awaits them, all of them. That is 'Jewish hatred,' and you should be proud of it." By "them," he did not mean only Fascists but all Italians, including the little boys and girls who teased us in the park. In this case, my father did not call on the Supreme Being with the unpronounceable tetragram but with more informal invocations, which did much to diminish the dramatic effect of his prophecy.

* Today this word is the subject of much discussion because of the many, and significant, differences that existed between National Socialism and Fascism. But I, as a child, often saw the two as one and the same.

That day in the park something irreversible happened in me. The words "Jewish hatred," my father's rushed but effective explanation, and the anger which I saw in him, effectively swept away the serenity of childhood, as far as serenity and childhood exist. My father appeared to me at that moment completely different from how I had imagined him until then: he was angry at the whole world. For years he had seen his life destroyed by the humiliation, indifference, and moral sloth of the people around him, and by the delirious notions which everyone seemed ready to accept. He knew that, by the time the insanity eventually disappeared back into the black hole of the minds which had conceived it, he would be an old man and finished as an artist. My father was a victim who dreamed of revenge but who, once the horror was ended, opted for justice for his own moral health, becoming one with the tragedy which had marked his life. That is how I remember him after that day at the Parco Valentino, a kind of Ivan from *The Brothers Karamazov* (ed. Barion, 1929).

I am not capable of judging whether revelatory moments truly exist or whether they are simply a nineteenth-century literary expedient. When one reads Balzac or Dostoyevsky, it is clear that they employed this literary trick in order to satisfy the requirements of publication by installment. But on the other hand, our lives too are lived in installments and form a story that we make up as we go along.

In any case, from that morning I was ashamed of being Italian, in addition to being ashamed of being Jewish. When

I walked to school on Sundays I was ashamed of myself and of my schoolbag with its meager contents, and I tried to hide it under my coat. I was convinced that passersby looked at me with disgust and contempt: "Look at that! A Jewish boy who goes to school on Sundays! And look at those ugly pencils he's carrying!"

But as there is no limit to misery, the Colonna e Finzi School (and our souls) held hidden even deeper conflicts that decades of assimilation had not been able to erase.

Papà came from a poor background. There had never been a ghetto in Livorno, but in the mid-nineteenth century, the city had received a wave of Jewish immigrants from the Arab Mediterranean countries. My father and his family belonged to the first generation of Italians from that wave of "Arabicized," Sephardic Jews. My grandfather spoke Spanish and Ladino, a Spanish-Hebrew dialect. He used to sing to me:

'Aina lo caprecico
che me compro me pare in plaza
por dos levanim . . .[9]

This nursery rhyme about a goat, which is sung in every language and dialect in the Jewish world, hides a Dantesque warning under its humorous exterior—*"Parva favilla gran fiamma seconda"* ("a small spark brings a large flame")—as well as the Jewish concept of the unity and numerability of the world. The goat knocks over some wine, is eaten by a wolf, who in turn is killed by a hunter, and so on until God himself intervenes and swiftly brings an end to the chaos. The modern version of this fable is represented by mathematical chaos theory and is called "the butterfly effect": under certain circumstances, it is enough for a butterfly to flutter its wings in the Amazonian jungle to touch off a sequence of events which will eventually lead to the destruction of Louisiana, South Carolina, and Texas by a hurricane. And so it is that my grandfather put me to sleep by acquainting me with the chaos of reality.

Pisa; the smallpox epidemic; Turin in 1901; elementary school to the third grade; the violin imposed by grandmother Ottavia as the only means to a brighter future; the Conservatory: these were my father's cultural building blocks. To these one must add a mystical and sentimental Judaism, the likes of which can only be found today in the Rome Ghetto, and even there not in its original form, because Israel has now existed for over half a century.

My father, who did not know a word of Hebrew and who only erratically and subjectively followed Judaism's rigid prescriptions on daily life, possessed a faith greater than I have ever had. His personality was rounded out by his success as a musician, which from his youth had given him access to the upper strata of Italian society; by his ability to understand the nuances of the culture that surrounded him; and by his extensive if haphazard reading. He was a large, elegant man who could swing from the most loving kindness, which I remember well, to the greatest cruelty, which I have forgotten. In some ways, he was like a beautiful woman who employs her physical graces to attain fame and fortune and then, in her later years, opens a cultural "salon." He defined himself proudly as an autodidact and asked me to explain everything I knew about philosophy. He was embarrassed that at the age of seventeen I still read Mandrake comics and would explain to the confused bookseller: "He's not as dumb as he looks, you know, he reads Spinoza and understands it better than you or I ever could!" He would affirm with a perhaps overly concise theosophism, "All wisdom comes from the Orient," but until the end remained completely Italian. After the war, he combined anti-Zionism with a great and childish enthusiasm for the dazzling successes of the *Haganah.** He died before he could understand that, to me, Mandrake the hypnotizer and Spinoza the crafter of lenses were two sides of the same coin.

My mother did not know Hebrew either; she was an atheist and a freethinker, with a slight, if skeptical, tendency toward spiritualism. Her family was Ashkenazi, Jews from the Rhineland who founded ancient communities in Italy

* The Jewish commandoes who won the 1948 War of Independence. My relation with my father was mediated by our readings of the daily papers. We argued often, and bitterly, over my Zionism, but one day on the tram, in 1949, he handed me *La Stampa* with his index finger pointed at the last words of an article ". . . and Israel's total victory is now an incontrovertible fact." And then he studied my face with a satisfied air as he thought to himself: "Look how happy he is, the fool!"

and conserved their original rites. They had settled in Verona, and their last name was, appropriately, Tedeschi, or "German"; they were highly educated but not especially well off. Her father, a cultivated man who had completed the classical course, had been forced to end his military career because he fought one too many duels in defense of Captain Dreyfus; he became a respected and successful entrepreneur in the painting business. He happily and confidently embraced his daughter's marriage to an artist of humble and Sephardic origins. And he was right to, because *mamma* and *papà* loved each other deeply and truly in those terrible years they experienced together: *papà,* who was elegant and good-looking, felt the deepest deference to and devotion for his not beautiful but wise companion. *Mamma*'s bible consisted of three prophets: Émile Zola, Anatole France, and, in her more optimistic moments, Jules Verne. And she argued—and took offense at my scorn of the idea—that in Pompeii, the ashes of Vesuvius had trapped not only the bodies but also the souls of the inhabitants. She was a convinced positivist, finding evidence of the soul in the material world, for example, in Hertzian waves and in radioactivity. How she would have embraced the recent studies of the brain which go beyond psychoanalysis: cognitive science, the discovery of neural networks! Her faith in progress expressed itself in her tales of eighteenth-century catastrophes, which, for her, along with family memories, took the place of fables: she told us over and over about the crossing of the Berezina, the plagues of London and Milan, and the sinking of the Medusa. In fact, when I finally saw the painting by Géricault in the Louvre, I had an intense feeling of déjà vu.

Mamma and *papà* had one thing in common with Miss Amar: they were intensely moralistic, especially about sex.

In Turin, the Jewish population hardly ever followed the usual dietary prescriptions—in my house, ham could be consumed any day but Saturday—and also adopted all of the Catholic, middle-class sexual taboos. A Judeo-Turinese sexual ethic had been created in which silence was the absolute, universal, and eternal rule. In the fall of 1943, a young man asked my cousin Pucci to run away with him to Switzerland; my mother and Pucci's mother, Aunt Rosetta, both declared the scheme "unseemly," and the matter ended there, or rather at Auschwitz.*

Left to my own devices, and already confused by the events going on around me, I was convinced that Jews were born circumcised and *goyim* were not, while the Greeks, like Laocoön and his sons, were born with strange members shaped like fig leaves, which I studied in reproductions, worried by what other possible variations might exist in nature. Who knew? Perhaps the natives of New Guinea had it in the shape of . . . colored feathers? I thought that this was the racial diversity that everyone talked about so much in those years, and the source of my disgrace, given that

* Tedeschi, Rosetta Rimini, and Tedeschi, Lidia (known as Pucci). See L. Picciotto Fargion, *Il libro della memoria,* pp. 504, 581.

in every other way I appeared to be identical to other children. My mother's reticent and evasive responses complicated rather than clarified this mystery of the plurality of sexual organs.

When the time came to explain to our class what exactly the sign of the pact between Abraham and God was which the males of the Chosen People carry in their flesh, poor Miss Amar was, as a Turinese, visibly flustered. She was so uncomfortable that when Giorgino asked her where *exactly* this sign was to be found, she answered brusquely and unpleasantly: "In the lower back." The teacher's authority and my unreflective nature, confused by the fig leaves, kept me from understanding that the foreskin of which I had been deprived was, in fact, the tangible sign of the love that God had for his people, who were ex-Bedouins.

As luck would have it, a little boy I often played with at the park was the natural son of Pitigrilli, the author of such risqué books as *Dolico Blonde* and *Luxurious Beasts,* and an OVRA spy.[10] This child, who, like me, was eight or nine years old, was living proof of the power of DNA: he was perfidious, insinuating, pornographic, fascist, and anti-Semitic. Just like his father. Thin, pale, neurotic, and elegant, he asked me one day, with a snakelike air, staring with his green eyes into my own and shaking his bifurcated tongue, "Do you know where you people are circumcised?" And I answered, "Of course I know. In the lower back." He whispered into my ear, "Stupid, they cut your thing. That's what they do to you people." And he went off snickering to himself, happy to have dealt me a knife to the sex, and to the heart. I think his treacherous intention was to make me even more ashamed of being Jewish, but instead he revealed to me that my vivid intelligence coexisted with enormous lacunae of ignorance and disingenuousness, and that Miss Amar was not only cruel and unpleasant but a liar.

Obviously, anti-Fascism did not exist in the school. We were constantly watched, and our condition spoke for itself. Even so, I did manage to decipher some small signs of dissatisfaction. When Miss Amar was encouraged—or, rather, forced; one should never let antipathy cloud one's judgment—by the Inspector of the "Raineri" public school to tell her students to bring in wool for the Italian soldiers on the Russian front, *mamma* extracted a tiny matted clump of wool the size of a thumbnail from the mattress out of which she had already made itchy woolen socks, undershirts worse than hair shirts, and gloves which developed holes before one even tried them on. As she muttered disconnected phrases to herself ("I'll give them wool for the Russian front, all right . . ."), she teased the clump hair by hair until it reached the dimensions of a giant sheep. She then wrapped it in a large sheet of wax paper, amid our snickers. The following morning I walked slowly and nervously to school, afraid that the slightest breeze might blow away the immense package and its buoyant contents.

Another time, we were assigned a composition, to write at home, entitled "The cover of my textbook." The Futurist cover showed a happy *Balilla* with an orange face and greenish hands holding a book and a gun up toward the sky. *Papà* exclaimed, "Don't worry. Tonight, Mother and I will write your composition for you." Their two heads leaned toward each other, discussing excitedly. "And add this . . . and say this as well . . . and, yes, that's a good one! But careful, don't go too far!" I don't remember exactly what they wrote, but when I copied it out in my unsteady hand it was something about how, as a Jew, I could never be a *Balilla,* and so I couldn't hold up my book to the sky, or my gun, or laugh as he did. I remember the last sentence, which read: "What a shame!!! It's really too bad!!! I am so sad, it makes me want to cry."

One morning, sometime around Passover of 1942, our teacher excitably announced an unexpected visit from the head rabbi. He was almost six-foot-six and wore a black frock coat, as some old-fashioned doctors still did at the time, with a white tie and a starched collar. Rabbi Disegni had bony hands and a long face adorned with almost invisible white fuzz, and he wore a Homburg which obscured sad, gray eyes that seemed to foretell a great tragedy. The Colonna e Finzi School was about to close, after my ten trimesters there; after the bombs, it experienced long years of silence and abandonment. The rabbi, with his slouching gait and his hat, seemed more like a judge from the far West than a Turinese prelate; he did not sit at the front of the class but on a chair among us as we stood or sat around him in reverent silence. He was no longer distant and imperious as when he had sat on the high chair in the golden temple; he smiled serenely, as if already infused with a prophecy. In a clear voice, he read the verses of Moses' hymn after the crossing of the Red Sea. He read in Hebrew and then translated into Italian, with the magical rhythm, the onomatopoeia, the sounds of war and the cries of triumph, the cadence of the unexpected victory.*

I will sing unto YHWH, for he hath triumphed
gloriously:
The horse and his rider hath he thrown into the
sea [. . .]**
YHWH is a man of war: YHWH is his name.
Pharaoh's chariots and his host hath he cast into
the sea: [. . .]

* Exodus, 15; M. Buber, *Mosè.* I have altered the translation by substituting the tetragram YHWH in the places where he read *Adonai.* I have done so in order to give the reader an idea, even if vague, of the original style. It would be best to read *Adonai* or Lord each time that YHWH appears in the text. In this way, the reader can accomplish two aims: first, the rhythm of the hymn will not seem uneven or jagged, and second, the reader will not run the risk of taking God's name in vain (Third Commandment).

** *Sūs ve'rokhvo rama ba'yam . . .* (The horse and his rider hath he thrown into the sea). I hope that even the most uninitiated reader of verses of this type will be able to hear the thumping of the tambourines, the muffled steps in the sand, the jingle of bells tied around ankles, the harsh sound of female voices, the pauses filled with gestures of open palms held high, and the obsessive expression of the inexhaustible desire for tribal justice. All of this in the limitless yellow of the desert.

The depths have covered them: they sank into the
bottom as a stone.
Thy right hand, YHWH, is become glorious in power:
Thy right hand, YHWH, hath dashed in pieces the
enemy [. . .]
The enemy said, [. . .] I will draw my sword, my hand
shall destroy them.
Thou didst blow with thy wind, the sea covered them:
They sank as lead in the mighty waters.
Who is like unto thee, YHWH, among the gods? [. . .]
Thou stretchedst out thy right hand, the earth
swallowed them [. . . .]
And Miriam the prophetess, the sister of Aaron, took
a timbrel in her hand;
And all the women went out after her with timbrels
and with dances.
And Miriam answered them, Sing ye to YHWH, for
he hath triumphed gloriously;
The horse and his rider hath he thrown into the sea.

In 1938, I was obliged by law to become a Jew, but in 1945, I saw it; I saw the right hand of the God of armies, the God of history, strike down the horse and his rider.

8 ※ Prison

*Vexilla regis prodeunt inferni.** The Salesian book of psalms melted the frost, the frost inside of us, the frost produced by the parade of SS entering Costigliole d'Asti in the first days of November 1943. Fifty or a hundred or more took part in this "friendly" entrance, in compact formation, unarmed and bareheaded, their fine, blond hair caressed by the autumn breeze (it was not cut short and was combed back and

* "The banners of the king of Hell come forth." This is the opening line of the 34th Canto of Dante's *Inferno.* In the icy regions of Cocito, Dante shivers in the wind of Lucifer's wings, and he is afraid. In the eternal night of parody, he describes this dark world with a caricature of a processional hymn by Venantius Fortunatus, *Vexilla regis prodeunt,* adding the genitive *inferni.*

wet, parted with a straight line from the brow to the back of the head); as they marched, they sang the National Socialist hymn, *Horst Wessel Lied,* in their silvery German voices. It was a beer-hall song and conjured images of white foam on bluish lips; perhaps they thought the winemakers of Asti might prefer it to *Deutschland über alles?* Their glassy (or icy) eyes stared ahead at the red flag with the hooked cross. What Glockenspiel had these automatons emerged from, and why hadn't Death cut them down with her scythe?

Around the Christmas holidays of 1943, Monsignor Cavasin, the director of the school in Cavaglià, approached me in the frigid courtyard as I sat by myself watching the "falcon game": one of the assistants would run around the courtyard, arms raised and cassock billowing, playing the falcon, and try to catch one of the one hundred thirty-two doves who ran around him. I was number one hundred thirty-one, Roberto number one hundred thirty-two, and these numbers were fast becoming our official nicknames. The nuns cut pieces of white ribbon marked with red numbers and sewed them onto our underwear, socks, shirts, and trousers. There were one hundred thirty-two children in the school that winter, and Roberto and I had arrived on December 2nd, after the school year had already started. Number one hundred thirty-three came later; he was Monticone, from Turin, and he had lost both of his parents in a bombing raid. He had been dug out of the debris, his bones broken, several days later. His eyes shining from excitement, he would describe how "the bricks were stuck between my legs and made 'it' swell up till it was big as a horse's, and all black." He would let go of his crutches and show us the size with his arms which were not fully healed, looking around at us and basking in our envy. Number one hundred thirty-four came in February or March; his name was Teodoro Paschi, or rather Theo Pasch. He was from Berlin, and you could tell.

In the game, when the falcon catches a dove, he in turn becomes a dove and the dove becomes the falcon, and the game continues ad infinitum against the grayish-pink background, our breath tracing long streaks in the cold air, like Dante-esque transmutations in a winter scene by Bruegel.

"Why don't you play with the others?" Perhaps the monsignor was worried by my appearance: already gaunt by nature, I had not shown any physical improvement in the last few months. "Because my feet hurt." He took me to the nurse, Ernesto, a skinny, pale young man with graying hair. Perhaps he wasn't so young, but he wore sporty clothes, played and joked with us, and was sweet and affectionate. He had to cut the boots—the famous boots bought on December first—off of my feet, only to discover that my chilblains had burst and soaked the mattress-wool socks my mother had made for me with blood and pus, making the wool stick to my toes and my toes to each other. He joked, "What's this?! Let's see what we have here," and began to attend to my frozen feet with scissors, hot water, and hydrogen peroxide. Once he had bandaged each individual, medicated toe, he contemplated his work and handed me a pair of oversize but warm clogs. He treated me patiently and with care, without hurting me or making me feel embarrassed, singing to himself and distracting me with funny stories. He cured me of my painful condition, and in the Christmas pageant he played Mephistopheles: he appeared and disappeared, darting in and out of a flaming trap door —the flames produced by a flash bulb—in red tights, with two black fabric horns dangling from his *mefisto.*

When Christmas came, the ruddy-cheeked farm children returned to their prosperous dairy farms—during the war, the farmers who managed to survive became rich—and twenty or so pupils were left behind at the school. These were the ones whose homes had been bombed, the feeble-minded, the orphans, the boys whose relatives remained beyond the Gothic Line, and the Jews. We were the fortunate beneficiaries of the Christmas spirit: no Mass at six in the morning, lunch and dinner, consisting of rice and milk, with the priests in their warm dining room, and a magic lantern show put on by Maestro Ferrara in the dormitory.

Maestro Ferrara's boots had a strange feature: instead of folding once at the toes like most people's, they formed three or four creases, ending at an upturned point. How many metatarsals did his feet contain? He wore heavy woolen black trousers cut short enough to reveal these strange appendages. Looking up from his feet, before reaching his red, pumpkin-like nose, one saw a heavyset torso with no visible neck, to which a large, doltish head was attached, covered with gray hair the texture of steel wool, à la Umberto I. Most revealing was the shaved nape of his neck: it spoke volumes about his uncompromising lay Catholicism, his absolute beliefs, and his total absence of imagination. He had almost no forehead and a broad face frozen in a sarcastic expression and traced with a latticework of red capillaries produced by the Barbera wine which he consumed in large quantities. His falsely jovial air belied a stubborn nature, his devotion to the Madonna, and his cruel sarcasm, which was communicated only by his small, piglike eyes; he was the terror of the fifth-grade class. His preferred form of punishment was forcing the offender to kneel with his arms held out until he could no longer withstand the pain and time came to a standstill. Out of sheer sadism, he would place grains of rice under the boy's knees. His students responded to his sadism with hatred, incurable ignorance, blank stares, and total indifference to his humiliations, even to his blows. I was immune to his corrective measures because I was well behaved and worked hard, having learned my lesson from the terrible Miss Amar, and because my physical state must have made him afraid he might do me serious harm. Maestro Ferrara's cruelty verged upon, but never reached, the lower echelons of evil: he was a drunk, a fervent Catholic, a *Canavesian,* and an elementary school teacher, no more, no less.

The spirit of Christian generosity reached its apex on Christmas Eve when, in order to keep us awake for Midnight Mass, the nurse entertained us for two or three hours. First, he impersonated a devil with horns and then a gluttonous farmer:

Today, I went down to the market
And bought myself a ton of chocolate,
And little by little, a ton I ate,
And now, by God, my belly aches!!

He rubbed the large stomach, fashioned out of a cushion which had been stuffed into the gardener's trousers. And then, dressed in a gray smock and a beret which made his ears stick out, he played a village charlatan singing the praises of an invincible flea powder:

Gather close, my friends,
I'll show and you'll see,
This powder's the thing, does the trick one-two-three!
First take some and dab where the flea's had his fill,
Then you grab him 'tween two fingers,
And squeeze till he's killed!
I guarantee he'll not bother you ever again,
Satisfaction guaranteed, I promise, Amen!

After the show, and several encores, we left the dusty little theater and walked through courtyard after courtyard, singing as loudly as we could:

You desce-end from the stars,
O Ki-ing of the heavens,
And co-ome into a grotto . . .

It was freezing in the white church where Mass was held.

Epiphany was the end of the holidays and also the end of the holiday spirit, and school resumed. Again, we ate our scarce, cold food in the freezing dining hall in silence to avoid being hit on the head for talking, stealing, pushing, or spilling. Again, we were constantly reminded of the need to renounce the "pleasures of this world" and opt for eternal life.

Toward the end of January or the beginning of February, two terrible realities hit me with equal force: my parents no longer came to visit, and the days were passing, inexorably. After the ten-o'clock bell every Thursday morning, I ran down to wait for *mamma* and *papà* under the cantilever roof of the main entrance, watched over by the Madonna in her blue dress and by Saint John Bosco[1] who was also polychrome and surrounded by little praying children, their pink faces turned toward heaven. I ran down and waited, but they didn't come and they didn't come. Time passed relentlessly, echoed by the services at the school and the sun's journey from the winter's solstice—window by window, day after day—toward the spring equinox. When it was time for our evening prayers, I recited what I remembered of the *Shema,** blending it into the chorus of Ave

* "Hear, O Israel, the Lord our God, the Lord is One . . ." Perhaps this is why I still hear this prayer as a whisper rather than as a proclamation?

Marias; I was becoming more and more Catholic in outward aspect—and even in more intimate ways—but remained Jewish in some even darker, more secret place. The skylights of the roofed-in courtyard went from total darkness to an ever-lighter blue in only a few weeks. The cold refused to loosen its grip—this reassured me somewhat—but the sky, which was now a light gray at six in the morning, whispered to me, "They haven't come in a long time. They will never come again," and on the following Thursday I would again patiently wait after the bell. The sadness grew from week to week. It was a terrible, tearing sadness, but it was not rooted in fear; and it was no longer as searing as on the night of December first, 1943, the night that my parents disappeared, never to return—for the first time—all because of me.

On that night, my eternal love was cut by the blade of my unforgivable guilt and disappeared, never to return again; in February, March, and perhaps April of 1944, those two beloved shadows slowly faded in the glare of the sun which now pitilessly showered over nature. In order to taste this particular form of suffering, I suggest listening to the first of Gustav Mahler's *Kindertotenlieder,* in which a mother sings of how she does not want the day to come because her child has died in the night, and of how the indifferent sun returns to shine on a world without meaning for all eternity. In this case, the child who had died was me.

And so I waited, every Thursday for three or four months, until one Thursday in April when they returned. But had they really returned? Was it really them? And how many more Thursdays would it have been until I forgot them?

"The number 13 tram was arriving at the Via Cernaia stop in front of the *carabinieri* station. I was waiting there with your mother," *papà* told us later, "when a short man with a three-day-old beard took me by the arm. He was drunk. Your mother was already on the tram, and, unfortunately, she got off because she saw what was going on. The driver was ringing the bell impatiently. The drunk man took me by the arm, and your mother saw what was happening and got off the tram. I told her to go ahead, but the tram left without her. The strange man held on to the arm of my jacket and *mamma* asked him, 'What do you want from us?' I tried to shake him off, but he held on, he wouldn't let go, and he said, 'I know you're Jews, you're Jews, and you should be in a concentration camp. You are the reason they are bombing Turin: you send messages to the Brits with your lights. Everyone else is killed, but not your kind. My mother is dead, and you killed her, and now you're going to pay! You killed my mother, and now you're going to go to a concentration camp. You should have thought twice before you called the Brits.' He spoke into my face, and I could smell the wine on his breath. He had been following us for five days, and, finally, he had built his courage up with drink. *Mamma* and I began to cry, we begged him, but he wouldn't listen and kept holding onto my sleeve and saying, 'You made them kill my mother, and now you'll pay!' We showed him a picture of the two of you, the one I always keep in my wallet, from when we went to the beach at Finalmarina, but he wouldn't even look at it.* He took your mother by the sleeve and dragged us into UNPA headquarters.[2] He was in the anti-aircraft brigade, and so he took us there."

The commander there brushed him off and snapped at him when he realized the terrible thing that he had done, as my parents quivered. "Idiot! Fool! Why did you bring them here? What do they have to do with us? Forget them!" he shouted, but the man kept saying, over and over, "They're Jews, and I've brought them in, now send them to the concentration camp!"

%

The "mild" Italian racial laws, combined with the suffering of the war and the revival of age-old superstitions, had created their desired effect: to most people, the Jews had become monsters. They thought that if the Jews disappeared, the war, the madness, and the devastation, of which the Jews were the infernal authors, would come to an end. I had the good fortune of catching a glimpse of Buffarini Guidi, the Minister of the Interior of the Republic of Salò, at the Cinema Corso in Turin. In the summer of 1945, the theater showed a newsreel of his death by shooting squad. This man was the author of the November 1943 pamphlet which

* The last time we had gone to the beach was in 1938, because after that the racial laws prohibited Jews from vacationing on the coast, in the mountains, and in thermal spas. The photo on the cover of this book is the one my father had in his wallet at the time of his arrest.

declared that all Jews were enemies of the state and were to be sent to concentration camps. And at the moment of his death, he had the benefit of alcohol and Lepetit: he had to be dragged, at dawn, trembling, his legs resisting, his eyes swollen shut from drink, fear, and bitterness. He allowed his flaccid, overweight body to be tied to a chair, his head flopping to one side and his tongue hanging out of his mouth. And despite all of this, he was not the worst. Giovanni Preziosi[3] and his lovely wife, who had dedicated their lives first to hatred of, and then to the extermination of, the Jews—and who had railed against Guidi, Alessandro Pavolini,[4] and even Mussolini for being (just imagine) protectors of the Jews—killed themselves before the slow hand of justice could give them the death they deserved. Today, Buffarini Guidi has been forgotten, while the paranoid Preziosi is sometimes described in the cultural pages as a "philosopher."

%

On that January day in 1944, no one was able to reason with the half-crazed militiaman, and, in the end, the commander, moved more by fear than by his sense of duty, called police headquarters.

Two officers arrived out of breath a few minutes later. They were Pandoli—a commander—and a regular police officer. They gave the commander of the UNPA a piece of their mind: "You know you're not supposed to call us, but here we are, and now they'll have to come with us. The hero who brought them in can come later to pick up his five lire reward. In fact, take ten! You brought in two of them. Good man! You two, get up and come with us." *Mamma* felt ill and collapsed to the ground. It was her collapse—but too late!—that brought the UNPA militiaman to his senses (the booze was wearing off) and made him realize that Buffarini Guidi and the others were simply gorging themselves on violence in their last days. He started to sob and ask for forgiveness. Because of this, and because his mother had been killed by the bombs, and because he never collected his reward, he was not sought out in 1945, in the days of long-awaited revenge. And that is also why *mamma* and *papà* told me his name but asked me never to repeat it; and I remember it, but I will not repeat it.

I respect, even if I cannot completely share, the odd belief of two people who lived through those terrible times and who accepted the troubling innocence of that desperate, murderous drunkard. After killing his brother, Cain was condemned to *live:* "Therefore whosoever slayeth Cain, vengeance shall be taken on him sevenfold." And he was "the father of such as dwell in tents, and of such as have cattle . . . of all such as handle the harp and organ." (Gen. 4:15–21.)

I don't know if *mamma* and *papà* were thinking of Cain —who in their eyes was innocent because he was not the inventor of death—but they were thinking as Jews. Just as they were thinking as Jews when they asked me to observe their silence of the just. After April 25, 1945, the UNPA militiaman fled, but no one followed or sought him out.

Perhaps he thought that his victims had never returned, and that he was safe from their vengeance and so could return to normal life. It is unlikely that he did not come to know sooner or later that those whom he believed dead were in fact living, working, raising their family, and that they had paid no mind to him or his destiny. "Could they have forgotten me?"

While a Victor-Hugoian tempest brewed in the consciousness of the informer, around him the outrage over the Shoah was growing.

Just after the end of the war, the dimensions of the project of extermination of the Jews became apparent, but proximity to the conflict and to the terrible events many people had experienced made it impossible to fully comprehend its most horrifying characteristics: the gratuity of the killing, the attention to detail of its authors, their complete absence of rage or fury, the intentional nature of every act. In addition, there was the sheer accumulation of the National Socialists' crimes: they had exterminated Gypsies and homosexuals; they had begun eliminating the mentally deranged; they had committed massacres in the civilian population. They had shot to death sailors from the ships that they had sunk as the sailors swam toward the German ships, sure of assistance in accordance with a centuries-old maritime tradition. They had exterminated their Soviet prisoners of war. But historical research confirms that the extermination of the Jews and the Gypsies is the lowest point ever reached by the human race. In the late fifties, this research led to a belated consciousness, and the Shoah became a symbol, the single unifying symbol, of the limitless blame of Nazi-Fascism.

The ex-militiaman must have felt as if his innocent victims had died but were still living, ignoring him as if nothing had happened at all, or worse, as if they had never returned. It is likely, or even certain, that in the course of his life he realized that the act of *not* taking revenge while not forgiving was in itself a condemnation: he carried in him an obscene, irremovable stain. And if his victims pronounced his name, which they might do at any moment, if they spoke to others of his infamy . . . Perhaps the world already knew of his crime, and, like Cain, he would no longer be able to hide the stain inside of him but would carry a mark on his forehead for all to see. Perhaps he carried it already, and they only pretended not to see it. In short, my parents' silence turned him into a man who could not look at his face in the mirror.

Justice was done. Of this I am almost convinced. Almost.

During the long walk to police headquarters, the officers assured my parents that the matter would be resolved quickly, that they shouldn't worry, and that it was simply a question of necessary bureaucratic practice: "These useless papers are our curse!" As soon as they arrived at Corso Vinzaglio, Pandoli brought them to the office of the police chief, who I believe was called Cipullo: "He's a Fascist, but he's not a bad person, and he's honest. Just talk to him, talk to him, and it'll be all right." Pandoli was not completely in good faith, even if he had already decided to do everything he could to help my parents. His mind was clouded with conflicting thoughts, more about the chief of police than about my parents. Pandoli was Neapolitan, anti-Fascist, short, elegant, and expansive, with slicked-back hair. I met him after the war, and he told me the whole story of their capture in his office. This was after my father had subjected him to a flurry of hugs and kisses—as he did with all the other Christians who had shown compassion and a sense of justice, all too rare at the time—on one of our regular visits.

The Turin police chief invited them to sit down and, while he filled out paperwork, listened to them distractedly without commenting or looking up, as they protested their honesty, patriotism, and lack of ill intent. My mother told him of her five brothers who had fought in the First World War, and of Uncle Roberto's medal in memoriam. *Papà* told him that he was a musician in an orchestra, a corporal on the Kras, sapper, pontooneer, decorated soldier, violinist, violist, father of two, faithful to his flag, friend of Brandimarte,* and a respectful, humble, and innocent man. As they rambled on, the police chief rang a bell; an officer ap-

* A member of a Fascist action squad from 1919 to 1922. He was, in fact, a friend of my father's, and he was not anti-Semitic, and, after the war, when he was an old man, he dressed like a character from the Risorgimento. He did not seem like the killer of unionists he had once been. He did not adhere to the Republic of Salò, but neither did he help anyone.

peared, so quickly that he must have been waiting behind the door the whole time. He placed a piece of paper on the table. Pandoli frowned. When the police chief decided that my parents had gone on long enough, and Mother was on the verge of upgrading her brother's medal from a Bronze Star to a Gold Star ("fallen heroically in the second battle of Montello"), he interrupted them with a sly smile and a simple gesture and said calmly, as if he were finishing their story, "But you wanted this war, and now you must pay for it," and he signed the paper, a warrant for their arrest.

Cipullo could not have known as he signed that piece of paper that he was also signing his own death warrant in the presence of the stone-faced Neapolitan. In 1945, Pandoli, the elegant, friendly policeman, told me in his office, bathed in the greenish light filtered through the trees on Corso Vinzaglio, "You listen to me, 'cause this is how it happened. I knew some people were planning an ambush on the Turin-Milan highway, and we were supposed to tell them when the chief left the station and what kind of car he was driving, and 'they' would be waiting for him. But I meant what I said when I took your parents to talk to him. I thought it was right to kill him, but I was upset by it, because he was my boss, and I was convinced that he was a good man even though he was a Fascist. But at the moment your father saw me frown—he doesn't miss a beat, that one!" he said, pinching my father's cheek, "at that moment all my doubts disappeared and I thought, 'This bastard has to go. He's a dead man.'" In an often-reproduced photograph, you can see several anti-Fascists dangling from a highway overpass: this was the reprisal for the attack in which, by his own hand, the Turin chief of police perished.

My parents were separated at the entrance of the Nuove Prison, which sits across from the even-more-sinister Turin slaughterhouse. *Papà*'s belt was taken, and he was led in to his cell, holding up his trousers with his left hand: the scarcities of the war had so thinned him, his trousers could not stay up on their own. His cell was inhabited by a young prisoner who stood up deferentially when he saw the desperate appearance of this man in his fifties holding up his trousers with his hand. With all the dignity he could muster, *papà* introduced himself: "Mario Zargani, musician, it's a pleasure to meet you." And his cellmate responded, "The pleasure is all mine, professor. Ugo Lini, burglar," and held out his right hand. As he did so, he let go of his trousers, which fell around his ankles. This humorous greeting turned a painful beginning into a sort of jest and made it clear to my father that his burglar cellmate was a good man, and a joker. On many mornings, his cellmate consoled him as he moaned and tore his hair out when he heard the whistle of the train to Cavaglià: "I'll never see my little ones again!" As he tore his hair out, I was standing at the station at school, dreading the approach of the spring equinox.

Though they did not know it at the time, Pandoli had already helped my parents by having them put in the disagreeable but relatively safe wing reserved for common criminals. Death was just beyond the wall in the political wing, under the control of the SS. The other side was lorded over by Schmid from his office in the Albergo Nazionale on the small Piazza Delle Due Chiese; he executed the orders he received from Berlin methodically and scrupulously.

Mamma always spoke with sympathy of her cellmates. Her friends were an unwed mother who was awaiting trial for having, in the spirit of the times, gassed her baby by placing it on the stove and covering it with a large pot; a smuggler; and a lost soul who worked the streets without the olive-green official police permit issued to prostitutes.

The only person who could calm my mother was Suor Giuseppina, the mother superior of the prison, and she did so by treating her, in good Catholic spirit, exactly in the same way she did the other inmates, except for a special compassion which she reserved for my mother during those long months. At least so my mother suspected.

Later, from April 25th to the first days of May of the only miraculous year of my life—1945—Suor Giuseppina rode around the city on the running board of a silver Aprilia full of partisans, her arm gripping the window frame. With her starched veil and billowing robes, she had become the temporary leader of a partisan troop. The Lancia, bristling with machine guns, sped about—running on gas and alcohol—under a hail of bullets, clearing the road with loud honks and preannouncing its arrival with the fluttering of her veil and the red flags in its windows. At her command, the car would come to a screeching stop to pick up a half-dead partisan who had been left in the street, her head shaved and breasts exposed, slimy with spit, resigned to the blind hatred directed toward her. Holding up their weapons and shooting in the air if necessary, the band would pick up this poor soul and bring her to the Nuove Prison, where she would be kept safe for a short time and then released. She was better off in the prison.

In 1944, Suor Giuseppina was earning her gold medal for bravery, little by little, day by day, saving lives, many of them, and plotting with Pandoli and the gaunt Monsignor Barale, the powerful secretary of His Eminence, and probably many others as well. "Stand up straight, you little hunchback, be a man!" These are the only words she said to me; it was 1945, and, beneath the terrifying skylights of the Nuove Prison, we had brought her a gigantic bouquet of gladioli "for the chapel, for the chapel."

Rabbi Disegni was equally affectionate: in 1945 we went to visit him in the semi-destroyed headquarters of the Jewish Community, and in order to give the occasion a religious tone, *papà* had made us wear the gold Stars of David which we had put away in 1940. The hook-nosed rabbi looked at us grimly and yanked the six-pointed stars from our necks with his bony hands, slapping them into my father's palm without the slightest shadow of indulgence: "These too are *chadoglie.*" *Chadoglia,* in the Jewish dialect of Livorno, means the fanatical idolatry of the Madonna.

In their police reports and declarations, Buffarini Guidi and the others had allowed themselves certain fanciful flourishes, in part to assuage their own consciences, but mostly in order to calm the Fascist masses and the "good souls" of the Italian people. And so it was written that the Jews would be sent to concentration camps, but only "during the war" and only if they were "fit to withstand the conditions of internment."* In general, however, the Jews who were captured by the Fascists were handed over to the SS without much discussion. The criminal lawmakers, conscious of the fact that any Jew was fit enough to "withstand" the gas chambers, had created, with their codicils and post-codicils, a conflict between the lawless actions of the Germans, which were dictated by their esoteric moral imperatives, and the immoral Italian laws, which were, however, still laws, hesitant, contradictory, incomplete, and inefficient as they were, and as such vulnerable to interpretation. The loophole was microscopic, but it allowed for some frantic efforts.

Mamma and *papà,* watched over in their frigid cells by the even colder Suor Giuseppina, languished day after day in an absurd state of semi-clandestinity, just steps away from Schmid's men, waiting for the opening to widen just a bit and hoping not to fall through the trap door before it did.

In their zeal to redeem humanity from the Jewish infection, the SS turned entire neighborhoods upside down.

* From the Verona Manifesto of the Fascist Republicans, November 14–16, 1943. The document was written by Mussolini in collaboration with Nicola Bombacci and Alessandro Pavolini.

They moved about in trucks with an entourage of military Volkswagens and motorcycles with sidecars, fulfilling the mission that they believed history, with the passing of time, would come to understand and admire. The population was forced to witness the capture of old people and paralytics and the terrified expressions on the faces of old ladies wearing aprons and slippers as they were put onto the military trucks of the Third Reich. People saw as the SS went into hospitals and dragged away the ill and dying. The musicologist Leone Sinigaglia, who was born in 1868, died on May 16, 1944, when he was arrested at the Mauriziano Hospital in Turin, where he was a patient. He died of cardiac arrest in the hallway, as he vainly begged the officers not to hurt his wife.* He was a gentle old man who loved the songs of Piedmont; he had a beard like Freud's, and he used to pat me lightly on the head, holding his hand motionless as if in a blessing.

After the air strikes of 1943, Turin was no longer a docile city—if it ever had been—and the Fascists and the Germans knew it. Its population could not tolerate, even in the context of this total war, these incomprehensible atrocities. The stupor of its citizens became horror, which, in the eyes of the Fascist authority, was a source of worry. The always-vigilant archbishop and the police department, minus Cipullo, perceived these shudders and decided to take advan-

* Sinigaglia, Leone. See L. Picciotto Fargion, *Il libro della memoria,* p. 767.

tage of the "favorable" moment to advance the cases of four Jews: Pescarolo, Alfredo; Zargani, Eugenia, née Tedeschi; Treves, Guido; and Zargani, Mario, all of whom were being held "incognito" at the Nuove Prison. There were meetings and discussions, and, in the end, after much hesitation, an objection was cautiously raised with the Nazis, based, on the one hand, on "gaffes" committed by SS men in the course of fulfilling their sacred duties and, on the other, on the words "fit to withstand the conditions of internment." Not even God, if he had wanted to interfere, could have saved the elderly and the sick once they were in the hands of the Germans and the Fascists and had embarked on the journey, the sole purpose of which was death on arrival at Auschwitz, instead of in their own beds. Nevertheless, this was the issue raised, based on a tactical or imprudent comment made by the banal Captain Schmid: "If the Italian police capture ailing Jews, they should do as they see fit, as is their right. As far as we are concerned, we shall continue to follow Berlin's orders."

Pandoli, who headed these negotiations, took note of Schmid's comment without batting an eye and, above all, without naming names.

The good Neapolitan officer later told me that this step led to the next, extremely dangerous step: that of getting the prisoners out of the Nuove Prison without attracting the attention of the Germans or the Fascists. This step was also extremely complicated: *mamma* and *papà,* who had been protected up to that point by their complete ignorance, would have to be informed and consulted, and then "prepared" for the medical visit. The physical examination would have to be undertaken, if possible, by a doctor friendly to the cause such as a certain Doctor Ciraldi. Pandoli went to the archbishop's palace, and the archbishop called Suor Giuseppina, and Suor Giuseppina called my mother into her office and, addressing her formally, said, "Madam. An unexpected but extremely risky opportunity has come to our attention. You must undergo a medical examination; the doctor is a friend of ours, he can be trusted, but we must be prudent. You must do as your cellmates tell you. They know what is to be done." And my mother, who, in her nineteenth-century way, believed that my father was in greater danger than she, a harmless woman, replied, "I won't leave here without my husband." Suor Giuseppina, an ardent "sexophobe," Catholic, and militant, bristled, "I believe you have two children, or am I wrong? Think of them, shut your mouth, do as you are told, and leave us to think about your little husband. We'll do everything we can to bring him back to you!"

My father did not talk much about his time in prison in 1944 or about the trenches back in 1917; he preferred to tell us about the jungle, the Indios, and about the great Paraná, Magdalena, and Amazon Rivers and his experiences in South America in 1925. But he did tell us one thing: before the medical visit, Ugo made him sleep naked and without covers in order to "cultivate" his bronchitis. *Mamma* underwent a more radical procedure, with more immediate effects: her cellmates had her swallow a bowl of tobacco extracted from cigarette butts and mixed with a few grams of sugar which they had been saving for that purpose.

As you can see from the medical report that follows, the prison doctor was in effect a good man. I met him in the period of thank-you visits in 1945, and so I can also tell you that he was very tall with a dark beard and shaggy eyebrows—he looked like Landru.[5] His pleasant office was on the Via Roma, just before the Piazza Castello.

Report: Police Headquarters for Turin Province, Sanitary Division

Subject: Report on medical visits for the Jews: Pescarolo, Alfredo di Natale; Zargani, Eugenia, née Tedeschi (father: Attilio, deceased); Treves, Guido (father: Graziadio, deceased); and Zargani, Mario (father: Eugenio, deceased).

In reference to the request made by the Turin police department on the 24th of February, I performed medical examinations of the following Jews on prison grounds:

Pescarolo, Alfredo di Natale—Reports that he suffered from bronchial pneumonia in 1918 with lingering effects of bronchial catarrh. For the past year he has experienced shortness of breath, especially at night, and an insistent cough with expectoration.

In my examination I found wheezing and whistling in the entire pulmonary area.

I judge therefore that Pescarolo, Alfredo di Natale, having the condition of bronchial asthma, is not fit to withstand the conditions of internment.

Zargani, Eugenia, née Tedeschi (father: Attilio, deceased) —Reports that she has suffered from arrhythmia since childhood. Currently suffers from palpitations, tremors, insomnia, pulsing in the forehead and fingers.

In my examination I found: hypertension, metallic cardiosis; pulse at 120 beats per minute. Blood pressure is noticeably high (max 210, min 120).

I judge therefore that Zargani, Eugenia, née Tedeschi (father, Attilio: deceased), Jew, having the condition of arterial hypertension, is not fit to withstand the conditions of internment.

Treves, Guido (father: Graziadio, deceased)—Lower left limb amputated at the upper thigh and lower right limb showing aftereffects of numerous fractures. For this reason, I judge that he is not fit to withstand the conditions of internment.

Zargani, Mario (father, Eugenio: deceased)—Suffering from pulmonary tuberculosis over the course of several years.

In my examination I found: Ipophonesia of the superior thoracic area and a resulting reduction of the vesicular murmur.

I judge therefore that Zargani, Mario (father, Eugenio: deceased) is not fit to withstand the conditions of internment.

Turin, March 4, 1944
XXII Adjunct Provincial Medical Examiner
Ciraldi, Salvatore.

Stamp: Police Headquarters, Turin—Office (illegible)—
Signature.

Of the two people who were liberated with my parents, I met only Treves, Guido (father, Graziadio: deceased). Before he was arrested, he was a beggar, and for a short time after the end of the war he returned to his sunny spot on the corner of Via Roma and Via Gramsci, where he exposed his stump, described in the document I have quoted here. My father often stopped to chat with him and give him some money.

As soon as the report was complete, Officer Pandoli took it and pushed until he had obtained a release order from the head office, signed also by His Eminence the Archbishop of Turin.

In the middle of the night, Suor Giuseppina went to the transit cell near the entrance of the prison to caution my mother, who was already dressed in civilian clothes including the fox—still biting its tail in rage at being killed. "Madam, the time has come. You are safe here with us, but out there, on the Corso Vittorio, the danger is real and great. The Fascists and the Germans crouch in wait for us to release their victims into their hands. Wait here a moment, and I'll take another look. I'll go around the block and come back, just in case. Pray if you can." When she returned, she was shivering. "There's a thick fog, and it's terribly cold for April! Madam, I saw only Pandoli with a tall, brown-haired man I don't know, on the corner near the tracks." My mother cried out, "It's him!" and in a moment she was outside, in the fog, embracing my father, as Pandoli whispered, "That's enough! Get out of here! It's too dangerous. Don't make me angry! Out of here, right now!"

After months of hesitation, Alfredo Pagani, the young doctor who, at what now seems like the immature age of twenty-five, had been bringing two packages of food to the prison every other day—one for my father and another for my mother—had decided that it was his duty to come to the school to visit us. He could not decide whether or not to tell us about the terrible thing that had happened. Suor Giuseppina never breathed a word to the young doctor with the gold-colored glasses about the stratagem that was being brewed. She merely observed, surmised, accepted the packages, and remained silent.

Alfredo waited for the train to Santhià and, as he ruminated over how he would explain to us that there was a high probability that we would soon be orphans, he thought he saw, he did see, and, incredulous, sputtered, "Mario . . . Eugenia?" "Yes, it's us," they answered. Given the condition of the two ghosts before him, they had to confirm their identity for him to be sure.

As on every Thursday, I was waiting for them under the cantilever roof at the entrance, without much hope, when I saw Alfredo and my mother, whom I recognized, and another man whom I was not immediately able to identify. I realized who he was by inference and was able to react accordingly. But it wasn't really my father. The last Thursday we had seen each other, three or four months earlier, I had embraced a man who was still young, and now I was standing in front of a wild-eyed old man, his cheeks fallen and sunken, who hugged and kissed me but no longer had his familiar, reassuring fragrance; he emanated the terrifying stench of prison.

Meanwhile, Monsignor Cavasin had located my brother, Roberto, who had been scratching about somewhere, and brought him to us; the Monsignor took part, at a distance, in that encounter which both he and Alfredo knew to be a miracle, to be recounted to future generations. *Mamma* and *papà* were behaving strangely, doing their best to contain their emotions; they had become unaccustomed to freedom. Even more than to embrace us, they wanted simply to look at us. They took us in their arms, released us, took a step back, and then took us in their arms once again. They didn't speak about their experiences in prison, but, as my mother looked on, *papà* pulled a grayish piece of bread out of the pocket of his wrinkled and torn gutta-percha raincoat, tore it in half, and said: "It tastes terrible, but you must eat all of it." The bread tasted of prison, and he had brought it to us so that we could experience that place with our mouths, even before we understood it with our minds, according to the Jewish custom. And we did.

9 ❧ The Salesians

Imitatio Christi: Man is halfway between God and the animals—a category that includes everything from beetles to elephants—and in order to escape his intrinsic bestiality, man must imitate Christ, the part of God who descended to Earth in order to redeem the lost identity of man.

After millennia of discussions and hypotheses, it turns out that Christianity is based on the duality of the soul and the body which it inhabits. Our physical being can be tamed through rigorous sport—for the young, tepid Catholics, or for moderate sinners—or with hair shirts or worse—for the rigid, sedentary, or those particularly inclined to repentance combined with suffering. Even illness is a welcome experience, because it outlines, with a blunt and rusty scalpel, the limits of the material out of which we are built. Judaism is not completely alien to the idea of a hereafter, even if the concept is never specified. This is surprising considering the Jewish people's long sojourns in Egypt, the kingdom of the dead, Babylon, the gates of Heaven, and Europe. But Jews are horrified by the idea of corporal punishment, hair shirts, suffering, and death. Our body is all that remains, it seems, of the Temple of Jerusalem, in addition, of course, to our moral duties and a little piece of the *Shekhinah,* or the immanent presence of the transcendent God, God on Earth, who—ever more disheartened and depressed—accompanies each one of us.

Perhaps I felt these things at the beginning of 1944, but only vaguely. In any case, the Christian notion of mortification of the flesh horrified me. But this duality, which through the ages became certain, even evident, to Christians, was a fascinating and exotic idea to the young, Jewish, "neutral monist" I had instinctually become. I was shocked to learn that inside each one of us, within this imperfect and pitiful machine, there exists a spirit that painstakingly runs the controls. A small, hesitant spirit which nevertheless is immortal and capable of deciding what it wants—independently of any God—through free will. This spirit must be saved, against its will. The body is but a shell, already in the first stages of decomposition, and the spirit inside is seduced and attracted by its putrefaction. It takes pleasure in the vices of the flesh.

Spiritual exercises, however, are not mortifying; they evoke the myth of the spirit. In three days of silence and prayer, Catholics—including children—can achieve a sense of inner spirituality.

The soul does not age in the same manner as the body; instead of wrinkles, it acquires sins. Inside of me, I am still ten years old, the same age as on the night of December first, 1943, when *mamma* and *papà* were delayed because of my request, *mea culpa, mea culpa, mea maxima culpa.* How I wish I could go back to that night, just before committing the mortal sin of asking them for those black boots and knickerbockers! Which, by the way, turned out to be of terrible quality.

The three days of spiritual exercises we held at the school in 1944 were a great discovery: silence in the courtyard, silent games, time to reflect and converse with one's transcendent inner self, contrite faces staring at each other mutely, conversations with God through prayer, and the language of signs to communicate with one another.

The traffic of images was also based on signs: there were cards with Saint John Bosco pointing out the sky to the inspired Saint Francis de Sales and, even better, cards with a little cellophane pouch containing a tiny piece of white cloth, a relic of the saint. The value of these objects of devotion was multiplied by their rarity; you could trade two of them for one of the Turin or Juventus soccer players. In addition to trading them, we used the cards to play a game called *"al mur,"* where you flick a card toward the wall and the card which comes closest, without touching, wins all of the others. Since I wasn't interested in soccer, I managed to put together an impressive collection of these relics, so many, in fact, that when my father unpacked my bag on the morning of October 15, 1944, in the partisan-controlled mountains, he exclaimed: "My word, son, you've got the saint's entire underpants in here!"

The language of signs was interrupted when one of the priests or their assistants called out the sacred command, *"Oremus,"* and all of us, with our hands together, would declaim the Our Father and the Ave Maria. The prayers became a grand event, as they were practically the only opportunity for us to speak. Every so often a yelp would ring out in the sacred silence when, with Olympic precision, the shoe of one of the assistants would reach the rear end of an undisciplined student. Other occasions for speech were the short sermons and discussions on such pressing themes as "God is everywhere."

One impertinent soul, nicknamed "Candelabra" because his nose perennially dripped long, waxlike streaks of snot, responded brazenly, "No, God can't be everywhere. He can't be in the bathroom, because dirty things go on in there." In my Jewish-Turinese ingenuousness, I assumed he was speaking of our ordinary evacuations, and with horror I visualized the comma-shaped shit stains on the bathroom wall, signs of the absence of God. When they went to the toilet, the most primitive farm children, unacquainted with toilet paper, did not bring along newspapers, wrapping paper, or, as I did, *faute de mieux,* the wax paper which my cough medicine came wrapped in.

But these fetid *orango virgulari** were not the object of the disciplinary investigation which began immediately after the three days of meditation on the self and the hereafter. In fact, it was the epidemic of homosexual practices, which horrified the priests as much as the more abstract lust for women. "Enough of dreams, it's time to act!" was the unuttered motto of those practicing homosexuality among the schoolboys. The investigation culminated in the public punishment of the confessed transgressors: they had to run ten laps around the courtyard followed by Maestro Ferrara on a bicycle with a willow branch in hand, inciting the two "athletes" to beat the school record for the kilometer dash while receiving a thrashing.

The priests sincerely believed that sport was the most effective antidote for the poison of sex, and in this they concurred with the opinion of sports trainers, who believe that sex poisons athletic ability. At my age, that was one of the biggest differences I could perceive between Judaism and Christianity. For many Jews, athleticism is not only linked to Fascism but also to Hellenism, the ancient enemy, and

* Piedmontese schoolboy Latin for the primates (*orango*) who make comma- (*virgola-*) shaped shit stains on bathroom partitions.

Hellenism to nudity, nudity to sex, and sex to idolatry and ritual prostitution under the terebinth trees, practically extinct in the last 3,500 years. But one must keep one's guard up, considering how the cult of the body returns every so often to replace that of the soul, in a sort of "idolatry of the here and now." It is the fear of sport, of the profanation of the Holy City by the ultimate idolatry, a football stadium, which induced the ultra-Orthodox Jews of the sect of the *Neturei Kartah* in Jerusalem to lie down in front of buses, throw stones at shop windows, and assault passersby. Now the stadium exists, and the Orthodox and anti-Zionist Jews have apparently resigned themselves to the fact. Perhaps they hope that the triumph of this immorality, or ignominy, as they call it, constitutes one of the dark signs announcing the coming of the Messiah.

Such Jewish superstitions seem to linger in the dark recesses of the spirits of the *goyim,* including those of most Italians; a few years ago, a group of normally reasonable people wrote, in tones which were on the surface ironic but in fact were rabbinically indignant, that the frenetic throngs who came to admire the Riace bronzes—masterpieces which the experts, in moments of delirium, ascribe to Phidias, or, more reasonably, to "Praxiteles, Lysippos . . . Lysippos, Praxiteles . . ."—were actually admiring an immodest exhibition of bronze masculine attributes, which, in fact, were anything but awe-inspiring and, frankly, out of scale.

Despite the efforts of the Salesians, I managed miraculously to intuit that Christianity is not synonymous with the abhorrence of sex, just as Judaism and Islam do not consist solely in the distaste for pork. And, as a child, I was able to spontaneously reenact the secular dispute over the true Jews: are the "real" Jews the Jews like myself or the ones who became Christians because they understood that the real Jews were no longer Jews because they had rejected Christ?

Christianity suddenly appeared to me in the full radiance of its imagery, of which colorful rituals, Mass, the perfume of incense, paintings, and statues are but a pale but significant shadow. I compared this abundance of color with the Jewish monochromaticism, based on the word, which, in the absence of images, abandons the mind to find its way in the disquieting algebra of history, oppression, survival, and justice, and which places the transcendent and moral God further and further away from the world of the real. For millennia, He has been tiptoeing away from us, and one can't blame Him, given the way He has bungled things in our history, both sacred and profane.

The logical, syntactic arabesques which are found in the Torah and the Talmud and which appear figuratively in Western synagogues—an art-nouveau imitation of Islamic mosques—may seem little adapted to the precocious imaginations of children, who do not distinguish well between internal and external worlds. The war between the Jews and the Romans stripped Judaism of its public rites,* which, as one can read, were sumptuous, intriguing, and mysterious enough to fascinate all of antiquity. See Josephus, *Jewish War.*

What remained were the familial rites that fill the heart with joy and place children at the center of ceremonies, but this warm splendor was almost unknown to me in 1943, because my family were not practicing Jews. I knew nothing of the setting sun which announces the quiet arrival of the Sabbath, or the beloved Queen who folds the world in her arms and listens, invisible, to the family's welcome around the candles and the sumptuously laid table: "Return, return, O Shulamite."[1] The Seder, the magical and joyous Passover meal in honor of justice and freedom, and during which Christ was arrested, was known to me only through the mimeographed sacred history pamphlets which were handed out at the Colonna e Finzi School. I remember a few flavors from the holidays; Judaism teaches us to experience the magic of holidays first through the taste buds. In 1938, I had been declared a Jew by Italian law, but I hardly felt Jewish at the Salesian school. Even so, I had eaten un-

* In his own account, in 70 A.D., Titus Vespasian watched powerlessly as his soldiers burned down the Temple. This act ushered in the Rabbinical period of Judaism, which continues to this day. In the Moscow synagogue, in far-off 1962, a few elderly Jews asked me worriedly about the state of anti-Semitism in Italy. When I responded that Italy was substantially free of anti-Semitism, they exclaimed, surprised: "How is it possible, after what the Emperor Titus did to us?"

leavened bread with its rough taste of wheat, and I had consumed dried figs and dates in a hut built out of drafty mulberry branches for Succoth, the autumn wind murmuring: "You were once nomads, and so you shall be again; you aren't like the rest of humanity, don't imagine you are. You do not belong to the present." And my ears rang with the obsessive call of the shofar, the ram's horn announcing the end of fasting during Yom Kippur and the arrival of forgiveness.

And before (or after?) the shofar we sang the final prayer: "Oh God Whose Deeds Are Awesome." In Hebrew, the opening words of this moving prayer are *"El nora 'alilah,"* and at that moment every year *papà* extracted his gold Longines pocket watch from his waistcoat and exclaimed, *"È l'ora"*—it's time—"the fasting is over, let's go eat!" It took me several Yom Kippurs to understand that *papà* thought, and had thought since childhood, that *El nora 'alilah* was a kind of Italian-Hebrew patois that meant *"È l'ora";* in other words, time to eat! When I explained this to him, *papà,* instead of being embarrassed, exclaimed enthusiastically, "My word, you're right! You're brilliant. I always said it! I never could have figured it out myself!"

In 1943, I knew without knowing that the food favored by the Jewish religion—the apples with honey for Rosh Hashanah, the *charosset,* tropical fruit preserves for the Seder, the unleavened sweets—is meant to remind us of another place: "You are not of this land, you are from the East, where the sun, with its pink rays, is born, and you hold your hands up to it to warm yourself in your morning prayers; that is where your heart is. Have your bags ready because one day, slowly, one pasture at a time, one gas station at a time, you will return . . . to Jerusalem! The impenetrable fortress of celestial peace . . . in the future, when the sacred past returns. Keep your bags ready, it may be in your life or your children's, or their children's. But the sacred will return, in the Orient."

What has been taking place for thousands of years in synagogues on Saturdays is not a ceremony but a lesson and a display in which the scrolls of the Torah, the Law, are lifted overhead by the rabbis. This act is completely different from the holding up of the communion wafer, which is literally transformed into the body of Christ. The holding up of the Torah is a judicial act, which is undertaken in order to allow the assembled faithful to observe the authenticity of the binding, as my father used to tell me; the drinking of wine, or *kiddush,* which is frequent in family ceremonies and in weddings, is more of a toast than a consecration, even if the prayer that the priest recites in Mass is the same: "Blessed are You, O Lord our God, creator of the fruit of the vine . . . which gladdens our hearts." But after *kiddush,* the wine is still wine; after it is held up by a priest, it becomes blood. And not a symbol for blood, but actual blood, and anyone who doesn't believe it is a heretic, even if he doesn't know it.

In Christianity, the sacred flows into the everyday through a thousand open channels, but in Judaism there is a wall separating the two, in which the heart of the believer can only very rarely perceive the tiniest cracks. The sacred is almost feared by the Jews, especially when it prematurely infiltrates the chaos of everyday life. This is why the scrolls of the Torah are sacred and one must wash one's hands after touching them; this is why the name of God cannot be pronounced, and why martyrs and heroes are impure. Auschwitz is also impure, and the esplanade of the Temple of Jerusalem is avoided fearfully by believers, because a stray fragment of the *Shekhinah* might still lie there.

Naturally, these were not my thoughts when, as a young boy, I began not to reject my undeveloped Judaism, which I was no longer ashamed of, but rather to love Christianity, in part because my infantile mind found it easier to understand, no offence to Saint Augustine and the other Fathers of the Church. But for Christians, the sacred and the real are parts of a whole, accessible to everyone, with the exception of the mysteries which no one, not even Saint Thomas Aquinas, can decipher. For the Jews, on the other hand, and I had had a taste of this at the Colonna e Finzi School, the only remedy to the inconsistency of life is the continual study of books which speak of the sacred, of a time when it existed, and a time in the future when it will return.

%

My brother, Roberto's, and my experience of Christianity began brusquely in our first days at the school. No one, except Monsignor Cavasin, could know, or even suspect, that we were Jewish. No precaution was considered excessive, and, in that spirit, the priest explained to us upon our arrival that we had to behave like all the other students and imitate them in everything. He did not take two important factors into consideration, however, the first being that the Roman Catholic Apostolic Church could seem as exotic and bewildering as the Tao or Shinto Buddhism to two apparently normal children from Turin. Before we entered the school, we knew next to nothing about the Madonna, which was only slightly more than we knew about the goddess Kali from Emilio Salgàri's *The Tigers of Mompracem* (ed. Vallardi, 1937). The second factor was that my brother was (and is) by nature divided into two extreme attitudes: either he follows instructions to the last detail or he ignores them completely. In that period, Roberto happened to be going through an extremely rare phase of blind obedience: when he saw that, at a certain point during the Mass, the others put their hands together and held them under their chins as they walked up to the altar and knelt, he did as he had been told. He went with the other children, simulating mystical devotion. I, on the other hand, noticed that a few of the other boys stayed back, and I did the same, without imagining that they could not take Communion because, heavy with sins both mortal and venial, they had not gone to confession. As we had not been baptized, my brother and I were guilty of the most terrible mortal sin of all: the original sin of Adam and Eve. We were human beings for the Church, which at the time was already an extremely comforting fact, but we were not Christian and so were terribly impure; our very souls were stained with sin.

After Mass, my brother came over to me and said, with the sleepy attitude he still affects when, in the face of some dramatic event, he wishes to manifest a self-control he does not feel, "Listen, something terrible happened. I kneeled down with everyone else, and I stuck out my tongue, and I saw the priest making everyone lick a piece of blotting paper. Even though it seemed disgusting, I left my tongue out, but when he got to me—I was the last one—the priest took the piece of blotting paper, which had been licked by everyone—even Maestro Ferrara, just think of it! with his warty purple tongue!—and left it in my mouth. I was so surprised that I swallowed it! I wanted to spit it out, but the priest was looking at me strangely, almost as if he were scared, and I just swallowed. I'm sure I'll get some infection. Maybe I should go to the Infirmary?" Bewildered by the strangeness of this unfamiliar ritual, and indifferent to whatever infection Roberto could have picked up, I convinced him not to say anything to anyone, and, furthermore, informed him that the blotting paper had been disinfected.

A moment later, Monsignor Cavasin came over to me with an expression which was not the least bit sleepy and squeezed my arm, whispering, "Is it true that your brother took Communion?" "I'm afraid so," I responded, with the concerned look of someone who is conscious of a grave occurrence which he has been powerless to stop and who, though innocent of any wrongdoing, is terribly afflicted by what has happened. Naturally, I had no idea what Communion was about, except what Roberto had told me, but I had learned to simulate understanding of matters which were beyond my comprehension and sentiments which I did not feel. "It's terrible," the priest moaned, "but you can't understand why, you don't know what it means. Just don't do it again." And that was the origin of the private catechism lessons that Monsignor Cavasin gave us in his office; he tried not to frighten us, while putting certain limits on our impersonation of young Catholics, which he believed to be as comprehensive as possible under the circumstances. Clandestinity presents one with a continuous stream of irremediable contradictions, and that it why it is so difficult and so fascinating.

On the following Sunday, Monsignor Cavasin himself gave the sermon, and he climbed up to the pulpit and explained to all of us that the taking of the sacred Communion wafer in a state of sin, without confessing, was like corrupting the living body of Christ, turning it into a decaying corpse. Only my brother and I understood who the rotting, fetid corpse was; the others took it to be simply another lesson, generically intended to induce them to behave in a manner which was less despicable than usual.

Monsignor Cavasin always treated me like an adult. Perhaps it was because he was sorely in need of someone to talk to; he seemed like someone destined for a more important position than that of director of a boarding school for country children. I immediately perceived this need and responded to it with affection and obedience. My father had a very high opinion of him. In fact, *papà* suspected that he was an illustrious prelate who had been sent to Cavaglià as punishment for some "mistake." In my opinion, whatever mistake had led Monignor Cavasin to that sad place must have been of a theological or perhaps amorous nature, because I can't imagine what other temptations could have led a man of such high moral fiber down the path of sin. He was young, refined, of medium stature, thin, and sullen, his thick, dark eyebrows always knit in a frown but his expression keen and penetrating.

One day in spring, Monsignor Barale, the cardinal's secretary, came to Cavaglià accompanied by Monsignor Pellegrini, head of the Salesian order and a living example of boy-scoutesque optimism; Saint John Bosco was a Catholic, Piedmontese version of Baden-Powell. They brought with them a very small boy, elegantly dressed in a blue overcoat with a velvet collar, knickerbockers, white knee socks, and a velvet cap with a visor and button. Barale and Pellegrini, with the majesty and benevolence typical of high prelates in the observance of their functions, visited the school and were satisfied with the order and hygiene they found there —which were as relative as the devotion—and left the elegant child behind. They also greeted my brother and me, as if at random, and we bowed and showed the requisite respect and awe.

After the big day had passed, Cavasin brought the small boy over to me and said, "His name is Teodoro Paschi. Look out for him, defend him, be nice to him, explain things to him. He is your little brother, younger even than Roberto. And while we're on the subject of Roberto . . ." I had long since lost interest in Roberto, having given him up to a confusing succession of transgressions and punishments, the result of his rebellious spirit. But I kept Teodoro with me, the better to study his getup. It all made sense to me when I saw a hand-written label inside his elegant but slightly tight overcoat with the name "Pasch" and the address of a tailor in Berlin, on the Friedrichstrasse; my heart jumped. I ran to the director, who immediately carried the boy off to the wardrobe, where the nuns removed every sign of his perilous identity. With a sigh of relief, Monsignor Cavasin thanked me as he would an equal, placing a hand on my shoulder and looking me in the eyes. Now the only danger was our circumcision, which the nuns could not alter with their sewing implements.

Theo Pasch was the son of a dentist who had somehow fled to Italy after her husband, also a dentist, was killed, probably in one of the first deportations of Jews from Berlin to Lithuania. When Theo's mother was captured in Turin, she managed, in the confusion, to hide her child in the concierge's apartment. But when Captain Schmid, who, as we know, believed in following orders, heard that the young boy had fled to a dairy farm with the concierge's wife, he had the concierge arrested and declared that he would have him killed unless the boy was returned. The poor woman gave the boy to the cardinal, saying, "Please take him and hide him somewhere, but don't tell me where. I want my husband back, and if I know where the boy is, I'll turn him over to the Germans." Even Alfredo Pagani, the doctor who was by now consumed with the desire to save as many Jews as he could, intervened in Theo's case. But I don't know the details.

His mother survived, after being transformed into one of those living skeletons from Bergen-Belsen whom we try to avoid looking at in the famous documentary by Hitchcock, an homage perhaps to Méliès's *Voyage dans la Lune*. The British took her to Tel Aviv, and from there she searched for her son across the ruins of Europe. In late 1945, as my father and Alfredo Pagani were struggling for custody of the orphan, his mother arrived at the airport in Mirafiori. Not long after, a Lancaster bomber took off from that same airport with Theo and his mother aboard—Theo looking like a hopeful puppy as he always did. With a growl it flew off, and the little boy disappeared from our lives, bound for the Promised Land, which was evidently populated with dentists who had survived the camps.

%

I managed to adapt completely at the Salesian school: I accepted the rules, withstood the hardships, escaped the bullies with whom Roberto was perennially fighting; I tried to understand, or at least appear to understand, what was going on around me, and to avoid punishment. As soon as I had learned the Latin prayers, which were as incomprehensible as Hebrew prayers, if somewhat easier to remember, I was made an altar boy by some quirk of the "universality of the church" combined with the director's desire that we should be fully integrated; I wore a red cassock and served at Vespers. I was an impeccable altar boy, except for the one time I dropped smoking embers from the censer onto the embroidered cloth laid out on the altar. On that occasion, the priest, who was performing a sung Mass, hissed commands toward the sacristy between the long notes of a Gregorian chant, meanwhile attempting to put out hundreds of small fires: "Do something, for charity's sake!" A nun hugged me on the way out, her face wet with tears. "Thank you, my child, I've never laughed so hard. Thank you!"

Even though I was somewhat clumsy, the fact that I assisted at Mass gave me the privilege of helping to serve meals and, consequently, of eating my fill of mashed potatoes and soup. I sat at a special table, glared at by hundreds of hungry children as I slowly ate a mountain of mashed potatoes, carving a path with my fork with plenty of twists and turns. One day, someone yelled out at me, "Make a tunnel!" That was my triumph.

In Cavaglià, I reaped the accumulated benefits of three years of hard training at the Colonna e Finzi School. Despite the director's precautions, the priests found out or at least suspected my secret. My intellectual abilities, which had seemed unexceptional in the urban, twentieth-century world I had escaped from, were extraordinary in the rural Middle Ages at the Salesian school, a place which struggled, like a decrepit hydroplane, to lift itself out of a mire of illiteracy. Very few boys in the fifth grade could read without breaking the words into syllables, even fewer could read with any semblance of animation, and I was the only one who made any attempt at interpretation. "Effeminate rubbish" was how Maestro Ferrara described my efforts. Perhaps so, but when I wasn't helping to serve lunch, I was often asked to read aloud from *The Phantom Prince* (ed. SEI, 1940), a violent, priestly novel in which shadowy, bearded Masons with hats and merciless swords kidnapped a small Christian child out of sheer malice and abhorrence for Christ. The infidels were vanquished by the ghost-prince through his acrobatic abilities, along with some help from the Virgin. My specialty, other than recitation and interpretation, was the tiny pen mark with which, in memory of Uncle Rino, I marked the stopping point of each reading session, thus avoiding the madness that broke loose when some unlucky soul mistakenly reread a passage.

This intellectual serenity, which I have never experienced since, was accentuated by the fact that I had already passed the entrance exams for middle school in Asti in the fall of 1943. I attended the fifth grade with a sense of total tranquility, impervious to day-to-day successes and failures; in fact, I did not have to study at all.

It was more comforting to be at the top of the class at the Salesian school than at the bottom of the class at the Colonna e Finzi, and I think that my academic successes there awakened great hope in the priests; of course, they would never have confessed such feelings, even to themselves. If destiny had wanted me to become a priest, or I had chosen that route, it would have been a success for the Church, which is like a giant tree with deep roots in the rural community but which feels the need to mingle its branches with the more exotic, less robust branches of its rival religions. Their silent hope was so evident, so pitifully clear, that to a certain point I gave in to the hypocrisy which is learned by all children who are struggling to survive.

The confessor was a humble, diaphanous, bald priest, probably a saint, who played the organ in church—in fact, he died at the keyboard; he wore half-gloves from which emerged pale, tapered artist's fingers. One day, he asked me what I wanted to be when I grew up, and I answered, "A theologian." I wasn't consciously committing the sin of hypocrisy: my Jewish half—if it still amounted to half—was trying to come to some sort of compromise with the half of me which had become Christian. Something told me that the most fruitful occupation for me would be one in which I dedicated myself to deciphering the mysteries of faith and seeking out all that is Jewish in Christianity. The confessor's casual, paternal question had elicited a forceful reaction, and, in fact, the good man seemed struck by this force. After that, the confessor, the counselor, the accountant, the catechism instructor, and the director asked me the same question, but no one ever thought to ask me why. They were happy to hear again and again that I wanted to become a theologian, and they were satisfied in their benevolent hope.

My enthusiasm for the cloth suffered a setback in the early fall of 1944. At the end of September, the priests gave us wicker baskets and led us to a forest to gather mushrooms. They pointed out the *porcini* mushrooms and asked us to pick those and only those. Toward nightfall, when we gathered at the roadside, all hundred and thirty-four of us had picked exclusively giant, lovely *porcini.* Meanwhile, the priests had gathered four or five jute-bags-full of *garitule, chiodini, manine, prataioli,* and *tamburini* mushrooms mixed together indiscriminately; in other words, the most vulgar varieties of edible mushrooms. These were served to us that night in foamy clumps in our slippery aluminum bowls, while from the priests' dining room emerged the delicious fragrance of the roasted tops of the *porcini* we had picked. It was an imprudent gesture on their part, because it reinforced the anticlerical feeling which was already rife at the school and which was practically innate in those children, and it killed any theological aspirations I might have harbored.

After *mamma* and *papà* were released from prison, they were taken by Pandoli or one of his anti-Fascist friends to the mountains in the area around Biella, where by May 1944 the partisan bands were consolidating their forces. Peace seemed to be within reach. My parents did not come often to see us that summer; it was better for them to avoid passing through the roadblocks in the valley too often with their unconvincing false papers. But they sent us colorful postcards in envelopes which the director destroyed so that we would not be able to tell their place of origin from the postmark. The cards were addressed to an imaginary child, Aldo Roberti, created out of our combined identities. *Papà* was proud of his invention, because it conserved our names while eliminating the Arab-Jewish last name, which could have been recognized by any of the Orientalists in the SS, some of whom had degrees from Heidelberg and Gottingen. They carefully and methodically went through communal archives, letters, and identity cards.

By summer the partisan-controlled areas had become more secure; *mamma* and *papà* were being hidden in the mountains near Biella, in a hospice run by the *Cottolengo*[2] of Bioglio, a place that housed all types, including fugitives, the sick, the elderly, the deficient, and the insane. The period of panic was slowly coming to an end, and from that hidden, relatively secure place, my parents looked down upon the plain, which was no longer tranquil as it had been in the winter. Lately, it had become a theater for ambushes, killings, and reprisals.

Our school outings in the fields had two purposes: we could bathe in the ponds by the embankment, and the soft-hearted farmers took pity on us and gave us fruit to eat. The farm wives, wearing heavy boots, their thick stockings around their ankles, would bring pails of clear, cold water from their wells. They gave it to us by the ladleful as we stood in line, sweaty and thirsty. And then the men would run over in their wooden clogs, carrying bags full of fruit.

This was a countrified version of the *tzedakah,* the act of justice of the prophets; to these country people, charity was an obligation. Whether these people were actually Christian, or pagan, or animistic, as I have always suspected, was a complex question that I'll leave to professional anthropologists.

It was difficult to decipher what was hidden in the thoughts of these people, who were still living in the Dark Ages. Signora Tecla, an old woman who took us in in October 1944 at her own risk and peril, asked my mother after Liberation, "Please explain to me, Madam, if you don't mind, how nice people like you can eat babies every year at Easter?"* These country people, straight out of a Grimm fairy tale, were willing to put their own lives in danger in order to safeguard those of a family of blood-sucking monsters!

Our school outings in the countryside—tormented by war and not yet done away with by peace, close by but invisible—had a geographic-didactic purpose as well, according to Maestro Ferrara: he enjoyed taking us to admire the border between the province of Turin and the province of Vercelli. There was nothing much there to see, and there were at least ten letters missing from the signs reading "Welcome to . . ." The only identifiable feature was the contrast in the quality of the road surface, which was brand

* See the account of Saint Simon of Trent, whose followers claimed he was bled to death in 1475 by Jews so they might make unleavened bread. Devotion to the saint, which had been fomented by Bernardino of Feltre, was abrogated by the Second Vatican Council.

new on the Turin side and tattered on the Vercelli side. Each time we went, our teacher made us admire the splendid Turinese pavement and then pointed with silent disdain at the state of the road on the other side. We would spend a few moments there meditating on the vastness of the world, the differences between peoples, customs, and civilizations, and then we would head back, singing and making a racket, our pockets full of shell casings and fruit.

During my last days in Cavaglià, I saw an event which became legendary; word of it reached the mountains, frightening my parents so much that they decided to come and get us as soon as possible. But how? And when?

The cool air of autumn had already arrived, and it rained on the grayish skylights of the courtyard. Grayness was returning to the Canavese, and the sky was leaden above the rice fields. A break in the clouds inspired the Salesians to take us to play on the soccer field, which was separated from the school by a country road. I saw everything because I was standing facing the school; there was just one small steel door on the road side, which we knew was always open, as it had no lock.

The first person I saw was a young man with a checkered shirt who was walking slowly, a petrol can in each hand. This was a system used by the Nazis to immobilize prisoners when they were short of rope and chains. The young man was a freshly captured partisan and an ex-student of the school. He knew about the small door which appeared to be locked but was not. He remembered the maze of corridors in the school and calculated that if he could make his way through the compound, on the other side he would find safety in the narrow, tortuous medieval streets of the village, an impenetrable labyrinth for the Huns. He was followed by four SS officers, tall and clanking, in pewter-colored rubberized raincoats slick with rain, machine guns ready, helmets dripping, grenades in each low boot, and many more on their belts and in their bandoliers.

When the young man in the checkered shirt reached the small door, he hurled the canisters at the two Germans nearest to him and, leaning against the door, disappeared into it. After a fraction of a second, when the clatter of the canisters and the creaking of the door had subsided, the gray giants dove into the doorway, their four helmets almost touching in the tiny opening. In order to imagine the scene, you should think back to the Teutonic knights in Eisenstein's *Alexander Nevsky,* accompanied by the music of Prokofiev. But I wasn't at the movies, and I felt no emotion, except surprise at the rapid, mechanical sequence of events which unfolded before my eyes. Moments later, we—especially the priests—were terrorized by fifteen minutes of shooting, guttural shouting, exploding grenades, shattering glass, shouting, and white smoke emerging from the bathroom window. "Stay calm, stay calm," the priests yelled at us, looking anything but calm, while like sheep dogs they herded us toward the furthest corner of the field, holding out their arms to shield us with their cassocks, those porcini-mushroom thieves. And then it was over.

When we went back inside, the school was in terrible shape; the beds were in shreds, shell casings lay everywhere—more for our collections—there were bullet holes in the walls, broken glass, nightstands knocked over and riddled with holes. There was no sign of the Germans nor, it goes without saying, of the young man in the checkered shirt. He had made his way to the covered courtyard, climbed up into the dormitories, navigated the zigzagging corridors, jumped out of a window onto the cantilever roof, walked precariously across the iron bars of the skylights, serenely guarded from below by the Holy Virgin Mary in her blue dress and Saint John Bosco with his devoted, ruddy-faced students. Then he had leapt ten feet down to the cobblestone street, where he had been greeted by an open door in that Christian Casbah and, with long strides, had disappeared over the horizon, through other windows, courtyards, and rooftops and into the Canavesian Dark Ages. Safe and sound. But the Germans in their raincoats did not realize this and continued to search for him in the dormitories he had long since left behind. They tried to scare him out by peppering the beds with bullets and tossing grenades into rooms he had never been in. For at least fifteen minutes, if not longer.

At the beginning of the 1944–45 school year, I was preparing to enter the fifth grade, pointlessly, for the third time. But one day, Monsignor Cavasin approached me with a serious look on his face. "I need to talk to you about something important, and you must listen to me very, very closely. As you know, the school goes only to the fifth grade, but it is not right for you not to start middle school. You mustn't miss a year, because you seem to be quite gifted. So the only choice we have is to put you provisionally in the diocesan seminary. Don't look at me that way, it's not in order to make a priest out of you, no one is asking that, even if you'll have to wear vestments, which, as you well know, is nothing to be ashamed of. In any case, every Sunday you could take the bus here and visit your brother."

Of all the clergy I came in contact with, only Suor Pierina of the *Cottolengo* of Bioglio ever expressed the ardent desire to see us convert. But that was after the war, amidst goodbyes and tears. "I hope we shall see each other one day, united in the holy Church, if and when our Lord desires it," she said. Priests know that Jews are hard to convert, that there is no way to convince them; it's already there in the Old Testament and confirmed in the New Testament.

But the night after my conversation with the monsignor, *mamma* swooped down on the plain like a falcon, to carry us away with her into the *Bandenkrieg*—the world of the partisan war. We were going to the mountains, with *papà,* to a safe place in the perilous world of partisans.

10 ❧ Temple

In 1939, or maybe 1938, misfortune befell my brother and me: *mamma* fell in love with a piece of yellowish-brown velvet cloth which she had bought at the market in Piazza Madama Cristina. She would drape it on one arm and then the other and dream of what to make out of the cloth. She often dropped by the dark, messy Tosi dressmaker's shop at 34, Via Berthollet, on the corner of Via Ormea; the dressmaker, who was old, slovenly, and crazy, and her nasal-voiced, lazy assistant, created audacious outfits for the ballerinas of the Politeama Chiarella Theater, or so they claimed. The dressmaker never delivered her creations on time, in part out of laziness, and in part because my mother's extravagant ideas required, in her words, "a lengthy pursuit of perfection." The dressmaker and her sleepy assistant kept the piece of fabric for months, but eventually she sewed us two little velvet outfits. If she had taken just a bit longer, the outfits would never have seen the light of day: on the night of November 18, 1942, the night of the leaflets that declared, "Tonight we were just playing around. Just wait and see what happens tomorrow!" justice came down from the heavens. The shop was leveled, along with the rest of 34, Via Berthollet, by two phosphorous bombs, three fragmentation bombs, and an unspecified number of incendiary bombs, all in one night. And so it was that I was forced to trot around town dressed like a clown, until the miracle of growth finally put an end to my misery. *Mamma* always dressed us up in these twin outfits when we went to visit relatives. After tea, our relatives would silently put a bank note in my mother's bag, perhaps a thousand lire, and *mamma* would turn bright red, all because her unemployed husband only knew how to be an artist. *Tzedakah.*

Along with the gratitude and love I feel for my mother, there is a slight tinge of bitterness for those Little Lord Fauntleroy outfits she had made for us à la *Misunderstood* (Florence Montgomery, ed. Brigola, 1881), and I keep it in the same drawer of my memory as the ugly, uncomfortable homemade underwear.

Mamma was an ex-capitalist who had been driven around in an Isotta-Fraschini[1] accompanied by her father wearing a bowler hat. After marrying my father, a penniless

Sephardic Jew and a slightly mad violinist, and after the events of the thirties, she moved from the comfortable middle class to abject poverty, but she always kept her "leftist" attitude, cultivating her own brand of personal philosophical pessimism. This allowed her to experience her submersion in the bog of misery like a British explorer delving into the mysteries and dangers of the Ganges delta. My mother, an adventurer in the world of poverty, was comforted daily by real-life parallels to the solitary readings of her privileged youth: *L'Assommoir, La Bête Humaine,* and the entire saga of Zola's Rougon-Macquart family, which my grandfather Attilio had given her when she was a young girl in order to cultivate her innate pessimism. "Well, what did you expect?" she seemed to be saying, like a tourist in the world of "we won't make it to the end of the month, who is that at the door, where can I hide the children?" At the end of the dark tunnel of horrors stood her beloved Zola, her dear Émile, who, bowing slightly and holding his dove-colored bowler against his large stomach, held open the door of the Isotta-Fraschini with a benevolent "leftist" air: *"J'accuse!"* (*L'aurore,* January 8, 1898).

Even if in 1945 *mamma* anticipated total victory and the arrival of Justice on Earth after we had barely escaped destruction at the hands of *The Iron Heel* (Jack London, ed. Modernissima, 1927), I still can't forgive her moralism, or the universal, supreme conclusions she derived from her singular, unhappy experience: "The cotton underwear you find in the neighborhood is far better than silk underwear from the Via Roma and incomparably superior in quality and durability to the wool-and-silk underwear on Via Lagrange. Those are just false elegances for pretentious people with money to burn, the stuff doesn't last! Honest people . . . ," et cetera, et cetera, et cetera.

With that piece of cloth the color of cat's excrement, the seamstress made two pairs of pants—one for my brother and one for me—with giant black buttons à la Mickey Mouse and no pockets: who cares about pockets, they're just two little figurines! Then two little bolero jackets with sailor collars and, with the leftover cloth, two Raphaelesque painters' berets—I wince at the mere thought—which furthermore were precursors of the ones worn by members of the *X Mas* flotilla, the underwater raiding unit of the Italian Navy. To complete the outfit, there were white stockings that never stayed up and black patent-leather shoes with little buttons and, to top it all off, little fawn-colored rayon shirts with the large bow built in, the knot sewn straight so it stayed neat. I can still picture it.

My brother and I were born a year apart, but people continually asked my mother, "Are they twins?" to which she responded, obliquely, "No, but they are only eleven months apart." The allusion, which *mamma* was too embarrassed to explain even to herself, was to Tolstoy, that silly, saintly man from the steppes who, because it was believed at the time that women were sterile while breast-feeding, could not bear the thought of intercourse with a woman who would "afterwards" fulfill the saintly task of feeding their miserable little angels.

Let it be known, then, that breast-feeding is not an effective form of contraception, because that was when Roberto was conceived and how I became a "twin."

My parents dressed us up on Saturdays and important feast days when we went to temple. It was a modest comfort to see that other parents did the same to their poor children, who were similarly depressed.

Even after we were forced to learn the Hebrew alphabet at the Colonna e Finzi School, it was impossible for us to understand the prayers in temple—which we did not even attempt to do—or even to follow them in the *tefillah,* an incomprehensible labyrinth which jumps from one page to another depending on the day and other lunar considerations. But it was fun to be with other children and relatives, and to look up at the mothers, aunts, and cousins perched in the women's gallery. "Perched" is the correct, if unfeminist, term, considering the number of feathers I could see sticking out of hats with little veils, straining to see the sea of talliths* below, all held within those golden walls.

For descriptions of the mystical feeling of persecution, I refer you to the many pages written on the subject. These were lovely, sad moments of premonition, when, under the wings of the tallith, grandfathers blessed fathers, and fa-

* The white shawl with blue stripes and four tassels on the corners, which Jewish men—pastors by right—wear during prayer.

thers blessed children, including daughters, who were sent scampering down from the galleries. The feathers above us fluttered about as the mothers strained their eyes to pick out their own family in the sea of shawls, and even orphans were blessed by religious and semi-religious uncles and grandfathers. If a complete lack of faith requires a great effort for Jews in times of peace, in 1938 it was practically an impossibility.

And so my cousins Pucci and Attilio, who had lost their father, would run over to my father to receive the blessing that is handed down from generation to generation of the chosen people, the *berakhah,* potent, universal, and ineffectual, like the Pope's *urbi et orbi* benediction in the Piazza San Pietro.

From under the tallith, the children and men sought out their mothers, wives, and other assorted relatives in the gallery. We could clearly see Aunt Rosetta, worried and teary-eyed, practically falling out of her seat to see her children in that sea of faded silk.

"Aunt Rosetta is no hawk," *mamma* used to joke. She was sweet, funny, exuberant, tall, with red cheeks and straight, light-colored hair put up in a chignon like the character Tordella in the comics I read in the *Corriere dei Piccoli* and like the mother of Bibì and Bibò, as the Katzenjammer Kids were known to me, except she didn't brandish a rolling pin. She was always flustered and spoke quickly in the Verona dialect, waving her arms about. Her specialties were everyday family events, like the preparation of delicious lunches

—as she demonstrated later in the long, calm summer of 1943 in Asti—and worrying about her children: "They're wild ones, they are. I'm at my wit's end as to what to do about them!"

She had married my mother's brother, and by 1940 she was already a widow with two children: Lidia, a rebellious teenager known to everyone as Pucci, and Attilio, who was our age. Attilio died in 1988 in Jerusalem, where for a long time he had held the honorable position of guardian of the false tomb of King David, actually a mausoleum constructed in the eighteenth century for an Arab sheik.

In 1943, Pucci was around eighteen years old; she was not a great beauty, but she was attractive and shapely and seemed prototypically "Italian" to the country bumpkins who were the mainstay of Hitler's army. She herself told me, with the thoughtless pride of a young girl *en fleur* who was also a chronic, imprudent complainer, that since September 8th, she had been followed several times by German soldiers all the way to temple, which she would enter with great ostentation simply for the pleasure of watching the horrified expressions on the faces of those unfortunate clowns of the *Wehrmacht.*

One day, she was picked up by a band of Fascists at the bank where she had gone to withdraw some money for her mother. They asked each customer what his or her race was because, as we all know, banks are full of usurers—*Pisan Cantos* (Ezra Pound, ed. Guanda). My cousin, who could have lied or at least kept silent, came forward arrogantly:

"I'm Jewish." That night, Aunt Rosetta telephoned everyone she knew and, finally, police headquarters; the officers implored her not to go to Schmid's offices at the Albergo Nazionale. But she went anyway, with our cousin Attilio, then eleven years old. When she reached the little *piazza* with the two churches, beneath the arches of Via Roma, she called one of our relatives from the Bar Augustus: she was going up, but she would leave Attilio downstairs in the street. He was saved by our uncle Vittorio, a shy member of the Valabrega clan with blue eyes (all Valabregas are shy and have blue eyes) and eyebrows so thick and long they seemed false, who arrived just as little Attilio, tired of waiting, was about to go up to look for his mother. Nothing more is known about Aunt Rosetta: she was killed on arrival, like Aunt Lina, like most of them.

Pucci was young and strong; she was able to face down Auschwitz, such was her nature, and she almost made it, and God knows she deserved to . . . In July 1945, a young woman by the name of Segre with an ashen, shriveled, and sardonic look, who was dying in a hospital bed at the Maria Vittorio Hospital in Turin, told my mother and me that my cousin had died of dysentery after Liberation, having seen with her own eyes the soldiers of the Red Army.

%

Names written on tombstones in a far-off cemetery: many of them I do not recognize, some of them I've forgotten, and all of them are destined to become simply names carved in stone, but some of them are still real people to me.

People I saw as a child and perhaps remember only slightly, but still alive to me, even if only for a short while longer. They will die with me. With every passing generation, each personal memory of that tragedy disappears, and the victims become faceless and ephemeral, less than shadows, moaning as they melt away in Hades or *Sheol.* The passage of time, while allowing for a reloading of the ammunition of horror, also allows for a "serene and equanimous" reexamination of the Shoah. Pushed by this serene equanimity of historical revisionism, many Jews are, like me, "packing up" before it is too late, trying to bury their memories in the minds of others in order to preserve them from the injuries of time and the efforts of those who actively seek to destroy them. Like an army of Emanuel Ringelblums,[2] we bury iron trunks full of documents and memories, hoping that the cognitive archeologists of the future, dressed in anti-radiation suits, will discover traces of our sinister thoughts in the minds of our descendants, led by Amos Oz.

Oz is the Israeli writer who defined the dangers of memory when its venoms alter perceptions of the present. But we are afraid that in the black night that falls behind us, as we run our last breathless steps to stay in the light, someone will take advantage of the darkness to wreak havoc with the tombstones in our graveyards. I don't mean the people who do their damage with black paint; these are pitiful dilettantes who confuse the reality of their thoughts with the meager abstraction represented by marble. But hordes of lies advance just beyond the waning light, and as we flee from the night—a black wall rising from the ground to the darkened stars—we throw a match into the darkness behind, turn back momentarily, and move on. There are many, lesser versions of Auschwitz, besides the real one: even one modeled after the Coliseum, with Carmelite nuns praying for Christian martyrs.

This is why I scour the names on the gravestones of the deported: I seek, often unsuccessfully, the real faces of the ones who never returned. Last month, in that dark cavern of the past illuminated by a solitary trembling candle, I discovered Mosè Poggetto,* a crotchety old man whose eyes were always red because of a chronic, noninfectious disease and whose droopy gray whiskers were stained yellow by snuff. I was afraid of him. I was afraid of him because of those red eyes that looked threatening to me at the time. People called him Barba Moise. *Barba* means "uncle" in Piedmontese, and so he had become everyone's uncle, and in reality he was the uncle of Lina and Rino. I used to see him often at their house in the late thirties. He was paralyzed and confined to a wheelchair, and when he went to temple, he had to be carried up the stairs by volunteers.

He was married to a Catholic, with whom he had a child, also Catholic, who had been arrested in Turin. On the advice of shadowy messengers, he was convinced that his half-

* Poggetto, Mosè. See L. Picciotto Fargion, *Il libro della memoria,* p. 490.

Jewish, Catholic daughter would be set free if he turned himself in in her place. And he was right.

Barba Moise went to the SS headquarters in his wheelchair, accompanied by his wife, who wanted to be taken with her husband. But, as was "logical," she was forced to leave him there alone.

He was carried onto one of the cattle cars in his wheelchair, in which he traveled all the way to Auschwitz; I don't know how he went to the gas chamber. Perhaps in his wheelchair.

%

Facing east in the golden temple, wrapped in our tallidths, we wiggled as we pronounced in unison, *"Kadosh, ḳadosh, ḳadosh,"* holy, holy, holy the Name be blessed in eternity. Everyone was there except the anti-Fascists who were in jail or in the camps, like Carlo Levi (*Christ Stopped at Eboli,* ed. Einaudi). He often went to temple in the days after the war was over, until he realized that he was more of an expert on southern Italian life than on being a Jew.

The superhero Bruno Jesi, mutilated in the Fascist war in Spain, hobbled on two black canes. On his release from the military hospital that had patched him together in 1938, he found himself to be a Jew and a cripple. He died happy before 1943 in the most elegant casino on Via Fratelli Calandra: he was with two naked girls who were trying to excite his shattered remains with the combined effects of their healthy, young flesh; halfway there, they had to switch their efforts to first aid. Before this enviable end, Bruno Jesi often visited the Colonna e Finzi School, a silent witness to his Italianness, gold medals dangling from his blue jacket, which covered a hollow, perhaps nonexistent chest. He didn't say much or sermonize; I think he knew what was about to happen. He just sat there and watched the class through thick glasses, which gave him a steady, vitreous gaze. His mere presence scared us out of our wits.

Then there was Ettore Ovazza with the mild, uncondescending look typical of members of his unimaginably wealthy family. He was a confirmed Fascist who founded *La Nostra Bandiera,* an anti-Zionist Jewish journal; he did not fully comprehend that his German and Fascist comrades were more than simple anti-Zionists until he was hacked to pieces by the Adolf Hitler Division of the SS and burned to a crisp in the furnace of the public school in Intra along with his wife and his daughter, who had been in school with me.*

They were all there, wrapped in their talliths: the Zionists, the liberals, the Communists, the ex-Fascists, the future

* See L. Picciotto Fargion, *Il libro della memoria,* p. 761. *La Nostra Bandiera* was the organ of Turin's Jewish Fascists, sworn enemies of the Zionists who published the magazine *Israel.* As anti-Semitism grew, *La Nostra Bandiera*'s Fascism became more virulent. Few people lamented its closing with the passing of the racial laws. In 1933, it published the following congratulatory message: "A Fascist salute to our comrade Mario Zargani on the birth of his *balilla* Aldo."

partisans, and the others, the majority, who were nothing in particular, just bewildered individuals.

The Saturday after June 14, 1940—the day the Germans marched on Paris—Signor Pfeiffer extracted his tallith from its embroidered bag with a satisfied, serene air, kissed it, placed it around his shoulders, and began to participate in the ceremony as he gazed at the *Aron ha-Kodesh,* the holy closet which holds the scrolls of the Law. He smiled to himself, proud of his stature as an Ashkenazi. *Papà* eyed him suspiciously, because as a German, he seemed insufficiently contrite about what was happening. Wrapped in the family tallith, my father asked him accusingly, "Haven't you read the papers today?" "Yes, I read them, and I tell you, despite everything, as someone who fought in the Battle of the Marne, the idea of Germans marching in Paris—I know, it's absurd, don't look at me that way, I myself am shocked by my own reaction—but the entrance of my compatriots in Paris is . . . well, a victory. Yes, a victory, a great victory." After a moment of silence, my father managed to compose himself and said, wrapped in the dignity of his eighteen months on the Kras and his French allies in their *bleu horizon*-colored uniforms, "I pity you," and turned his back, swearing never to speak to him again. He did speak to him again, because the events of the next few months and years erased any sign of "Germanness" from poor Signor Pfeiffer.

"Kadosh, ḳadosh, ḳadosh," they repeated, and when, after the reading, the scrolls of the Torah were brought around

triumphantly, silver crowns shimmering and bells jingling—after they are read, the goat-leather-bound scrolls are dressed up in royal pomp—Rabbi Disegni angrily pushed back the hands which reached up toward the sacred scrolls to touch them and then touch their fingers to their lips, a sign of mystical devotion. "Leave that to the *goyim,*" he would say, between prayers, staring disdainfully at the poor idolaters.

Kadosh, ḳadosh, ḳadosh . . . Even I was an idolater as a child: I would have given anything to be allowed to enter, in my velvet outfit, the dimly lit space where the scrolls were stored after their triumphal journey and uncover the mystery of their holiness. For a long time I believed this holiness to be the source of the dark call of the shofar, until one day I saw the rabbi blow into the horn. It was holiness that shone from above, through an alabaster panel, pierced by the Kabbalistic rays of the Oriental sun, emanating from far-off Jerusalem, that hilly, earthy, blue city. I thought that perhaps the unpronounceable YHWH, God himself, might be found behind that sparkling, opalescent slab.

Instead, beyond it lay the roof of the Politeama Chiarella Theater.

11 ⁂ Asti

Mamma kept repeating, over and over again, "I'm telling you, your Aunt Rosetta, poor thing, she can't possibly imagine your finicky tastes. Now she's here in Asti, she thinks she's back in Verona. No two ways about it, she can't stop talking about her *polenta e osei,*[1] and I'm telling you, you won't like it, but I'm telling you, if she makes it, I don't care if you like it or not, you're going to eat it, no complaining, because there are limits, even to the whims of stubborn children. But I'm warning you, you won't like it. As soon as she says she's going to make *polenta e osei*—and I don't know why she insists, as if it were some great delicacy—just say, 'Yes! Yes! We want *polenta e osei!*' But be forewarned: you won't like it! Count your lucky stars she hasn't found all the ingredients yet, it's not even the right season, but she will, I guarantee it!" *Mamma* didn't provide any further information, and we didn't really know what *osei* were anyway.

I'm not sure when or how, but sometime around the beginning of 1943, Aunt Rosetta, Pucci, and Attilio came to live with us. I can only clearly remember them being there in the summer, during the hot months, and I saw them for the last time at the celebration on September 8th, Armistice Day, the night we prematurely celebrated the end of the war. By the end of that winter, half of the party had been incinerated and scattered in the mud of Silesia.

The provincial, sinful Asti has its season, and what a season it is. In summer, between May and September, its cobblestone streets, empty of passersby and vehicles, and its squat brick *palazzi,* normally darkened by sloping eaves and roofs, are sharply lit by the sun. They stand in stark silence under an implacable dark-blue sky, which in turn reflects the blackish-green ocean of vineyards surrounding the city. The disorderly sloping roofs reflect the golden light of the sun; the scene is tinged by a warm glow of memory even when it is real and present.

Our relatives had become fast friends with a neighbor who had been living there alone for years before they arrived: an elderly American tourist—she seemed ancient to me—who had been caught unawares in 1941 in San Gimignano by a side effect of the bombing of Pearl Harbor. Because of her advanced age, she had been spared the camps and was confined to Asti, where she serenely waited for the end of the cruelest and vastest war in history: her travel agent was really going to get a piece of her mind when she got back! We never found out what she told people about her five years in an obscure town in the Po River Valley when she returned to her mythical New England, where a single tree is large enough to cover half of medieval Asti with its foliage: "It's beeeautiful, beeeautiful like you can't imagine, not quite as beautiful as San Gimignano, but really lovely. I had the nicest neighbors, a big family, and now I don't see them anymore . . ." She was very thin, with white, frizzy hair and lots of teeth like Eleanor Roosevelt. In 1943, she had not yet mastered much of a vocabulary; in fact, she used the same word, *pipa,* when referring to the heater, the stove, or anything else used for burning, heating, or cooking. So we called her "La Pipa," a nickname she tolerated with Anglo-Saxon good humor as she went about her business smoking one cigarette after another, calm and slouching in her heavy woolen black-and-white-checked dressing gown that reached down to her large slippers with tiny checks. As none of us spoke a word of English, and she barely knew ten words of Italian, our friendship was based on a mutual, visceral, sentimental sympathy: she appeared to like our aunt and her rabble-rousing children as well as us, and she used to smile at us broadly, hug us, and caress us with her diaphanous, blue-veined hands. She would abandon herself to long soliloquies, especially with seventeen-year-old Pucci. She considered Pucci a confidante and would entrust her memories and secrets to her. Perhaps she told stories about the young men of Newton, Massachusetts, and about herself as a young girl, which none of us could understand and to which we responded with smiles, nods, the pressing of hands, and consoling gestures when she cried.

%

The Corso Alfieri cut the small city in half, and it was along this street that the residents of Asti went for their leisurely Sunday stroll, rendered even more leisurely by the shortness of the street. We lived on the Piazza Umberto I, at number 1 on the narrow Stradina della Cattedrale, near the Palazzo Alfieri, ancestral home of the tragedian who as a child, the story goes, asked to be tied to a chair in order to be forced to study. From Piazza Umberto I, the Corso Alfieri ran alongside several elegant *palazzi* renovated in the seventeen and eighteen hundreds, and then the houses became more dismal, badly in need of repair. The street ended abruptly in a formless *piazza* with a few trees where livestock auctions were held; in it were scattered seemingly at random a guardhouse, some urinals, the public weighing house, and the Palazzo del Fascio with its giant *fascio* —a bundle of rods with a projecting axe blade, the symbol of Fascism—as tall as the building itself. The *fascio* was built out of tubes of glass in which bubbles constantly rose through white-, red-, and green-tinted water. It wasn't really a *piazza,* but it was known as the Piazza del Littorio and was the ill-conceived outer limit of the city. This *piazza* was used as a park, a threshing floor, and even as a train platform. It was the rear end of Asti, the end from which one entered the city.*

✠

Toward the middle of February of 1943, I became an auditor in the fourth-grade class at the Vittorio Alfieri School on Corso Alfieri. Not even the fifth grade at the Salesian school the following year was as empty of substance: the teacher, who had messy gray hair and one leg shorter than the other, moved slowly and could not keep up with the spirited children she would have liked to strangle. Next to her desk, she kept a long rod with a wooden sphere the size of an orange attached to the end. In the late forties, I saw this instrument of repression used by the mounted police of the AMG** in Trieste. They were the famous *cerini*—or matches—so called because their helmets, similar to those worn by London "bobbies," reminded the people of Trieste of match heads.

* Please do not compare this description to any city map; it does not correspond to the reality you would have found there at the time, and, fortunately, the urban design of Asti has since changed.

** The Allied Military Government. After the Second World War, Trieste was in the hands of the AMG while a peace treaty was hammered out. I was a member of a small group that hoped that Trieste would go neither to Italy nor to Yugoslavia but rather become an independent city-state, a crossroads of races, peoples, civilizations, cultures, and economies. I had been contaminated by the utopian teachings of Ballarin, my father's viola teacher and a passionate Triestian secessionist. That was not the only lapse of political judgment in my life. Until the fall of the Berlin Wall, I always referred to East Germany as the German Democratic Republic . . . *panta rei.*

The teacher would bellow at the class, waving her weapon over the heads of the children, who cowered under their desks. That was nothing. When, on more rare occasions, her nerves gave out completely, she would stare straight at the offender and continue her lesson, while slowly, without altering her gaze, picking up her weapon. Then, still speaking evenly, she would place it as close as possible to the miscreant, who, hypnotized by the monotony of her voice, would be caught unaware by a terrible blow to the head.

At first I was frightened by the teacher's ferocity and decided that she was worse even than Miss Amar, who almost never took recourse in violence; her preferred weapon was humiliation. But, in fact, a blissful year awaited me because, for racial reasons, the teacher loved me from my first day in class. She was an ardent anti-Fascist, and she could no longer tolerate the world we were living in, and now, miracle of miracles, there was a little Jewish boy in her class, a persecuted innocent to be loved and protected. She took me aside on my first day to assure me that I would never suffer punishment from her: I needn't worry; her enemies knew who they were. And she gnashed her rotten teeth.

Whatever I said in class, the teacher would look at me adoringly and ask me to stand and repeat it several times for all to note and learn from. "Got that?!" she would ask threateningly after I finished, and was answered by growls and mumbles, the product of her psychological thrashing and physical violence.

The teacher had a group of sworn enemies, who, commanded by the most bestial among them, always did the same thing, driving her out of her mind: they ostentatiously drank the ink out of their inkwells, allowing it to drip down their chins, and laughed, their teeth completely blue. There were only three or four offenders, but they were persistent in their battle, which was probably in part a war of ideologies, considering that their leader, the class dunce, was the son of the Fascist *Federale*[2] in Asti. I am not surprised that the son of a Fascist *Federale* could be an intellectual zero, but I can't help suspecting, or rather believing, that the battle originated with the teacher; I cannot judge the intellectual capacities of the ink-drinkers, but I'm sure that I did not deserve the top score on every single test, every homework assignment, in every subject: Italian, history, geography, and even, to add insult to injury, arithmetic! The teacher, blinded by her political passions, was as unfair to me as she was to the son of the *Federale*. She had probably lost her mind many years earlier, perhaps even as far back as the Ethiopian campaign, but certainly since the Spanish Civil War.

Later, in 1949, at the Camillo Benso Conte di Cavour School in Turin, a sweet, gentle, and lovely literature teacher who had been a militant in the Italian Women's Union heard a friend of mine innocently call me "big-nose" and lost her head, a very rare occurrence. She decided to dedicate an entire lesson to my nose. She made me stand next to the lectern in front of the class as she compared my profile to those found in twenty-or-forty-pounds-worth of art books which she had leafed through feverishly the night before: profiles by Masaccio, Piero della Francesco, Giotto, Duccio di Buoninsegna. She lingered of course on the drawn features of Christ, my fellow countryman, but also pointed out the exotic nobility of my profile with the aid of photographs of ancient Mayan, Aztec, Inca, and Hindu sculptures. Good artistic reproductions and the Skira e Lionello Venturi Publishing House had made this lucid delirium possible. This horrifying lesson in nasal racism ended with a comparison (!) between myself and a photograph of Sitting Bull. Being Jewish has a price even in the best of times.

Fortunately, the attitude of my teacher in Asti did not cause any resentment among my classmates, who were not aware of the fact that I was Jewish. And perhaps the son of the Fascist was not a Fascist himself and, even more likely, was unaware of why he was being singled out.

At the end of the school year, almost two months before the unbelievable events of July 25th, my father was called in by the superintendent of schools. *Papà* was worried before the meeting, and he returned from it perhaps even more worried but also proud. The superintendent took his time, taking credit for Roberto's and my performance in school, and inviting well-deserved thanks for his brilliant idea of having us attend the school as auditors. Then he cut to the chase, dramatically: the teacher had handed in her grades and had given me a 10 in every subject, including religion.

But more important, she had failed the son of the *Federale.* She refused to listen to reason. She had failed him in every subject, including gymnastics, and had given him a 6 in conduct, so that poor unfortunate delinquent would have to repeat the fourth grade.

The superintendent was desperate, because after he had tried to convince the teacher through reason, he had decided to threaten her, in vain; "that crazy woman," as the superintendent described her, had calmly indicated that she intended to sacrifice herself for the right to fail "that delinquent."

"The superintendent told me," *papà* concluded, "that he will hold back her grades as long as possible so we can try to convince her to let the fool pass!" It wasn't easy; we had to go to her house more than once, and we invited her to our house for dinner, but in the end she was persuaded for two reasons: first, because her "self-sacrifice," while fully justified, would have reflected badly on the superintendent, who was clearly not a Fascist, and on us. And second, because my parents asked her to tutor me over the summer so that I could take the middle school entrance examination and skip the fifth grade. And so I was forced to study all of July and August of 1943 and take the exam on September 8th, Armistice Day, the beginning of the period of panic.

At the end of the summer, Aunt Rosetta, after much searching and effort, managed one day to prepare the infamous *polenta e osei:* it is not possible to avoid every pitfall.

Both doors flew open—fortunately, the French doors at my aunt's house did not lead to a scandalous bedroom but rather to a very respectable kitchen—and my aunt entered, beaming—one of her two possible states, the other being utter desolation. She looked like an ad for *polenta e osei:* radiant and speaking with a particularly strong Veronese accent, she held up the mountain of polenta spotted with the tiny cadavers of birds—these were the *osei*—which looked like the skeletons of mountain climbers who hadn't quite made it to the top. We were about to take a bite out of the *Piccolo Alpino* (Salvator Gotta, ed. SEI), wondering if the climber's ropes had worn out or been cut clean, when Pucci arrived to save us. She normally paid scant attention to what was going on around her, and in particular took little notice of my brother and me, whom she equated with her infernal brother Attilio.

Attilio was not quite right in the head from when he was a small child. He was nervous, intolerant, and unkind, and would sometimes start gasping violently for air for no apparent reason, perhaps for a laugh—and it was definitely not funny, though he seemed to think it was. In Asti, he was a fun companion, and with him we acquired our basic musical formation, using the records of the Cetra Quartet, a popular singing group of the time. In my mind, the warm light of that summer is accompanied by the musical soundtrack:

The Viscount of Castelfombrone,
The ancestor of Buglione,

Challenged Count Lomanto,
And with his glove called for a fight . . .

But even when it came to music, he was frenetic and anxious: he listened to the records, with us and on his own, hundreds and hundreds of times, ad nauseam, until one day he decided to scratch them all with a nail. He could not come to an internal decision without immediately applying it to the real world. *Mamma* and *papà* watched us for any signs of Attilio-like behavior; they believed that we might be "infected" by what they considered a kind of mental illness.

Attilio's mind—rendered fascinating by its inventiveness—was unable to understand, filter, and rationalize the greatest collective madness in history, of which he became a direct victim. When his mother and sister were taken away, his mind stopped working altogether, or almost, and he was not able to finish even middle school. After 1945, no one could look after him, because he would get up three or four times a night yelling out disconnected phrases. It was impossible to wake him, even by shaking him strenuously for long periods of time. In the morning he would say it had all been a joke.

It doesn't take much to make life with a young man who has lost his marbles impossible. In 1949, when he left for a kibbutz, all of Turin gave a none-too-generous sigh of relief. I don't think that it was the kibbutz or Israel itself which lessened—but could not cure—his suffering but rather the long, melancholy silence of the Sheik's Tomb in the shade of the cypress trees and the Hebrew language, which is like a magnificent maze for laboratory rats.

I saw Attilio for the last time in 1987, in Jerusalem, near the walls of the old city, pink and luminous at sundown as designed by Suleiman's architects in honor of Islam. He was dressed like a rabbi, which he was not; in fact, he did not even believe in God. He seemed less anxious and—perhaps as a result of the Hebrew language and its sumptuous, primordial cadences—spoke like an ancient wise man, in proverbs and religious sayings, which perhaps lent his brain a modicum of order. Every so often, always unannounced, a blue streak of angst would illuminate his face as he asked, in the middle of a talmudic citation, "Remember when my mother made *polenta e osei* . . . Remember when you stole Pucci's bicycle and broke it, and she got mad at you? . . . Sing me the song by the Cetra Quartet, the one that went, '*the Viscount of Castelfombrone,*' no, the other one, '*oh, woodcutter, come back to your homestead . . .*'"

Pucci saved us on the day of the *osei* in 1943, momentarily shaking off her adolescent "autism," into which she quickly receded again, picking up an old fashion magazine. She had perceived our desperate glances and the menace in my mother's eyes and said to Aunt Rosetta, in her perennially lazy, tired air, copied from Marlene Dietrich and Jean Arthur, "Can't you see, *mammina,* that these two are disgusted by your polenta?"

Papà, who struggled to feed his six-foot-two-inch frame with the meager war rations, swallowed little birds like pills, loudly thanking his lucky stars for our finicky tastes, partly to comfort Aunt Rosetta. Spitting out the tiny bones, he exclaimed: *"Ai chamorim non piacciono confetti."** *Papà*'s simulated or real insensitivity to the destinies of those tiny winged animals—meant to flit across the infinite blue sky and instead floating dead in red sauce, legs stiff and eyes closed—was put to the test on the night of September 30, 1943. Lina had been arrested on the 28th, and on the 29th there were rumors of roundups in Asti and all around. On the 30th we decided to flee, on the advice, or pressure, of our kind neighbors. They were a husband and wife with four children, two sons around our age and two older girls, who lived serenely but vigilantly in the house on the corner of Piazza Umberto I.

That night we put together the bare essentials we would need when we departed the next day; we had to travel light so that we could hop across Piedmont, without a precise destination, and cover our tracks; this is the real function of panic in the natural world. Some time later, when we were in Cotigliole or Acqui, we attempted to return to Asti because we no longer knew where to go. Our neighbors, look-

* A Jewish-Livornese proverb which means "mules don't eat sugar-covered almonds." It is usually used in a figurative sense, for example if a person does not appreciate a beautiful woman, an interesting play, or a good book . . .

ing out over the *piazza* from their house—which, in addition to real windows and doors, had two doors and two windows painted in trompe l'oeil—saw us crossing the *piazza* with our suitcases in the direction of our house and rushed down, all six of them, to block our path. "Don't go there, don't even slow down! They're looking for you, get out of here now, take the train, go anywhere, but don't stay here one minute longer!"

The night of the 30th, about fifteen or twenty days earlier, we had packed our bags and paid our debts in preparation for our flight to Costigliole and Turin, Casale Monferrato, Borgone di Susa, then back to Turin, and finally to Bioglio once the partisan struggle had begun in earnest: a great moment in Italian history and a stroke of good fortune for hundreds, thousands of Jews.

One of the problems we had to solve before the period of panic and aimless flight—which lasted until the middle of 1944, when it was replaced by a more normal level of terror—was what to do with two yellow ducklings that *papà* had given us back in the now remote month of August. They were adorable, with their little billed faces, their innocent, kind eyes, their waddling gait, and their downy feathers; we let them swim in the laundry basin. But no one wanted to look after them for us, and, as my father suffered terribly from hunger, he announced in a thundering voice like the rumble of the approaching storm which was about to turn my life upside down: "I'm going to eat them." He went to the butcher's with the two little creatures, one in each hand, their feet curled under them, looking calmly ahead, and he came back with a bloody package containing the plucked and decapitated corpses of his victims. He wasn't able to eat them, though, because Roberto, Mother, and I cried and stared at his plate. He sat with his chin in one hand, playing with the scraps, turning his plate, until finally he pushed it away and exclaimed: "I can't eat them, and it's your fault. I'll just stay hungry."

Papà would have qualified to go to Paradise, if that place ever existed, but instead he, together with *mamma,* survives in my mind, in a cramped paradise where I play God. He must tolerate, without much say in the matter, the most outlandish fragments of memory that keep introducing themselves into my consciousness, which is his disorderly and not-so-eternal resting place.

Pucci also continues to float in my brain, appearing from time to time in Piazza Umberto I on her aluminum bicycle with white tires and pedal-brakes. And after the *polenta e osei,* Aunt Rosetta enters—beaming and carrying a huge bowl from the kitchen door—with *succa barucca,** and then, on September 8th, *gnocchi alla bava,* full of butter and cheese.

Early on the morning of July 26th, the window of my room opened above me in the courtyard and *papà* appeared, crying out, "Aldino, Mussolini has fallen!" I went with him

* In Jewish-Veronese dialect, a dish called "blessed pumpkin": it is a poor-man's dish, cooked in the oven after the bread is baked, and eaten as a dessert, with a spoon. It's nothing to write home about.

to the station, where we saw the trains of the *Wehrmacht* with their tanks and long-barreled guns going by, one after the other, speeding towards Genoa and the Thyrrhenian Sea. *Papà* left for Turin to see if he could get back his seat in the orchestra: they didn't give it to him; they hemmed and hawed, reassuring him, courteously, even cordially, but they sent him away. He went back several times, and each time he would say: "They said to come back in a week or two." His silver medal from the First World War showing the helmet from the Great War on a background of blue enamel reappeared on his lapel. It was a useless gesture, and he knew it, but it gave him hope and made him feel in step with the brief tenure of Badoglio's military coup. Everything changed, except the racial laws.

I took part in marches with him, and on the night of July 26th, I watched with my parents as a crowd knocked down the tricolor *fascio* on the Piazza Littorio in Asti. It resisted, leaking colored water from the little glass tubes of its cardiovascular system. On September 8th, Pucci shouted from the courtyard, dressed in a trouser-skirt, "The war is over! The war is over!" putting her foot on the brake and then abandoning her bicycle on the ground in order to jump up and down and hug everyone she saw. She embraced the soldiers on Corso Alfieri in the encroaching darkness, running from one to the next, celebrating her impending death the following February. The light in Pucci's eyes was already fading when Segre brought two Mongolian soldiers from the Siberian army—the "fresh troops" who eventually arrived in the Unter den Linden and the Kurfurstendamm in Berlin—but she raised her dehydrated hands a tiny bit, and she knew then that she was free. And according to Segre, she held the soldiers' dark hands as they stared at each other, perplexed by the mysteries of the West.

After the debacle of September 8th, events rushed headlong, but the evening stroll on Corso Alfieri persevered at its usual, leisurely pace every evening at sunset. The faces changed, appearing and disappearing in an instant, transmitting messages, and then they disappeared forever. One evening there was a soldier sitting on the sidewalk, his legbands loose, his beard long, and his gun leaning against his thigh; he used his bayonet to cut pieces of meat, which he devoured. The passersby continued their slow stroll, crossing over to the other side, because the meat was spoiled and crawling with worms. *Papà* didn't cross over; he squatted down in front of the soldier, his colleague-at-arms, and looked him in the eyes, saying softly, "Don't eat that, it's bad, it will make you sick." And with his delicate, strong hand, he pushed the soldier's hand toward the gutter, his eyes jumping back and forth from the soldier's desperate, fierce eyes to the bayonet he gripped in his right hand. The soldier grunted, his mouth full of meat and worms, and my father spoke to him as to a child, and the soldier was a child, a child bewildered by hunger, with a shaggy blue beard and dark eyes full of hatred, fear, and suspicion. In the end, the rotten meat went into the gutter, and *papà* gave him some money so he could at least buy himself some bread. Then we continued our evening stroll. *Papà* had been frightened because he knew that hungry men turn into beasts; sometimes they let themselves be cajoled, and other times they attack.

We had other neighbors on Corso Umberto I. There was a blonde, skinny woman, neither old nor ugly, who seldom acknowledged us, and when she did, did so with a stiff nod; she usually avoided the dilemma by walking with her nose in the air, turned the other direction. *Papà* had nicknamed her "Miss Green-in-the-Gills" because her complexion was a sort of moldy green. We never spoke to her, nor she to us, but she seemed hostile and antagonistic as she watched us in silence from her balcony while we played in the courtyard.

One day *papà* called us to the table and said, "Listen to me, all of you. It's a good thing to see the errors in your ways in order to learn from them and better understand the world we live in, which is complicated and mysterious. Today I heard from our nice neighbors with the trompe l'oeil house that Miss Green-in-the-Gills is very, very ill. She has cancer and doesn't have long to live. See how you can be wrong in life? Please, from now on, be nice to her when you see her, even if she doesn't respond. She is not a bad person, she doesn't hate us, she's just ill."

As soon as she was well enough, this poor, unfortunate soul went to the SS and turned us in, took part in the distribution of our possessions to the "most needy," and then promptly died, serene in the knowledge that she had done her duty. On our brief return to Asti, when we barely set down our suitcases thanks to the vigilance of our neighbors, our house had just been emptied, under the instructions of that dutiful, dying woman.

Man's imperfection is perhaps not moral at all, as we believe or even hope, but connected to the very structure of his thought. Prejudice is vulnerable to confrontation with reality, but superstition lies hidden in the most ancient recesses of our mind, a remnant of forgotten modes of thinking. Or, perhaps, the destruction of the all-encompassing mirror of mythology may have left these shards of shimmering glass in our mind, cutting as razors.

The Asti period was coming to an end, and we were about to take flight once again, driven away by panic, but that night in the interminable summer of 1943, we continued our slow stroll up the Corso Alfieri.

There was a dimly lit bookstore halfway down the *corso;* in its cluttered window, the owner exhibited what he considered to be the latest titles. For months I stopped to gaze at a large, expensive book which loomed above all the others; on the shiny cover there was an enlarged photograph of a strange spiral, in which one could distinguish incandescent suns and isolated stars in a gravitational vortex millions of years old. The hurricane of stars remained a mystery to us because we couldn't afford to buy such an expensive book, and because the murky window of the shop accentuated the dark night around the incandescent spiral. The title of the book was *Outer Galaxies.*

After September 8th, the Fascists began to return, anxious to reveal to the world and to themselves the nothingness they were made of, as my mother used to say. They wished to be seen as concrete and fierce. On one of our long strolls, in the middle of September, I believe, or perhaps after the 20th, a Fascist in leggings and a black colonial shirt, angry-faced and pugnacious, stood in the middle of Corso Alfieri—his legs apart, his hand on the pistol in his waistband—and insulted the passersby for taking part in the mild, nonviolent protests of July 25th and September 8th. With a nasty, ferocious air, he glared at the people in the street, who looked down at the ground penitently, hoping that no one had seen them in their moment of rebellion, tearing down posters of *il Duce* and dancing hand in hand around a bonfire of his complete works. I seem to remember joyful singing on that occasion.

Who's afraid of the big bad wolf?

But then I realize I'm confusing our joyful celebration on July 25th with Walt Disney's *The Three Little Pigs,* which I saw at the Cinema Nazionale in Turin in 1939. On the program that afternoon there was another cartoon: a jury of evil cats tried Pluto and sentenced him to death for being a dog before he realized—lucky dog!—that it was all a bad dream.

For a moment that felt like an eternity, our eyes crossed the Fascist's angry gaze. He started, as did my father, and then looked past us at the people who followed on the sidewalk. It was the *Federale,* and he knew, because the superintendent had told him, that if it hadn't been for my father, his son would have had to repeat the fourth grade.

12 ※ Tarcisio

If someone had been walking among the rice fields in the blinding sun of the Vercellese on the morning of October 15, 1944, along the long, straight, and deserted road leading from Cavaglià to Salussola—a tiny station on the Turin-Biella line—he would have seen a woman, small, middle-aged, and plump—within the limitations on plumpness during wartime—accompanied by two children as tall as she was, with shaved heads—school regulations—and bare-chested because of the unseasonable heat, their shirts tied about their waists and their sweaters stuffed into their mother's two large bags, one on each arm, which contained everything, including afternoon snacks.

The sky was streaked with Flying Fortresses—armored planes fitted with machine guns on the front, the tail, the wings, the top, the belly, as well as cannons, a crew of ten to twelve airmen, and bombs—flying north to crush Germany on my behalf. Entire fleets of armored planes flew by us: it was the powerful hand of an industrial nation larger than the world had ever seen, extending its white fingers across the sky. The white hand in the sky was allied with the Bolsheviks: the Hegelian right was finally being crushed between the jaws of Anglo-Saxon empiricism and the Hegelian left. We were invisible to the crowds of American pilots who looked down on the plain distractedly, bored by the long flight from the Mediterranean to a Germany in flames and onward toward the North to the wintry islands of Scotland.

I saw my first American soldier after Liberation, on a tepid May 7, 1945, at 10:00 P.M.; he was bored, mortally so, and he was driving one of those bumper cars with an antenna that gives off sparks against the electric wires above. We were in Biella, free and on our way home, waiting for a night train to Turin. He was all alone in the deserted rink, and he drove around and around, unobserved, yawning joylessly, his long legs sticking out of the bumper car; the owner had fallen asleep on the bench behind the ticket counter. *Papà* decided, in a flash of joy brighter than the lights in the rink, which were like the lamps in *Quai Des Brumes* (Cinema Nazionale, Turin, 1940), that it was time for a gesture, a joyful proclamation of our newly recovered safety—we were ten hours away from Germany's unconditional surrender. With his typically regal attitude, he declared in this brief moment of license before the return to normalcy that we could go around as many times as we liked, each in his own car. "You decide how much I should spend. Have fun." The American was overjoyed—and he wasn't even drunk—and he crashed into us again and again, screaming like a Mohican, laughing his loud American laugh and speaking in his incomprehensible dialect from West Virginia or New Hampshire. He let us crash into him, and then, selecting the least protected one of us, attacked astutely and fiercely, yelping in terror at our two-pronged retaliation. This went on for countless turns, until Roberto and I were completely exhausted. The American, who was just starting to have fun, ran after us and begged my father, his compartmentalized American wallet in his hands: "Signore, hey, Signore, I'll pay! Signore! Just a few more rounds, *dobbiamo giocare, giocare tutti, pago io!!*" And he returned disappointedly and long-leggedly to his bumper car, and into our memory, where he could only crash into his own boredom.

%

Mamma and *papà* wanted us to be happy because we had a future and, they hoped, no past. For them it was more difficult, because their future was already largely used up. They were alive and that was enough, but their youth was gone, and they grieved for people they had loved who had been murdered. Their time was up, and they had used it to save their two children. They had won the battle, but like all survivors, they were alone; their large family, a typically Jewish and Italian institution, had been destroyed by the war. The institution of the large family had come to an end for all Italians, but for the Jews the reassuring and warm way of life which it represented—which had seemed eternal—had disappeared in twenty months with the crushing massacre of the Shoah. Still ahead were the sad days of futile searching, the interviews with survivors and witnesses, and the lost causes, like the trial of the banal Captain Schmid. Months and years of legal justice, incomplete, but justice all the same.

Civil justice came late but was truly impeccable: The Federal Republic of Germany (the German Democratic Republic proclaimed itself to be a victim of the Nazis and asked for reparations!) gave the heirs, when there were any, compensation equivalent to three months of an unskilled worker's salary for every relative who had died in the camps, using tables of average income provided by insurance experts. This financial effort (22 percent of the GDP in 1954 and 30 percent in 1966) contributed to German forgetfulness and rewarded history's winners: the Jews and the Gypsies.

%

It is October 1944, and we are in the middle of the war, walking among the rice fields. We were not invisible to the Mosquitoes, tiny fighter-bombers made out of wood whose motors sounded like insects; they circled above our heads and the endless Po River Valley, skimming the treetops. Dazzling rice fields, rows of poplars, and the road with three dots—us—another flash of the burning mirror of the rice fields, poplars, flash, train tracks, curve, three dots. But what are those dots? The three of us! Us! Happy to be leaving behind Christianity and eternal life at the school, dazzled by the hot, yellow sun, happy to hear the roar of the armored planes, the buzzing of the Mosquitoes watching over and protecting us: "Come this way, we know you are Jews, there's no danger, we'll take care of you, don't be afraid, we have to go fast so they don't get us, but we'll be back, so just keep moving along . . ."

That October, France had been liberated, and the partisan republics were created. The Americans were almost, but not quite, in Bologna; the air was full of friendly airplanes, and millions of Russians, Tartars, Mongolians, and Kalmucks were arriving from the opposite end of the Earth, from the edge of the frozen Pacific, at train stations in German cities. The war was "practically" over. But we still had a winter ahead of us—in fact, we had autumn, a terrible winter, and spring—but luckily we did not know it yet. The real future, the one that loomed ahead of us to everyone's great surprise after so many years of false hopes, was still beyond grasp. The present and the past are devoid of laws or rules to indicate the path or illuminate the night of what is still to come. We had no idea whether we would be saved; otherwise, we would have taken pictures, signed autographs, and written letters to our present selves.

Meanwhile, we crossed the semimaritime plain of the rice fields, without a thought for the future.

When Radetzky's imperial army arrived in the Ticino in 1849, his troops had moved so quickly from the Peschiera Quadrilateral—the area demarcated by the fortresses of Mantua, Verona, Legnago, and Peschiera—that the army of Hungarians, Czechs, and Slovaks mistook the rice fields for the sea: before them they saw a series of blue mirrors framed by poplars, dusty roads, and lakes that reflected the swollen white clouds, the sky, and the silent, immobile farmhouses.

We wandered through this sea of mud—in 1944, the abandoned rice fields had become swamps—Mother weighed down by her bags and by a "marsupial," her invention, a small pouch hidden under her girdle containing the treasury bonds she had received as a wedding gift (100,000 lire), the family jewels, and three gold pocket watches—my father's and two grandfathers'—with their chains, on which were hung little coral charms and medals won in *bocce* tournaments.

Roberto scampered back and forth like a puppy, picking flowers and running after his beloved toads and the *preive* butterflies, or "priests," the Piedmontese name for the small yellow-and-black *Amata phegea.* These butterflies fly stuck together in pairs, in primordial orgasms that last hours and hours, lucky beasts. At one point he stopped short, like a hound who has caught a whiff of his prey; he had recognized the farmhouse where he had been served stuffed zucchini on the day in July when he ran away from school because of a complicated situation in which, I must admit, he was the wounded party. He found a turtle and carried it under his right arm like a package, leaning way over to the left to counterbalance its weight. The reptile was adopted by our family as a potential portable safe, with the crazy idea that we might bury father's giant diamond ring in its armhole; this ring was our greatest treasure and our only hope for salvation *in extremis. Mamma* could feel it shimmering dangerously through her girdle, slip, undershirt, and dress, all of which were black.

Suddenly, behind us, we heard the growl of an engine, and all three of us turned around, including Roberto with his giant turtle which, having already adopted him, no longer looked like a package and had stuck out its elephant-like legs, fish-like arms, and lettuce-like head and was gazing toward the flat horizon of the rice field with its not-quite-human but harmless, myopic, astigmatic eyes. After a moment or two, our mother-commander said: "They must be from the *X Mas.*" A greenish armored vehicle careened down the straight road from the west, skidding right and left, tilting as it did, jostling a dozen heads which we could see sticking out of it in the distance. "We're against the light, and those people are crazy," *mamma* declared, pushing us to the side of the road with her bags; we stood there in single file looking like people who are hoping, after all, to be picked up. The armored vehicle had spotted us as well and started to slow down until it almost came to a stop, but when the blinding effect of the light had been eliminated, and they saw that my mother was not Assia Noris, the berets looked down and sneered, and they did not have arms, hands, or fingers enough to make all the most common vulgar gestures. Once their vast repertoire was exhausted—directed more at the dispelled mirage of the diva of white-telephone dramas than at our mother—the diesel amphibious vehicle expelled some fumes, and the heavy craft began its slow takeoff. Before it had reached the opposite horizon, it was careening down the road again, swinging back and forth, into the light. The disappointed exiles had hoped to find Luisa Ferida or Alida Valli on that road through the rice fields of the Vercellese, and instead they found my brother and his toads.[1]

We walked on, unfazed by the "absolutely uncouth"—my mother's words—but not unexpected behavior of the enemy soldiers, until our general halted once again, put down her bags, and gazed into the light, shading her eyes with her hand. "Those idiots went off the side of the road, and they deserve it, if only for their terrible manners, but now they're dangerous, so if you want to laugh, laugh inside but don't say a word, and don't look at them. I'll talk to them. I want you to be completely silent, no laughing, and try not to look at them."

We filed past the scene in silence: the amphibious vehicle had slammed headfirst into a rice field and spilled its cargo into the mud and water. The twelve berets were now searching in the *pauta*—Piedmontese for soft mud—for their rucksacks, machine guns, and packages of food, which they had to dry out on the side of the road, while they stared angrily at the horizon. "Is anyone hurt?" *mamma* asked, with the sweetest and steadiest tone she could muster, already expecting the "Get out of here! Get lost!" which effectively came her way, but not so fiercely as expected, because now they faced the task of pulling that giant steel object with its huge propeller out of the mud, with no oxen or horses or even white telephones in sight, only rice weeders, but even they were out of season.

We were the only people waiting for a train in the tiny station at Salussola, so tiny it did not even have a roof; we were blinded by the double brightness of sky and rice field, and we couldn't talk because of the deafening noise of the grasshoppers, in addition to the trilling of hundreds of thousands of cicadas out of season, and the silent retort of the laborious ants: "Serves you right! What did you expect?" This terrible din is what I've since heard described as the "silence of the countryside." The "silence" was interrupted by black smoke from the locomotive, which pulled three or four cattle cars, elegantly furnished with green benches picked up from some public park. After we automatically pulled ourselves and our bags onto the train, the few passengers took up their conversation about the latest roundup, telling a story—legend or reality?—about a dog who picked up the head of his master and went looking for the rest of the body, scratching disconsolately near the train tracks.

Tarcisio Moss was waiting for us at the Biella train station. Moss was not his real name but had become it over time; in the Biellese dialect it means idiot, and Tarcisio was a half-wit. He was the trusted simpleton of the priests in the Biella *Cottolengo,* and he had a beloved mule which bit him at every opportunity, in order to get back at him for the blows he dealt it. Before going up the hill, it took Tarcisio a quarter of an hour to convince the mule to move; the animal's head, ears, and eyes were cast downward, and the only way to get him to go was by hitting him and yelling into his ear.

I don't even remember the Nazi-Fascist* roadblock: the usual uniforms, distracted officers, and false documents. Two turns in the road, perhaps less than 200 yards further on, beyond the sign that read *"Achtung! Bandengebiet!"* ("Danger! Watch out for partisan bands!"—did this sign really exist?) lay the future, in other words, our distant past.

This was the advance roadblock of the partisans of the Garibaldi Divisions let by Cino Moscatelli, political commissioner and strategist in the Hellenic sense of the word. (Imagine a Piedmontese rhetorical approximation of Leonidas at Thermopylae or Quintus Fabius Maximus.) They were wearing their summer uniforms, perhaps for the last time, hoping beyond hope that the almost victorious summer of 1944 would not come to an end. They didn't want to let us through; perhaps they were bored and wanted to waste some time. After having dreamt about them for months, I was terrified of them—they looked different in

* Here the use of this word is correct and pertinent: the roadblock was made up of both Germans and Italians.

my dreams—and watched them from the cart, gripping the railing because the mule, frightened by their slaps and pats, kept stepping forward and backward. In fact, they didn't really want to turn us away—they didn't give a damn about us—but they wanted to poke fun at Tarcisio, because he was a half-wit and because he worked for the priests; they said terrible, mostly sexual things, hoping he would go repeat them to the nuns. These were innocuous games among temporary allies: the priests and the partisans. They knew that Tarcisio repeated everything he heard—he was like a cross between a loudspeaker and a cassette recorder. He could not be silent or lie, and this was the disease that had led him to the priests, after a few useless years in boarding school. His parents were dead.

He was tall and strong, as rough-hewn as his mule, with a tiny head as round as a billiard ball; even his flap-ears were round, and his eyes, oblique as an Oriental's, were blue. His small, ageless face was covered with laugh lines; he had laughed all day long every day from the day he was born, perhaps forty years earlier. He obeyed only Suor Pierina, the mother superior of the *Cottolengo,* who would repeat her instructions to him ten times, sticking her index finger right in his face, and threatening him with blows which she never inflicted. He listened, his large red hands and elbows sticking out of a small jacket he had inherited from an old dwarf years earlier; when he had understood the instructions, he would turn around and do exactly as he had been told.

I was afraid of the partisans: because of the way they laughed, because of the red stars they wore—just like in *We the Living* and *Good-Bye Kira* with Alida Valli (Cinema Nazionale, Turin, 1942)—because they wore short shorts and thick socks folded over their spiked boots, making their legs look even more obscenely bare. Especially bare and immodest were the legs of the young partisan women, who lavished attention on Tarcisio. There was one in particular, perhaps the leader, the most military-looking of the group, a real "tough" with curls and heart-shaped blood-red lips, a pistol resting against her round bottom, and a shoulder belt, the better to accentuate her breasts compressed under the military shirt, its little pockets sticking up (as well as, I imagined, her nipples). Eventually, she yelled, "That's enough! Stop screwing around! Can't you see you're scaring the *gorba,* the children? You can go through. But Tarcisio, heh, heh, tell Suor Pierina, heh, heh, that her ass . . ."

It was dark when we reached Urì. Only one car, a silver Aprilia with bright headlights, had passed us, its engine roaring on a mixture of alcohol and gas. *Papà* had anxiously awaited our arrival, looking only slightly less ghostly than on that day at the Salesian school, sitting in the half-light of the kitchen, the dark night all around him. We all climbed into bed and waited for morning, the first morning of the icy winter of 1944–1945.

Mamma and *papà* were better now; they seemed less panicked and gray, their eyes less glassy. They had made some friends at the *Cottolengo* and in the village. We lived in a kind of alpine hut which belonged to Tecla, a sweet-tempered innkeeper who was a friend of some friends of Pandoli's.

Other than the kitchen and the stairs, we had one bedroom with a floor of wooden boards which also served as the ceiling of the kitchen. It had low beams and two windows that froze in winter, despite the fact that they faced the tepid southern winds from Mount Monviso, which was framed by one of the two windows like a caricature of the typical Neapolitan postcard—a white Vesuvius overlooking a white gulf of icy mountains and the gray, foggy sea. Above the bed, which was made of iron and beige marbleized sheet-metal, decorated with scenes of bare-legged shepherdesses gazing off into the distance, and piled with covers, there was a crucifix with a dried-out olive branch wound tightly around it, a souvenir from a Low Sunday in 1941 or 1942. All through the winter, before Christ's one-thousand-nine-hundred-and-twelfth return to Jerusalem on a white mule, greeted by crowds carrying palm fronds and olive branches, Roberto and I smoked the dry olive leaves as cigars. The decoration of the room was completed by two cots set against the wall for my brother and me. There was nothing else, because the beds took up the entire space, but the room was warm; warm air rose from the heater in the kitchen through the cracks in the wooden beams. We often took our food up there and ate in bed in order to feel warm and protected from the moral, psychic, and meteorologic storm raging around us. There was no running water in the houses or outside, and no toilet. In Urì, the well water and the hygienic facilities were public and had been since time immemorial.

The Sunday after our arrival, when we went down to Mass at the *Cottolengo*—the first of countless Sundays until Liberation—Roberto and I were embraced and caressed by Nuccio de Filippis, the doctor and general (on leave) from Messina, and his "lovely consort," the "dear companion of my life, I'm the luckiest man on earth." She was Signora Olga, a handsome, elderly, and elegant Sicilian lady, the benevolent second-in-command to her strange husband: a soldier, a doctor, and a madman.

In order to give a quick sketch of the tall, dark-skinned, aristocratic, retired officer, with white whiskers sticking up and short hair—parted, of course—I will say that he resembled Crispi,[2] a Southern gentleman and a good man, if a bit rigid and suspicious—which is, as we know, a characteristic of military doctors. My impression of my father when I saw him at the school at the end of April or beginning of May was not subjective. His physical state inspired pity in those who knew of his recent travails and fear in those who didn't. Suor Pierina decided it was best to say to everyone that *papà* was on early holiday because of an illness: he could pass for a sick officer rather than an old caporal with Israelite origins. He coughed and coughed, especially at night, a result of the chronic bronchitis cultivated so lovingly at the Nuove Prison by his cellmate, the sardonic *cambrioleur*—or burglar, in layman's terms.

The general, awakened night after night from his shallow old-man's slumber by my father's coughing, combined cough and mountain retreat, mountain retreat and officer on holiday, officer on holiday and desperate, bewildered expression, and came up with his irrevocable diagnosis: an acute case of tuberculosis.

Papà's appearance was rather more military than Jewish; this was indirectly the result of the grandiose attitude of King Fuad of Egypt and the atmosphere surrounding Verdi's *Aida,* performed under the stars at the foot of the Pyramid of Cheops in the 1931 opera season. *Papà* was first viola in the Regio di Torino Orchestra, and at the time, he had the bent posture often identified with Semitic peoples. Two German orchestra members, friends of his, decided to straighten him up and did so with a quick system learned from the Prussian army: when they saw him sitting with bent posture, they would strike him in the back when he least expected it, whether it was in the street, in front of his music stand, or in the hotel, museums, or on buses in Cairo, Alexandria, and Assuan. The terror of being struck eventually straightened out his six-foot-two-inch frame, and for the rest of his life he was as rigid as Erich von Stroheim. Perhaps he took things to an extreme, because when he kissed ladies' hands, he clicked his heels and folded his body in half. His appearance was softened by bright-colored silk bow ties, which, if he had grown old, would have made him look like Furtwängler, the marvelous, if slightly Nazi, conductor.

The general's diagnosis was rough but not altogether off target. In addition to the cough and his sickly appearance, my father had suffered from pleurisy in the trenches from which he was cured, but not completely, in 1919. Our valley had the advantage of being home to a clinic in our section of the Urì, but *papà* hid a much more terrible, inadmissible illness: he was Jewish.

The general rushed down to complain to Suor Pierina that it was "unacceptable that a gravely sick, contagious person be living in close proximity to other people who are paying guests, and it's not cheap either! As a doctor, I should know!" The sister's clumsy lies and assurances that *papà* wasn't contagious—and in fact, Judaism is almost never contagious—did not convince the doctor from the Royal Army, who continued to live his nightmare, rendered more acute by his anticlericalism which led him to believe that priests are capable of any abomination imaginable in their craze to help the ill at the cost of the healthy, respectable public. After several pointless meetings, she saw the general with his straw hat and bamboo cane setting off down the valley toward Biella to lay out his reasonable complaints to the General Headquarters: the consumptive had to go.

In her desperation, Suor Pierina ran over to the general and pressed him up against a wall of the *Cottolengo:* she told him everything, holding him tightly by the arms and shaking him slightly as if to awake him to reason: "For the love of God, don't do this, don't go down to Biella, they are . . . they are . . . Jewish." She whispered the syllables of the last word in a dramatic crescendo, her eyes open wide. The general became as pale as was possible for him and raised his snow-white eyebrows: "Oh my! . . . Goodness! . . . God! . . . but I . . . I was about to . . . Good God!" He turned around and ran back toward the building, his black alpaca jacket flapping in the breeze.

Mamma and *papà* were at home, unaware of these events going on just steps away from them. They sat on the bed, probably meditating on the progressive deterioration of conditions in the valley and the consequent need to take us out of school, when suddenly the door burst open and the old man appeared, gasping from exertion, and hugged *papà,* kissed him on both cheeks as if he had just received a medal. "Brother, friend . . . what dangers we face . . . (gasp) . . . I was about to turn you in . . . (gasp) . . . and all because of a faulty diagnosis and . . . (gasp) . . . because of the lies of the priests . . . (gasp) . . . but why, why didn't you tell me? Why didn't you trust me? When will this end? What can I do for you? I'm going to fetch my dear Olga, so she learns of the honor you are doing us . . . Yes, honor, a tremendous honor. But please, please look after that bronchitis. I'll give you Guaiacol drops!"

I don't know the details of what happened next, but I know that for years after that General de Filippis sent us letters and postcards written in old-fashioned sepia ink, full of affection, exclamation points, and happy news about his family. In the late summer of 1944, before Roberto and I arrived in the liberated valley—liberated by bits—when the Nazi-Fascists had caught their second wind and were attacking the contiguous Republic of Ossola, there was a raid, and the general went to my father and confessed his secret: "I have a pair of dueling pistols hidden in my closet. What should I do?"

When he found out that my father was neither an officer nor a consumptive, the general had immediately promoted him from corporal to at least colonel, considering him not only a friend but a colleague. But my father wasn't really a military man, and the revelation of the existence of these pistols filled him with terror. Germans, pistols, and generals, even retired generals: it was all too much for him, and he came to an ill-considered and unfair decision, and imposed a heartbreaking sacrifice. "The pistols were in a black morocco-leather case; they were precious objects, the butts inlaid with mother-of-pearl." *Papà,* in his abyss of terror, was determined; and in the end, the night before the raid, he and the general wrapped the case in rags—more to make the pistols "disappear" than to protect them, and, whispering under the light of a full moon, threw the pistols into the *Cottolengo* well. When the sound of splashing was heard, *papà* felt an immediate sense of relief, but not the general: a shadow had descended upon his recently acquired feeling of trust and friendship. Antique pistols, family relics, thrown down a well for the peace of mind of the persecuted.

"What harm could they have done? An old man, almost eighty years old, with two dueling pistols from the eighteenth century, in my family for generations?" The general, with his aristocratic self-control, never again mentioned the pistols, but from that moment on my father could sense his regret when they took walks in the park, discussing the imminent end of the war, the fall of Nazi Germany, and the inevitable punishment that would befall the Fascists. Sometimes the old man would stop short, looking with sad eyes at the well where he had sacrificed so much, and sigh. Then he would look at my father from under his shaggy eyebrows, sigh once more, and remain silent.

13 ⁂ Bandenkrieg!

In the winter of 1944, Urì was a cluster of gray stone huts with chimney pots doing their best to protect the inhabitants from the frost, gray roofs made from slabs of gneiss stained with lichen, and long, wooden balconies. The road ended at the edge of a forest of chestnuts on the slope of the Caplùn. This was the local name, meaning "shaggy-head," for Mount Rovella because it was covered with trees—chestnuts and birches and firs, then shrubs, and finally bare rock. On the other side lay the Val Sesia, Valle Mosso, Mosso Santa Maria, the Ossola, and just beyond, but unattainable, Switzerland.

The houses, balancing precariously on the overhanging rock, perched on the mountainside with their backs to this "world's end"—the forest of chestnuts—looking out over the misty plain. Toward the south and directly beneath us was Bioglio with its white bell tower, and further down, hidden from view, Biella with its factories. To the left was Valle San Nicolao with its false Neo-Gothic castle tower, and to the right, on clear days, we could make out the frozen craters and peaks of the Alps and Mount Monviso set against pale, pinkish sunsets. The road from Bioglio to Urì climbed up to a small, impenetrable valley of elder trees near an invisible torrent known simply as the Rì, the brook. It was steep and paved only up to the hospital, where it crossed the road to Valsesia; from there on it clambered up, even more steeply and roughly, to the covered washbasin, where it passed under an arcade of dark, mossy rock formations and finally disappeared in front of our house, near the waters of the Rì, which drenched the field under the chestnut grove. This field was full of crows, moles, squirrels, and—during raids—concealed partisans.

Our house, with its ground floor kitchen and small bedroom upstairs, was wedged between that of the Dragos, "rich" farmers and seasonal weavers, and that of the destitute Barca family, immigrants from the Veneto with no work, money, or clothes, who ate cats and stolen goats. The family consisted of a husband, a wife, and five children, the youngest of whom was two years old and always ran around naked, in winter as in summer: "After all, at that age they don't feel the cold." None of the Barcas had shoes, and they were all half-starved and forced to steal to stay alive. Signor Barca had mongoloid features; he captured cats by the neck, impervious to their scratches, and killed them with a hammer-stroke to the head. *Mamma* and *papà* were suspicious of the Barcas and watched them closely; they were afraid that desperation might lead them to cruelty, and one mustn't forget that we were worth twenty-thousand lire, which was more money than those poor people had ever seen. But they never did anything to hurt us, unless you count the time they stole a handful of coarse salt, which the eldest daughter grabbed one day when we left the box on the kitchen table and the door open. It was a small handful because the thief was only ten years old and wasn't even a real thief, more like a ferret: she had seen the white salt, which that year in the mountain was like gold, and she had taken a little handful and run home in a flash, leaving behind a path of white grains. My mother yelled "Thief!" having caught a glimpse of the child's white dress over the bare, muddy feet. She started after her but gave up, falling heavily onto a rickety chair, her hand to her forehead. "For a handful of salt! Is it possible that I, Eugenia, have been reduced to this?" Émile Zola had saved her once again.

Among the horrors of the war, one of the worst—besides the fear which never left us day or night, at home or in the street—was the contrast of our hunger with that of these people who had suffered more hunger and more misery than us, and not only for months or years, but since time immemorial. No one felt sorry for them because in addition to being poor and ignorant, they were ugly and dirty: the women wore no undergarments and peed standing up, their legs apart, as they held their naked baby in their arms, staring blankly into space.

The Barcas were so despised by the people of the village that they were not even allowed to use the public toilet in Urì. This was a small hut with a roof of cement and asbestos with wooden planks and hay on the ground; the door was kept closed by a rope that you held in your hand. You had to squat on two boards, balancing above a pit full of shit; when it was full, the hole was covered with two shovelfuls of dirt, and the cabin was moved a few yards over. I would hold the rope with one hand, and with the other I would hold up newspaper cuttings I had brought to read and then use as toilet paper. It was in this position that I savored Mussolini's Teatro Lirico speech of the 16th of December[1] (twenty degrees below zero); "If You're With Us Beat a Drum" by Concetto Pettinato* (ten degrees below); and the Fascist condolences to the American people on the occasion of the death of their "Commander," Franklin Delano Roosevelt, at the beginning of April 1945 (five degrees above zero).

The Drago family was well off; they owned the chestnut grove, two cows, some land, and a few rows of grapevines lower down in the valley. Piero and Dante let us into their

* This article was published in *La Stampa* in February or March of 1945, and the spirit that was supposed to beat its drum was the government of the "Little Republic" (the Fascist Republic of Salò), which, in the name of the fatherland, was called upon to cease all aggression toward the Socialist and Communist resistance, and vice-versa, in order to save Italy from the invasion of the foreigners.

world: they were fourteen and seventeen, or perhaps thirteen and eighteen. Dante looked like a man, and he even got drunk sometimes: he was strong and ill-tempered. Piero, on the other hand, was sweet and mild; but they were both our friends. They taught us how to place traps under dry leaves or snow and how to raise crows. We raised crows in cages: the relationship you form with a crow in a cage is fascinating, because the bird remains savage—I still have marks on my fingers to prove it—but also toys with your affection. It stays in the cage provocatively, seemingly tame, but as soon as it has the chance, it escapes to join its brothers in the Convent of the Chestnuts. Roberto is convinced that he had actually tamed his pet crow; I suspect that the animal led him on. Roberto claims that after it escaped, it still recognized him and made signs to him.

We learned how to skin moles and kill cats by placing them in a bag and beating them to death—I cringe at the memory—and how to smoke chestnuts and apple slices on trellises in the attic, and how to roast Biellese chestnuts, which you don't cut but moisten with a brush as they're roasting and then peel by repeatedly flinging them in the air and catching them in a wicker basket until the thin, burned skin flies off, revealing the ivory chestnut. A chestnut prepared in this way is better than any *marron glacé*. The Drago brothers taught us how to steal trees: you cut acacias and birches at ground level so the owner won't be able to tell from far away, and then you cut off the branches and tie them to the trunk and sled down the snow-covered mountainside toward Urì, yelping in fear and joy. We kept warm all winter long thanks to Dante and Piero. And you could tell from our chimney that we, like the Barcas, were acacia thieves, because when acacias burn, they release a greenish smoke against the gray winter sky. It was the Dragos who taught us how to use the hollow branches of elder trees—metaphoric male members—to shoot water at the appetizing rear ends of women bending over wash basins full of clothes. If you weren't quick, the furious woman would slap you so hard with an article of wet clothing that you would be knocked out cold on the pavement, to be awoken with bucketfuls of freezing water, a snickering, feminine vengeance.

We stole wood, and others stole salt from us; we didn't really need new clothes, because elegance was not a factor in those remote regions. We wore clogs, and the house and electricity were provided by Tecla, our hostess. We got our food from the *Cottolengo. Papà* almost always went to fetch it with *mamma*'s shopping bag, made out of pieces of different-colored leather, stuffed full of pots and pans. He walked carefully in order not to spill anything on the icy paths.

The nuns specialized in a "homeopathic" soup made with puréed potatoes diluted many times over. Juniper berries added a woodsy taste to the repulsive mixture. In the kitchen, we kept a bag of dried chestnuts and another full of corn flour. Along with the milk given to us by the Dragos and by Giusèp, the story-telling shepherd, these were the elements of our hypernutritious meals: chestnuts and milk, polenta and milk . . . it was enough to make you sick. When the salt and the *Liebig* bouillon cubes were gone, we salted the polenta with seawater from two demijohns we bought from salesmen who came from Savona with a caravan of mules, selling liters of brackish water in towns like Bioglio, on mountaintops, and along other stops on the seawater trail, which has been forgotten for centuries, like the Silk Road.

Medieval pathways had reappeared, because the more modern roads were dangerous to travel. When the Fort of Saint-Tropez fell to the Saracens in the eleventh century, the Arabs followed mountain paths over the Alps to Alessandria della Paglia (in Piedmont), or rather to the spot where the city would one day stand. You can still see them today in the Mandrogna,[2] with their sparkling Moorish eyes.

Papà worked for our food in a hundred ways. Having been the official barber for his regiment back in 1915, he performed this craft with steady violinist's hands at the *Cottolengo;* on Sundays before Mass, he went down ahead of us to trim the beards and hair of the half-wits. His smooth-faced customers would line up and then sit down in the barber's chair without saying a word, and he would soap up their faces and shave them attentively as if they had facial hair. When he was done, he would shake out the towel and fold it over his arm, bow, and say, "The gentleman is served." The idiots would look at themselves in the mirror, feeling handsome and normal, and then leave, as silently as they had come. The elegance with which my father accomplished this task ingratiated him with the sisters, who were already drawn to his wistful air.

My father, who had seen the world, including the naked and beardless natives of the Amazon region, had depths of patience coupled with great intelligence; he also had an irrational, serene faith that justice was compatible with the essence of this world. He was not of the Lévi-Strauss school of thought, and remembered the naked peoples of his distant youth with the amazement of a discoverer from past times who believes he has seen the mysteries of the furthest reaches of the world. He used to tell us about the horrible penetrating flea, the *Tunga penetrans,* which had gotten under the nails of his big toes and bored through him like a woodworm through a chest of drawers. He couldn't sleep at night because of the shrieking of the cutters grinding their way between the flesh and the nail. There were no doctors in the rainforest, and he couldn't walk because of the pain. The greatest danger was infection: if a flea dies under the nail, gangrene sets in. There was no other solution, so his musician colleagues carried him to an Indian, naked of course, who smiled and caressed his cheeks, which were cold and sweaty from *sgiai.** He plucked a long thorn from a wild rose and, with this natural scalpel, captured the parasites one by one from beneath the nail, pulling them out carefully and

* A very specialized Piedmontese word which describes a shudder of the entire nervous system (central and peripheral) caused by the scraping of knives against metal, the sight of blood or open wounds, and stories about ghosts, witches, or violent death. It is impossible to enumerate all of the situations which cause *sgiai.* The guillotine causes *sgiai;* death by shooting does not.

without hurting my father, singing to himself and comforting my father in his incomprehensible language composed for the most part of clicks and explosive lip consonants.

At the *Cottolengo,* the nuns were drawn to my father because he was nothing like the Jews in the gospel, the only Jews they were acquainted with. For all they knew, Jews really did yell, "Crucify him! Crucify him!" at every possible occasion, or "Barabbas was a good man!" They put him in charge of music at the solemn sung Mass which was to take place in March for the feast of San Giuseppe.

Another of my father's tasks was giving piano lessons to a youngish old maid, the blind daughter of the *Podestà,*[3] a textiles man who "had one foot in each camp," which means that on the one hand he gave money to the partisans and helped out a family of Jews—my family—while on the other he did not formally break with the dying regime. He paid for these lessons in part with an invitation to the four of us for tea on Sunday afternoons in the luxurious art deco bay window of his villa just above the *Cottolengo.* This invitation to tea was an implied recognition of our social rank which, at the time, was rather frayed. On Saturday evenings, after having gone to collect the juniper-laced soup at the *Cottolengo,* father stopped by the *Podestà*'s house for a pot of sausage broth, offered by the *Podestà*'s wife. The first thing he did as soon as he reached our little kitchen was fish around in the pot with his fork, hoping beyond hope that this week, given the downright unfavorable news from the front, the *Podestà*'s wife might have "forgotten" the sausage in the broth. She never did. After giving up his vain efforts, he would pull out the empty sausage skin by its string, dripping with fat, and show it to us, exclaiming: "Nothing. Can you believe it?"

In November, it began to snow, and it didn't stop until the end of March. It also snowed out of season on May 2, 1945, but November and December were the worst months because along with the cold came General Alexander's proclamation that the war would last the winter, and that the Germans had begun a counteroffensive in the Ardennes.

Now that the people who lived through the battles of the Marne, Caporetto, and Verdun are no longer with us, and few can remember the Ardennes, the words "German counteroffensive" no longer have the same concrete significance. In brief, a German counteroffensive meant unbelievable, hopeless anguish for those who experienced it and for those who followed it from a distance. *Papà* knew that the Prussians concentrate men and firepower at a single breakthrough point, a few hundred meters wide and kilometers deep: in the first hours, the forces under attack are killed like flies, and very few of the attacking forces survive. The Germanic peoples seem to be indifferent to death in war, a fact that is apparent even in Tacitus. A roar rises up in the front line, along with a wave of panic, and flight, escape, becomes the soldiers' only goal; they drop their weapons at random in order to cover their ears and run as fast as they can. But where are the Germans? They are everywhere, even behind enemy lines, running through the plains and climbing mountains. If you stay behind, you lose; if you run, you lose. "There's nothing to do, we're lost! It's the end!" The German counteroffensive produces the fear of a rout in order to produce a rout. In 1917, my father turned back once or twice as he ran down the valley, weighed down with hammer, chisels, and tubes full of explosives. He wanted to understand what the gray German shadows that already dotted the crest which had been deserted only minutes earlier were yelling as they raised their guns. They yelled in a dissonant chorus that we have all heard in our dreams, and which history has seen before: *"Die See, die See,"* with their silvery voices, the sea, the sea, *Thalassa, Thalassa.* And in 1917 what they saw, albeit at a considerable distance, was the Adriatic.

In December of 1944, as he listened trembling to news of the Ardennes on the radio, *papà* said, "All it takes is a day, one day, and then that's the end of it. I know. I saw it in '17. Last week it looked like the Americans were about to invade Germany, and now, on Monday, the Germans are in Paris again, they're in Paris and it's all over for us. I guarantee it!" *Mamma,* who was no strategist but who understood geopolitics and philosophy better than *papà* did from her reading Balzac and Victor Hugo, consoled him. "Mario, they're fighting on two fronts, and now it's all over for them. They win on the West and lose on the East. They're trapped and have no way out, and this is what they've been trying to do from the beginning: demonstrate that they are fighting alone against the whole world, that they've almost won the war, but in the end they'll lose, and how. They always do, and they will this time as well, you'll see. And this time it will go worse for them. This time we'll make them pay." And then she raised her voice. "Enough, Mario. Don't act this way in front of the children, just stop it!" She didn't say it to calm father; in fact, she thought that fear was highly educational. Her tone was accusing, as if *papà* had shown cowardice in the face of the enemy, and—worse yet!—he had done so in front of the troops.

I, on the other hand, was quite serene about the end of the war. *Papà* was conservative, a Republican and a Mason, and he did not trust the partisans. He didn't think that wars are won by the people and didn't trust in the power of being in the right. Evil can never conquer, so it should not be feared; if you don't fear it, it doesn't exist. Evil does not exist. Sometimes I muttered my borrowed philosophy, quite the contrary of my father's. But he was proud that at my age I could understand and expound on such mistaken, Leftist ideas. And he would pick me up on his lap and talk about my brilliant future, gently poking fun at me. He would put one hand on my thin shoulder, and, waving the other in a grandiose gesture, proclaim: "Supreme Soviet of the year 1960: The Delegate Aldo Zargani, representative of the Soviet of the Jews of Europe, enters, wearing a red scarf with the Star of David across his chest covered with medals . . ." This unlikely image seemed to distract him from the terror of the German counteroffensive in the Ardennes.

Roberto did not participate in these political-messianic meetings. He was more interested in other subjects: Where to put the half-frozen crickets he had in his pocket? How to cure the cat who hadn't digested its last mouse and was having convulsions, her expression still smiling but her eyes unhappy, salivating and ears down? And how to save his friends the frogs, fugitives from the San Nicolao Valley? Thinking back, the frogs must have been on his mind for a long time before the "big event" that came later. In November and December of 1944, our hopes slipped through our fingers, and we realized how much suffering and danger was still ahead of us in these last days of endless manhunts which had so impoverished and humiliated us. The partisans, warming themselves with military blankets, were moving back to their mountain hideouts, holes in the snow, the "houses" where they hibernated. The semivictories of the summer had not brought real victory, but rather the "November retreat."

Tarcisio, who had heard from one of the nuns or from someone else that *papà* was not a "real" teacher but a "music teacher," had taken to picking him up by the armpits like a doll and mocking him: *"Ciau, prufesur, ti t'ses prufesur cume mi."** His compulsion for the truth got him into trouble. One day, Suor Pierina sent him off to paint the house of a very old

* In Piedmontese dialect: "Hey, professor, if you're a professor, so am I!"

lady in the Valle San Nicolao who had written a will leaving all of her belongings to the *Cottolengo.* While he painted the top of the stairs, as she sat on a chair overseeing his work, he exclaimed: *"Tì, che t'ses tantu veia, quand ch'it meuire, che nui l'uma pì gnente da mangé?"** And the *Cottolengo* was disinherited. One day, as he was going around with his mule, he came across a member of the fascist Black Brigades, and from his cart, he yelled: *"I l'eve finila 'd rie, che adess à l'è rivà 'co la vostra ura."*** As they say, he who laughs last . . . because those monsters killed his mule and smashed his face with their rifle butts until he was unrecognizable. After a month in bed, he sat in the courtyard with the other halfwits, his hands hanging limp between his knees, silently staring into space. When Suor Pierina saw him in this condition, she would turn away so that he wouldn't see her cry: "My poor Tarcisio, my poor Tarcisio." His childhood was over, suddenly, at the age of forty. His adulthood was characterized by utter prudence: he said nothing, to anybody.

The *Cottolengo,* where we went every day for our soup and on Sundays for Mass, was not a happy place, even for people like us, accustomed to our snowed-in hovel. I felt oppressed by the ever-present skylights and the white silence of the corridors, by the primitive, servile Christianity I thought I had left behind at the school. *Papà* wasn't con-

* In Piedmontese dialect: "You're so old, why don't you die, because we have nothing to eat!"

** In Piedmontese dialect: "The laughing is over now, your time has come!"

vinced that my Christian tendencies had been erased; every Sunday, when the local women returned to their seats with their hands folded in front of them and their eyes down, inspired by having taken the body and blood of Christ, he would whisper in my ear: "It's all fanaticism and ignorance, of the lowest kind."

Mass was often accompanied by a wailing that came down from the dormitories, magnified by the stairs. It was a woman who had been dying for months from a brain cancer and whose cries, which reached almost unbelievably high notes, had inspired the nickname "the Siren." *Mamma* and *papà* were horrified by the sound, but when they asked Suor Pierina, "When will she die?" she answered with the terrifying serenity of the faithful, "When Our Lord decides to call her to him." And then she turned and walked away, deflecting any reply to her affirmation, her robes swishing as she went, her nose in the air, conscious of her superiority.

Suor Pierina, who in truth was anything but serene, lost her patience with me on two occasions. The first was when she found me lying on the floor of the visiting room, talking to a mouse who scampered off as soon as he saw her; he knew her all too well. The second time, I was standing in the soup line with the partisans, who, at the first hint of good weather, were wearing short shorts. Their machine guns, decorated with red stars, were lying about; by now I was used to seeing them. They were about to carry out the huge pot, when Suor Pierina, who had been simmering for a while like the soup, erupted in reproaches against their "lack of decency": "How dare you come here with bare legs! Shameless louts! Next time, I won't give you anything!" "And don't you laugh," she said, pointing at me, "or else you won't get any either."

The partisans liked uniforms but couldn't afford them, so they resorted to anything that looked faintly military. The most geared-up among them had spiked boots with external flaps to keep out snow and mud, the utmost in partisan chic. Each person invented his own outfit and took pride in it, and the result was a confusing mismatch of styles. Not even the Germans or the Fascists were identically dressed, when you saw them close-up during the raids. They ranged from the style of the resigned, exhausted soldier from the *Wehrmacht* to the impeccable SS officer, to the crumpled, nasty fifteen-year-old member of the Black Brigade, to the blue-uniformed airman who stopped by on his skis one day and, leaning on his poles, asked ironically why there were only women and children in the village. *Mamma* answered disingenuously: "Our men are all on the front, like you."

The partisans held only a few German prisoners in December of '44. On the other hand, there were far too many partisans being held prisoner. In order to correct this imbalance, Moscatelli—*The Phantom* (ed. Nerbini)—sent out one of the operatives he had saved for just this sort of difficult project. Disguised as a member of the Black Brigade, the partisan boarded a local bus, glaring at the unknowing passengers, and got off at Biella, where he knocked on the door of the apartment where the German Vice-commander, a major, lived with his wife. The operative stuck the barrel of his Beretta up the major's nose when they were in private and between his buttocks once they were outside—out of an instinctual sense of decorum—and led him onto the bus. The major's depressed face contrasted strangely with the martial appearance of the Fascist brigadier and the curious stares of the passengers, who were surprised at the presence of the two comrades in the heart of partisan territory. When, after a few days of negotiations mediated by the local priest, it was decided that the German major was worth twenty-seven partisans, the humbled official was returned to his wife.

For the most part, life in the valley was almost normal. The herds on the mountain, along with the corn and chestnuts, gave people something to live on, and the farmers always shared their food with us. Industry was making inroads in the mountains of the Biellese, and many of the people there worked seasonally in textiles. Often, when there was a bit of sunlight, one could see fragments of decatized twill and Prince of Wales fabric hanging out to dry from the Dragos' wooden balconies; this work rounded out their income.

The partisans were not particularly feared or disliked, but neither were they held in high regard by the residents. During periods of normalcy, they made rude attempts at civil government in order to win over the population.

After they shot a spy and left his corpse, along with that of his Irish setter, on the side of the road for all to see, they distributed meat from the man's cow, which had been executed along with its owner. *Mamma* arrived late and returned with a piece of udder. It was disgusting and tasted of soap, but it was the only meat we had eaten in five months other than Tarcisio's poor mule—which was delicious and tasted like pork, and which had been killed by the bayonets of the furious Black Brigade. He was a good mule, and his name was Mascherino, "Little Mask."

In our valley, the partisan police was composed of Briga and Pippo, a brigadier and a lance corporal of the military police, the *carabinieri.* In order to honor their oath to the King, the two Royal *Carabinieri* had remained in their station, joining forces with the Garibaldi division of the partisans and Moscatelli, the Bolshevik. Dressed as civilians, their machine guns under their coats, they kept watch over the locals and the partisans. Briga and Pippo hid with the renegades, perhaps hoping for the return of Richard the Lion-Hearted, or rather His Majesty Vittorio Emanuele III.

Moscatelli, the strategist of partisan warfare, was invisible. He moved his troops in a world without walkie-talkies, or even telephones, with speedy messengers on bicycles in an eternal cycle of hit-and-run. We could hear them yell: "Moscatelli! Moscatelli!" And then there was the rumbling of the engine of a silver Aprilia, running on a mixture of gas and alcohol; he was inside, we all saw him, the leader. Or perhaps it wasn't him? He almost never, if ever, appeared in public. He concealed himself behind his legend, conducting a strange war: a war of minimal efforts, with few battles, inflicting as much damage as possible on the enemy while avoiding, as much as possible, damaging the partisan forces and the local population. It was a war of nonappearances, of being and not being, a Hamletlike war.

Even *papà* was a strategist, because it had been his idea to escape to the battlefield, to slip, unseen, unrecognized, with wife and children, into the blood-soaked mountains, to go toward death in order to escape its grasp in the Glockenspiel of the valleys, emerging from one trapdoor just in time to slip into another. Meanwhile, Moscatelli was hidden in an underground den, from which he directed his invisible, infernal, ungraspable army. Two German Stukas dove down into the valleys to bomb and destroy what was not there with the sinister whistling of their sirens. Once they had reached the bottom of the next valley, they would climb back up along the mountainside and reappear, loud and huge, behind the sanatorium, one shooting, the other climbing. When Secondina, the eldest Drago, an unmarried ninety-year-old who had not been to the village in seventy years because "they had teased her when she was in love" and who was now completely deaf, saw the Stukas, she exclaimed: *"Oh Santa Madunina d'Oropa, ma che useí à sun cui lì?"*[4]

Even *papà* was a strategist, because he had learned in jail that the ice of the mountains was our friend, that the people who lived there, neither Christian nor pagan, had protected Fra' Dolcino, groups of bandits, and clusters of terrified Jews for centuries upon centuries. Otherwise, how could the Treves, the Segres, the Valabregas, and the Fubini have escaped to Turin from the dark night of Saint Bartholomew and Provence? Otherwise, how could Peter Waldo have managed with his Waldenses, or Hannibal with his elephants? When the inhabitants of the Urì came to visit us for the last time after Liberation, they said: "We knew you were Jews, but we pretended not to; we didn't want to frighten you." On May 7, 1945, we descended toward the plain in a silver Aprilia which ran half on gas, half on alcohol, and on either side of us were people who were happy for us, who clapped and shook our hands through the windows.

14 ✻ Winter

On January 20, 1945, or perhaps a few days later, history made a stop at our kitchen in Urì. Moscatelli had heard that the Jews who dotted the valleys lived in abject poverty, eking out an existence from Christian charity, and so he sent two partisans to ask us what we might need in the way of secular assistance, which since 1938 had been scarce if not nonexistent for Italian Jews.

Papà listened to them, petrified with fear and, to my great embarrassment, did nothing to hide his terror: his bewildered eyes wished those two friendly, armed, and obsequious beings away with all their might. He feared that the Germans and the Fascists would find us more easily if we were identified as friends of the partisans and not just concealed Jews—*stermà** as we were known—without contacts with the outside world other than the priests, nuns, and half-wits. The young men, embarrassed by the charitable task which had fallen to them as the intellectuals of the band, did what they could to reassure him that he could turn to them whenever he needed help, but he continued to guide them toward the door, sweating with fear: "Thank you, thank you. We don't need anything, we have everything we need, tell your commander Cino not to worry about us. We sincerely thank him, but tell him not to worry about us, with everything else he has on his mind."

It was so obvious that he was lying, and he lied so poorly, that the two did not give up and in the end managed to convince him to accept two pairs of warm boots for my brother and me before again finding themselves in three feet of snow. This is how we acquired our very own marvelous spiked boots with external flaps to keep out the snow.

What the two partisans had seen in our kitchen was neither a happy sight nor a new one: it was *Les Mangeurs de Pommes de Terre* by Van Gogh. In place of potatoes, we ate polenta. An ancient light bulb hung from the wood ceiling, whose beams had been painted pink many years before—

* The condition of being a *stermà*—"hidden," in Piedmontese—Jew affected entire families, or in some cases groups of families. In some places it became so typical as to become part of the topography, even after the war: "The Drago's house? No, the one after it, the *ca' dji ebreu stermà* [the house of the Jews in hiding]."

the rest was pale blue. The light from the bulb, which was originally reddish, struggled to shine through glass that was blackened with flies; it barely illuminated the sky-blue, windowless room, already dark during the day if the door was closed. In Piedmont, between November and mid-March, between clouds, fog, the solstice, and eclipses, the "day" is no more than a grayish sigh.

When one entered from the snowy mud, *paciara* in Piedmontese, into this dark room, one could make out the *potagé,* a nineteenth-century marvel. It was a cast-iron stove for cooking *potages,* or soups. It must be said that without Bismarck, the Iron Chancellor, the Krupp steel mills, the Franco-Prussian War, and the subsequent conversion of the war machine, we would never have had our *potagé,* this wonder from the past. On the sticky, blackish dirt floor stood a table, two chairs, the sacks of dried chestnuts and cornmeal, the demijohns of seawater, and a heap of stolen wood, under which the turtle my brother had brought back from the rice fields slept through the winter, never to wake up again.

Our benevolent messengers took their leave, and Roberto and I marched around the kitchen in our new boots, enjoying the clicking of the spikes; father made us promise—on fear of severe punishment—to say that the boots were a present from our grandmother.

Having to claim that these marvelous boots were a present from our grandmother Ottavia rather than from the larger-than-life partisans was one of the greatest sacrifices imposed by our clandestine life; it was a tribute to our love for our father, who threatened serious consequences "if the truth gets out."

The partisans felt sorry for *papà* and wanted to help him. Through mysterious methods, they convinced the local merchants to open an infinite line of credit for us. "The brigades will pay after the war, don't you trust them?" *Papà* would go into a store, ask for three eggs, and the owner would give him a dozen. "Why twelve? I asked for three!" "That way you save a trip." "OK, how much is it, then?" "Don't worry, we'll put it on your account." "What account?" He was afraid that a coalition of angry shopkeepers would turn us in at the first opportunity, "I'm sure of it!" And he began paying in cash, using decoys: "Dante, when you go down to the village, could you buy me an egg? Here's the money, but don't tell them it's for me!"

News arrived on the radio and by word of mouth across the valleys and up the mountainside. This is how my parents heard in September of 1944 of the gunbattle which had taken place at the school, and how we heard about people captured by the Nazis.

After a year or so, we heard about Uncle Carlo Morais and his family. They were our relatives from Milan, and we had visited them before the war and during the first calm months after the beginning of the hostilities. The Turin-Milan line was one of the last to be switched to electric power, and so half the trip was spent cleaning bits of coal dust from each other's eyes with the corner of a handkerchief. When we arrived in Milan, we visited one relative after another, and I would eagerly await the hour when I would see my cousin, and friend, Albert.

Albert was a year older than I was and first in his class. His father, Carlo, was much younger than mine and had an irritable personality, a fairly common characteristic of people who have studied too much and can no longer tolerate the senseless chaos of daily life. He was an engineer, and before the war he had worked as a manager at Pirelli, a high rank considering his age. He was small and thin—because of his nerves—and had straight, light-colored hair that flopped onto his forehead; he would push it back with a brusque gesture, simultaneously tossing his head back. He was even less Jewish than my parents and completely assimilated into the bourgeoisie of Milan, which was not particularly cosmopolitan but very urban. His joblessness had not affected his economic situation because he had family money and because of his know-how in the field of tires, which permitted him to start a business in retreading and vulcanization of rubber tires, a useful occupation at a time of national self-sufficiency and war, when nothing was built and it was necessary to fix things when they broke down. He was protected from the feeling of isolation and menace which was felt instinctively by those who could remember the ghetto and the anti-Jewish laws and thus were able to conceive of subhuman living conditions: in 1593, the Jews of Bologna were thrown out of the city and had to disinter their dead from the cemetery and carry them off in their suitcases.

Carlo, along with many others, tried to convince my father that western Europe, especially Italy, would never follow in the footsteps of the barbaric East, and that the Germans, an imperial people, behaved in each country according to the national customs they found there. It was a kind of *cuius regio, eius damnatio,* applied to the senseless horrors of the time. My father had few concrete arguments to counter these refined and reassuring theories, except for the horrible tales he had heard from a few Croatian Jews who had miraculously escaped the tortures of Ante Pavelic's *Ustasi.* It was his conviction that no one was safe, even in Turin or Milan, when reason had been eclipsed in the world.

The Jews who were hit the hardest in western Europe were those who were too poor to survive and those, like Uncle Carlo, who were too removed from ancestral terrors to understand what was happening around them.

Aunt Mafalda, Alberto's mother, was thin and graceful and young, much younger than my mother. She was one of the youngest of ten brothers and sisters. All five brothers had gone to the front in '15–'18, and one, Uncle Roberto, had been killed at the battle of Mount Montello. My mother had taught my brother from a tender age to recite, "My name is Roberto in honor of my uncle, who died as a hero in defense of the fatherland," like a parrot.

⁂

The origin of my name is less heroic: I was named after my uncle Aldo, my father's older brother, who died in Pisa in one of the last epidemics of smallpox at the end of the nineteenth century. It was not a major epidemic, just one of the final, tired returns of the scourge in Italy before it was annihilated by the vaccine. Uncle Aldo was only five years old when he died, but he has lain for 104 years in a glorious seaside tomb in the Jewish cemetery in Pisa. In the thirteenth century, before the construction of the Christian cemetery, the powerful city-state of Pisa sent a fleet of ships to bring back soil from the Golgotha on the orders of the Archbishop Ubaldo de' Lanfranchi. The mission was financed by the Pisan Jews, who in return received a piece of property on the precise spot of the Crucifixion, which to the Jews is almost as valuable as the Promised Land. Behind what was left of the cemetery after the American bombings of July 27, 1944, behind the fresco of the Last Judgment depicting Lucifer in the act of biting Nebuchadnezzar, as well as Julian the Apostate and Attila, behind the Triumph of Death, rise the embattled walls of Pisa. Next to the Christian cemetery, directly behind the fresco but outside of the severe walls, in the dark shadows of the secular cypress trees, separate but adjacent to the Christians, lie the Jews who subsidized the purchase of this plot and their descendants.* Poor Uncle Aldo lies in Israeli soil in the Piazza dei Miracoli, in Pisa.

%

Aunt Mafalda was nothing like our mother: she was tense and vulnerable, her hair was always slightly messy, and she did not seem beautiful to me, though she was, with an indolent beauty that I could not appreciate as a child. She had one visible defect which was mostly noticeable in her eyes but which permeated her entire being; it was a Jewish defect, common to Jewish women: a kind of languidness, verging on sloth. Perhaps it is not even a defect but rather a characteristic which can sometimes be positive rather than lethal: in a harem, for example. My mother was endowed with a powerful drive and moral energy, while Aunt Mafalda was defenseless in the adversities of the early forties. The passage from comfortable childhood to well-off married life had cultivated this dark flaw in her, a flaw she shared with Leah of the red eyes, who pretended to be Rachel in order to appease Laban, her father, with the betrayal of Jacob. Aunt Mafalda possessed no moral energy because she was not meant to require it; it was Carlo, her

* I've described here the Jewish cemetery as I saw it as a child in 1948. Today it has been devastated, in part by a post-mortem tourist trade made up mostly of American Jews. The cypress trees are skeletal, and I am told that the most ancient part of the cemetery has been sold; the tombstones have been redistributed, as well as possible, to the other section. I am also told that a gas station has been built in the section that was sold. Amen.

husband and master, who judged the world and made decisions with an irritated swiftness which was ill-suited to the chaos of the time.

Alberto's sister Graziella was a lethargic "young lady," dressed in lace and velvet like an infanta, and everyone said she looked just like her mother. She didn't play with me because she was older, but she always treated me with smiling affection.

In Milan we would ride the tram and get off a few stops from the Stazione Centrale on a tree-lined street. The attractive multistoried buildings had gardens, which were reserved for the inhabitants of the ground floor. And the Morais family lived in a large, sunny apartment on the ground floor.

Alberto and I would shut ourselves in his room and study the hypermodern *Enciclopedia del Tesoro,*[1] complete with physics experiments you could do at home. He was a studious child, beloved of his Jewish teachers who don't fall for children like me. He was studious and calm, but he used to completely lose control when I came to visit.

One day when he was trying to explain to me that glass is not a solid, as it appears, but rather an extremely viscous liquid, he picked up a crystal goblet from the table, which had been elegantly laid out for our lunch, submerged it in water in the sink, and explained that crystal can be cut like paper when the vibrations are deadened by water. The goblet shattered, and his parents said nothing, while my mother gave me her typical dirty look. Alberto's parents were so surprised that their wise child could behave so strangely that they didn't even dare scold him. My mother knew that I had put him up to it, in order to test his scientific assertions. The theory is actually correct, despite the negative results of his experiment, in case you would like to repeat it with your own fine crystal.

The luxurious and, today, antiquated *Enciclopedia del Tesoro* is now in my library, in the section where I keep my books related to the Shoah, near Bruegel's *Triumph of Death.*

It is difficult to describe the image of my dear Alberto. I remember a complex mixture of events, words, postures, expressions, and reflexes which are my own fleeting, indistinct creations, as ephemeral as ghosts. Alberto's ghost reminds me a bit of the precocious and stolid face of the nuclear physicist Bruno Pontecorvo in his youth.

After December first, 1943, my uncle decided to flee with his family to Switzerland and paid a smuggler who betrayed them, robbed them, and abandoned them in the snow. Aunt Mafalda sobbed and begged her husband to take them back home. My uncle was furious, and, before returning to Milan, he decided, I think "rashly" would be putting it mildly, to file a complaint with the police. He showed up at the *carabinieri* station in Tirano near the Swiss border with his wife and children. The marshal arrested them—he could not do otherwise after Buffarini Guidi's order—but tried to help them by calling some of their Catholic relatives in Milan. My uncle Alfredo Di Matteo, an entrepreneur and lyric tenor in his spare time, rushed to the village and, helped by the marshal, tried to convince his brother-in-law to entrust his children to him; they could be marked down as having escaped before the arrest. But my uncle refused: "The family must stay together," he said. "After all, it is only a question of staying in an internment camp in Germany for a few months. Germany is a civilized country."

"All or nothing," was the exact phrase he used, several times. My mind bridles at the thought.

At the end of their long voyage, the train stopped at Auschwitz, and an SS officer explained to the new arrivals that the old, the ill, and children could take the few trucks available to go to nearby Birkenau. The others would have to walk the two or three kilometers.

Uncle Carlo found space on the truck for his wife and children and, half an hour later upon his arrival in Birkenau, asked a prisoner where his family was. He spoke German, the lingua franca of the camps, quite well. "They're up there," the old man answered, pointing at the dark smoke rising from the chimneys of the crematoria. The trucks were the first form of selection upon arrival at the camp, before people realized that they were in an extermination camp; it was a way to minimize natural defensive reactions and panic in order to optimize the yield of the system. That is how Mafalda, Alberto, and Graziella ended their lives, after five minutes of breathing Zyklon B. Farewell Milan, the Jewish school on Via della Spiga, the French fries on Via Borgospesso, parties with cousins, bathing in the Lago Maggiore . . .

The flames, which shot up six yards because of the power of the kerosene and the natural combustion of the bodies, were visible from miles away. Passengers on the German railway line, which sped up at this point, crowded around the windows to comment on the extraordinary sight. A tourist pamphlet announced: "Come to the East, the new land of the Reich! See the world of the future!"

Uncle Carlo survived until the first transfers from Auschwitz, when the Russians and the roar of cannons were approaching. At this point, the stories differ. According to one survivor, he committed his third and final error: he joined the herd which was led to die elsewhere. He was shot on one of the forced marches, "one of the many who just couldn't go any longer; but by then, he was probably unconscious of what was happening around him." According to another survivor, he wandered around the camp on his last legs after the arrival of the Russians. But the two stories agree on one point: my uncle never stopped asking every single person he met if they had seen his wife and children.

After 1945, by combining police reports and the testimony of survivors, we were able to piece together details of the last days of Carlo and a few others. In December of 1944, we had received an oral cable, transmitted from person to person: "They've picked up Mafalda, Carlo, and the children. They're gone."

Our miserable but serene life in the mountains was interrupted by news of upcoming raids. How did we know a raid was about to take place? Perhaps the movements of the relatively scarce forces of the Nazi-Fascists revealed their next move, confirmed by the mustering of militiamen from the local barracks and the constant information from partisan spies, both lay and ecclesiastical. Ten or twenty hours before a raid, the valley prepared itself, like a person who sees dark, menacing clouds and takes steps to protect property and family. The partisans and the young men set out for the mountaintops, beyond the last houses in Urì, and hid in the forests. The sick and wounded were hidden away, as were Roberto and I, in the houses of others. *Papà* disappeared as well, sometimes with the partisans, and *mamma* joined the women of the village, chattering, knitting, and standing guard. On less serious occasions *papà* would go to the *Podestà*'s to give violin lessons or engage in deep theological discussion with the priest at the *Cottolengo.* The Bioglio priest, Don Giovanni—that was really his name—hid with the partisans, and quickly, because he had long since compromised himself. The priest at the *Cottolengo* was so taken with my father that he lent him the complete set of his sermons, written by hand on rice paper: more than sixty sermons, one for each Sunday plus feast days. *Papà* said they were not bad, and he would ask the priest to explain the most interesting passages during the raids. But he rolled his eyes at me as he flipped through the pages of the priest's leather-bound volume: "Do you realize, Aldino, he's been reading the same sermons every year for forty years, without moving a comma! Forty years! As soon as he finished the seminary, he wrote out exactly what he would be saying for the rest of his life! Bah!"

Right before the raid, our *carabinieri,* Briga and Pippo, calmly stopped at every household which they suspected of Fascist sympathies and reminded the inhabitants of the presence of partisans and Jewish fugitives hidden around the village, admonishing them that if any of the "aforementioned" were picked up during the raid, the price would be the immediate execution, without investigation or trial, of all those who had been thus forewarned. Then Briga and Pippo would disappear, and the valley would lie in wait, apparently tranquil and harmless, for the announced strike. The Fascists locked their doors, closed their shutters, and, to the untrained eye, appeared in every way to be true enemies of the army that was climbing up from the plains.

Once, during preparation for a raid, a terrible incident occurred. A twenty-year-old man and his eighteen-year-old girlfriend* had been stealing money and jewels, golden chains and crucifixes, rings, earrings, and similar objects that the local inhabitants kept for a rainy day (what day could be rainier than the ones we were living, I wonder?).

* These ages are the result of a compromise between my memory and Roberto's. I remember them as being eighteen and fifteen, whereas Roberto argues that he was thirty-five and she was twenty-seven. Roberto believes that the partisans were right, and I think that unfortunately they had no choice but to do what they did.

The thieves had disguised themselves as partisans, and this fact marked them for death, even though the truth is that they didn't hurt people, only frightened them.

Their execution was rendered all the more brutal by the lack of munitions and the imminence of a raid. The Americans had discarded shell cases that, oddly, contained no bullets, and the partisans had only old, humid, homemade gunpowder to fill them with. I had seen the partisans experiment with these, with the help of poachers; they would attach a pistol to a sawhorse in an empty horse stall or barn and then pull the trigger by means of a long string, in order to avoid having the gun explode in their hands. The bullets were made of soft, unmolded lead, placed carefully in the cartridges and carefully sanded so as not to block the barrel. The experiment seemed to work: the round bullets could perforate one or two boards, but no one knew what their effect would be on human flesh.

Unable to take the criminals with them, and afraid that they would "talk" in the hands of the Germans or the Fascists, the partisans hurriedly tried the couple and condemned them to death. They were confessed by the priest from the *Cottolengo,* who told my father and me that the girl, instead of praying, asked him, "Please help me get away, Father, help me!" and kept staring at a door behind his back. It was the door to a closet, but in her terror it had come to represent the door to life. Briga and Pippo took them behind the cemetery wall and started to shoot with their homemade munitions, which, because of the combination of defective powder and unmolded bullets, were less effective than the hammer that the Barcas used to kill cats. From the doorstep, I could hear shooting, then silence, and then more shooting; next to me, Signor Barca stopped his ears and said over and over: "They're really killing them good!" He must have been afraid for himself and his brother; they didn't mug people but were known to steal goats. They were goat thieves, and that's what they looked like too.

After what seemed like endless shooting, I went down to the town to find out what had happened. The gravedigger kept guard over the corpses in front of the cemetery chapel, wanting and not wanting to show them to a group of women who wanted and did not want to see them and make the inevitable sign of the cross which, inevitably, they made. After having said no a few times, and after having perhaps accepted a few "donations," he picked up the shroud for just a moment and displayed the two faces, which had been washed but were covered in large blue bruises from the lead pellets. The faces were sallow and sweaty, and the eyes had been closed by someone who was still capable of pity. As he covered the corpses, the gravedigger jested coldly, "Tonight they can be as dirty as they like," perhaps to poke fun at the piety of the ladies or perhaps to demonstrate his great professional distance. The next morning I awoke with a fever of 104 degrees and jaundice. I was as yellow as a canary in accordance with a Piedmontese superstition: *giaunisa*—turning yellow—is caused by looking at the dead.

The most memorable raid was on January 10, 1945. Roberto and I had been given to the care of the girlfriend of a partisan who had been forced to flee in a great hurry, with the snow up to his knees. He was a Latin teacher from Palermo, Nino Bolone, an ex-lieutenant from the Royal Army, who sporadically gave us Latin lessons. He was tall and had a mustache and, except for the Sicilian accent, was just like Errol Flynn in *Objective, Burma!* When we walked through the mountains, with him ahead and us behind, picking primroses, he wasn't sure of where he was going, but wherever he went, he went with an air of total self-assurance.

On the other hand, Gigi *"Al Fulatun"*—the madman—knew exactly where he was going: he went from one forest to another on his red Guzzi motorbike with rubber handle grips for himself and a passenger. But he never carried a passenger, because no one in his right mind would ride with him: he flew over roads, which seemed to be his only obstacles. One day, when we were descending toward Valle San Nicolao behind Nino Bolone, carrying primroses in one hand and our schoolbags in the other, *Al Fulatun* came up behind us on the path, silently, with his motor off, driving with one hand and holding a grenade in the other. "Better change path," he said to Nino as he passed us, "I'm about to throw a little party, heh, heh." A few minutes later, as we clambered up the path we had descended so calmly, our primroses trembling, Gigi *Al Fulatun* stood up, cranked up his Guzzi, pulled out the safety from the grenade, and leapt over the road while simultaneously throwing the bomb into a truck full of Fascists which was climbing up from Cossato. Then he disappeared into the forest beneath the road, on a 60 percent incline, his motorbike screaming, running on half gas, half alcohol.

Gigi *Al Fulatun* came from a good family; he had pomaded hair parted on the side. He was the son of a lawyer from Biella, and he didn't give a damn about uniforms. He rode around on his motorcycle in his sports jacket with a half-belt and darts up to his shoulders. I don't know why he liked the partisans so much or why he was so brave: he was a dirt-biking pioneer.

In the early afternoon of the January 10th raid, I was upset about the separation from my parents, which was yet another reenactment of the one I had experienced at the school. Everyone around us was consumed by a deep, atavistic fear and stayed in small groups in their houses, their hands covering their eyes, mouth, forehead, or cheeks, telling stories about the ancestral violence of the Cossacks and the Mongols.

There were no Cossacks or Mongols in Bioglio, however, and on that occasion there were no excesses that I know of, and I saw only Germans. At around three o'clock in the afternoon, someone came to the future Signora Bolone's door and announced that the raid had been postponed. The coast was clear in Valdengo, where he had come from, as well as in Piatto, further up the mountain. Hoping for the best, I ran up the steep road toward Urì and found my father with a group of partisans above Campore near the chestnut wood. When he saw me, he hissed, "Get out of here!" He was hiding with the partisans behind a pile of snow, and he wiped sweat from his brow, despite the cold. Biting his handkerchief, he mumbled, "Idiot! What do you mean there's no raid! Turn around and look, and then scram!" I turned around and saw, to my great shame and terror, hundreds of Germans (or perhaps only ten or twenty) skiing down the mountain, slaloming across the valley in silence, with their machine guns slung across their backs or chests. They were coming toward Bioglio from above. They had climbed up the Pettinengo road on the other side as far as they could and were now descending fast and spreading out, hoping to take the village by surprise with all of the partisans trapped like fools. Still staring at them, and deafened by the pounding of my heart, I ran desperately toward Bioglio.

On my return, the town was already full of Germans dressed in grayish-green. The ones who dressed in white were special elite mountain troops, and they had returned to Biella by bus, their skis strapped onto the roof. The others were regular soldiers of the *Wehrmacht* who had quickly climbed up the road from Valdengo. They occupied the entire valley, the streets in the village, and all around, and they seemed to number in the thousands. They didn't go into the houses, but we could see them through the windows with their wolfhounds in the white snow, their rifles leaning together in bunches. They beat their feet together to keep warm around the bonfire, preparing for a disagreeable night in the open. The surprise had failed, and the two-pronged attack had produced no results. The partisans, who were also sleeping *à la belle étoile,* shivered a few hundred yards up the mountain. No violence, no combat, no searches, no fires, just silvery German voices in the night: an impeccable maneuver gone wrong, one of many such episodes in the guerilla war. Late that night, however, one hungry German soldier knocked on the door, and, when Nino's girlfriend opened it, he asked if she would kindly give him an egg, *bitte*! She answered that she had none, closed and bolted the door, grabbed a basket full of eggs, and ran with Roberto and me to the toilet. We broke all of them. She threw four or five of them into the toilet, and I pulled the chain, until the basket was empty. *Dankeshön*!

The last raid, in March of 1945, was undertaken by the melodramatic *Republicchini,* who simply wanted to demonstrate that they were still able to do as they pleased. We underestimated the danger. They began killing chickens with their machine guns and wreaked so much destruction that the partisans were forced to give battle, if only to protect their honor. I believe that the new balance of power led Moscatelli to give free reign to the repressed fighting instinct in his men, who could now let themselves go without putting the cause in danger. From November to the end of January 1945, while massacres and fierce battles were going on in the valleys, in Moscatelli's area, as far as I know, there were only skirmishes, no battles.

Papà and I were coming up from Bioglio when suddenly we heard bullets whistling over our heads like telephone wires in the wind. *Papà* took me by the hand and shielded me as we walked a few, seemingly endless, yards to a group of houses. I did not realize the danger we were in, probably because of my father's protection and calm; he knew there were no snipers on either side and that only by fleeing would we be in danger. It is possible to pass by unnoticed in the middle of a battle. *Mamma,* who was above, had asked the partisans not to shoot until we had returned, and they had obeyed, begrudgingly, until they saw us a few yards away from the shelter of the houses.

When we arrived, *mamma* was crying, as she had cried on other occasions when we had been caught in dangerous situations. A slight delay was enough, just a few minutes, for *mamma* to start pacing back and forth in the kitchen yelling, "They've taken him! This time, they've got him!" or *papà* would go out to look for us in the fields, or Roberto and I would stare out the window with sad orphan eyes because our parents had not yet shown up at the curve in the road. "What's keeping them?"

The world was becoming less hostile, but we could not see it yet; it seemed more dangerous than ever because we were terribly tired, of the misery, the waiting, the powerlessness, the vulnerability, and even of the theorizing. I heard my parents talk endlessly about the destinies of captured Jews, perhaps in order to exorcise the evidence. *Papà* suggested, "Perhaps they sterilize the men," but *mamma* rejected this flight of fancy because the very manner in which the hunt was undertaken revealed its ends. Why did they take entire families, old people, why such a waste of energy in the immense continent of Europe, why the massacre at the Lago d'Orta,* why the old people from the Jewish Hospice in Trieste? What were these horrible crimes that the London radio spoke of which would be paid for when the war was over? Where were our uncles and cousins? Where had they been taken? And why had we never had a single letter or message from them, or any sign of life?

This was not the only political disagreement between my mother and father. They disagreed about many things, because my father was sentimental and my mother was not. In 1942 when the Vichy government imposed the yellow Star of David on French Jews, father predicted, even hoped, that the Italian government would do the same; we would have gone out proudly with our lovely yellow stars. *Mamma,* on the other hand, expressed her distaste for the idea and hoped that the yellow star never found its way to Italy. "Mario, you think people are normal and good, but it's not true, and you don't want to believe it. As soon as they pin

* It wasn't the Lago d'Orta, as was then believed. In December 1943, a band of SS from the Adolf Hitler Division drowned several Jewish families they had discovered in the hotels of Arona, Meina, and Intra in the Lago Maggiore. The tale circulated all over Italy. Among the twenty corpses brought to shore by the waves was an old man tied to his two grandchildren with wire. The total number of victims was fifty-four.

that yellow star to our collars, people will avoid us, and worse." The yellow star never came, but the "worse" happened anyway.

One Sunday at the beginning of February, or perhaps at the end of January 1945, we were having tea at the house of the *Podestà,* and, as usual, we were trying to tune into Radio London. The alternatives, when there was too much interference, were Radio Monteceneri, from the Italian part of Switzerland, and Vatican Radio. Those two transmitters were so circumspect, however, that it was difficult to understand what was going on. Moscow Radio was even more difficult to hear than Radio London, and the victories that it announced, all true, were so extraordinary and couched in so much rhetoric as to seem false. Transmissions started with a few notes of the Soviet Hymn and a voice that declared: "Death to Fascism and liberty to the people!"

That February evening, we were only able to get Moscow Radio. The voice came and went, but it revealed, clearly, what had occurred to the Jews of Europe: "thousands . . . corpses . . . smoke . . . millions of dead . . . Fascist animals . . . burned . . . Aus . . . a giant camp . . . we denounce in the eyes of the world . . . this morning the Soviet troops liberated . . . Aus . . . itz . . . urgent care . . . need assistance . . . train cars . . . fires everywhere . . . piles of corpses burning . . . extermination of a population . . . In their victorious advance, the Soviet troops today discovered a huge camp, surrounded by barbed wire . . . In eastern Silesia . . . the beast's den . . . the anti-Fascist Jewish Committee has declared . . .

the extermination of the Jewish population . . ." *Mamma* cried out, her voice strangled with sobs, "No one is coming back! Mafalda is dead!" The *Podestà*'s wife stared blankly, looking as blind as her daughter. "I think we should go home, Eugenia," *papà* whispered as he lifted *mamma* out of her chair by both shoulders, and the *Podestà*'s wife and daughter, both with blank stares, walked us silently to the door. Outside, in the cold, *mamma* muttered "Austerlitz" over and over as she stomped through the snow. "Why Austerlitz?" Only the names remained a mystery to us that night, and the reason behind it all. The means, the numbers, and the irrevocability of the crimes were revealed to us at the beginning of 1945.

15 ※ Roberto

In the desperate late spring of 1943, Felicino Ottolenghi disappeared nonchalantly into the Caffè degli Specchi, and the mirrors disappeared with him, as well as the café. All this is of the past. Meanwhile, we crossed the Sambuy Gardens to ask Ersilia Rossi for help. She was a friend of my father's, the first woman engineer in Europe, and the first woman pilot in Italy. "Will the heavier one win?"[1] Ersilia answered yes, around 1909.

This pioneer, who with the years had become a fat old lady with whiskers, breathed heavily as she guided us through her fantastic apartment, complete with eighteenth-century frescoes, onto the terrace above the arches of Piazza Carlo Felice, which led to the next, identical building, separated only by a neo-classical railing depicting lances, quivers, arrows, and bronze liturgical-cisalpine ribbons. From this elevated *piazza*-like terrace, with the tram running underneath, ringing its bell, we could see the Sambuy Gardens on the left, the trees in fall colors of red, violet, yellow, and the backdrop of the buildings arrayed to defend the military capital of the Kingdom of Sardinia. To the right, almost within reach, was a bronze statue of the Savoy bookkeeper Signor Paleocapa, seated in a little *piazza* named after him on a bronze easy chair a story high, reading his bronze book-newspaper. Terraces, tram, park, arches, *piazza,* hanging gardens, monuments: the *esprit de géométrie* at the service of the idealization of eternity.

For more than a hundred years, the Porta Nuova Station has formed one of the sides of the eighteenth-century ellipse of Piazza Carlo Felice. Before then, the architectural structure of the park opened toward the boundless countryside, like the other parks on the four sides of the city. They were like mouths that devoured the people who came into the city and spit out those who left. It was the tension of urban imperiousness against the singsong of the parochial countryside. Conceived in the false assurance that the world does not change, these *piazze* have now been swallowed up by the city.

From the other side of the elaborate Sambuy Gardens, beyond the paroxysm of heavy machinery, cars, buses, tanks, trains, and giant motors, on the other side of all this are the arches, the tram, and the breathtaking terraces. Beyond lies the little Piazza Lagrange, a twin of the Piazza Paleocapa, with a statue that exhibits a kind of deformity in a place where symmetry is a religion: Signor Lagrange is standing, anomalously upright, with his bronze newspaper in hand. Green, angular trams run down the Via Lagrange (mechanical analysis) and the Via Volta (electrostatic induction machines), and cross the identical arches holding up terraces that are cultivated as gardens with butcher's broom, rhododendrons, gardenias with blue shadows, and azaleas.*

Roberto maneuvered insouciantly through this dangerous mechanism; he picked up a small stone and placed it inside an empty bandage tin in his pocket. The small cylindrical box of "Leucoplast" bandages was made out of a light metal, and Roberto enjoyed shaking it, making a ticking noise. The armoire-shaped woman, with her stammering, intellectual, toothless, salivating voice, led us through her apartment—tic-tic went the little box—nonchalantly pointing out the paintings by Delleani and Fattori—tic-tic—and bringing our attention to the polished wooden propeller of her beloved Caproni jet airplane and to the photograph—tic-tic—in which she stood smiling—yes, smiling!—with her hand confidently resting on the wing of her flying machine constructed of fabric and bits of wood. She made it

* This description, like that of Asti, contradicts reality. For example, Signor Paleocapa and Signor Lagrange may have been made of stone, not bronze. And everyone knows there was never a tram line on Via Volta, but I think it's a shame considering that Volta was a pioneer in electricity.

understood that she could do nothing more for us—tic-tic—and when we were on the terrace, handed my father the usual little envelope—tic-tic—as Roberto, the monster, kept making the little rock go tic-tic, for goodness' sake! After she had handed my father the subsidy, the ex-pilot walked us to the dark, elegant, old-fashioned landing—tic-tic—and unlocked the door to the Stigler elevator. Thus we disappeared from view in an illuminated cabin decorated with mirrors, brass, and small, creaky red benches—tic-tic—waving our right hands in an affectionate, grateful salute: a thousand lire! And Roberto kept at it: tic-tic.

Our condition emanated anxiety, panic, and shame; as she closed the door, that poor, deaf old woman found herself in a state of turmoil and confusion: we existed, and she had seen us.

Once we turn seventy, or perhaps—unfortunately—earlier, the external world appears to us as it really is: an incomprehensible, chilling puzzle of death. On the street, we freeze anxiously at the sight of a group of children playing ball, hoping that they will be encouraged to stop by the funereal expression on our faces. And when we see shameless youths loitering outside a dance hall with lubricious looks on their faces, we prudently cross over to the other side of the street, because "you never know . . ."

We had disturbed the serenity of the old lady. Her house, in that reassuring, geometric location, had been occupied for a few moments by nonhumans: nonhumans to the SS, and less-than-humans to everyone else—even, though not exaggeratedly so, to aviation pioneers. She closed the door, and, instead of going back to tending her camellias (tic-tic) or to organizing her scrapbooks, the old woman wandered around her vast apartment, followed by her servant, opening and closing drawers (tic-tic) with a growing sense of anxiety and fear.

Endogenous anxiety and the exogenous memory of our panic intermingled and grew in the pilot's confused mind, amplified by the hammering of Roberto's tic-ticking. She remembered, or thought she remembered, or imagined that she remembered hiding her engagement ring—from the previous century—in a bandage tin. She ran to the drawer and found the box was gone (if such a box ever existed): this explained the ticking. And she sent her servant after us with a note asking *papà* to "kindly return for an urgent communication following our interview." *Papà* ran back, imagining a dairy farm in the woods or a patrician villa just for us, and the old lady, whiskers and scarf fluttering in the wind, pointing out the words "Confederatio Helvetica" to us as we crowded into the back seat of her biplane.

He returned, gloomy and trembling, and gripped Roberto by his little arm, relieved to see that he still held the box in his other hand and continued to shake it: tic-tic. My brother was dragged, tin in hand, to Piazza Carlo Felice. He held out his right hand, in which he held the box between his thumb and index finger. "Go tic-tic," my father ordered, working his other arm like a water pump, and Roberto, after a minute of reflection, shook his right hand and made the ticking sound. "There, Madam. Here is the little box . . . please look inside." The old lady took the box and looked inside: "But it's a pebble. Mine had cotton wool in it; did you throw it out with the ring, my little angel?" My father answered for him: "But, Madam, if there had been cotton wool inside, it wouldn't have gone tic-tic; it would only have gone tic." And the armoire-lady said, not rudely but unthinkingly: "Don't worry, Maestro. If the ring is here, we'll find it. But it was the same box, or at least I think so; anyway, if it's still there, we'll find it . . . sooner or later."

This tic-ticking was my brother's only war crime that might have had irreversible consequences, if one excludes the scandal of the San Nicolao frogs.

Many months later, for personal reasons, Roberto came to the highly justifiable decision that he would run away from school, and that is precisely what he did on July 15, 1944. He had had enough, after three days without lunch or dinner, plus periodic canings. Spiritually, he had reached his limit; even he, who had long since become used to punishment, had reached the end of the line. He had become a target, it's true; he had been singled out by his teacher, the *Consigliere,* who was perhaps the meanest of all the priests. This one had a round face with stiff cheeks and blue—or rather gray-blue—eyes. His soul had been replaced by a sarcasm that we surely deserved, but that he, as a priest, should have at least attempted to repress. He was a nasty man, and Roberto, with his usual bad luck, was stuck with him.

⸸

In the catechistic progression of infamous religions, Jews were far from the top: they fought for distant third place behind the Anglicans and the Protestants. More recent betrayals burned brighter than our far-off deicide, which, however, still loomed as an undeniable act of insubordination and continued to be bathed in an aura of free will and rituality, which placed it in the category of founding crimes. The Salesians had little else to add to our list of faults and limited themselves to the heavy account of events in the Gospels every Sunday: The Jew . . . and the Apostles feared the Jews . . . the Jews this, the Jews that. . . . The Jews had not understood in time that the Messiah had come . . . and that was it. But the Anglicans had truly betrayed, and recently, just a few centuries earlier, and all because of some vulgar women. Henry VIII represented a sexual criminality at least on the same level as that of His Repugnancy Martin Luther, an unpriestly priest married to an unnunly nun. The Russian and Greek Orthodox churches came out reasonably well, filling the last spot in the list of reprobates, after the Jews. Their many "insults" were tempered by the recognition of good conduct and hopes of reconciliation, recomposition, and reunification under the loving guidance of the Roman Catholic Apostolic Holy Father, Pius XII, a saint—they would see reason sooner or later. Hindus, Buddhists, Confucians, Taoists, and Muslims: these people didn't even exist and were simply to be pitied. They were distant savages in loincloths, unknowing of the true path, to be redeemed by missionaries by any means.

Roberto's teacher, the *Consigliere,* specialized in hatred for Anglicans, not because Italy was at war with England—a secondary fact, given that we were allied with Lutheran Germany—but because these obtuse islanders, their brains filled with the same fog as their streets, insisted on a false and evil religion, its wickedness revealed by the names they gave their children: "Tommy, Jimmy, Jackie, Bobby, Teddy, Fred—just like the dogs they love so much, you hear that? Those idiots baptize their children with such names, if you can call that baptism," the *Consigliere* would rant to his captive audience of boys, who were desperate to scamper off and play *tùt al trùc* in the courtyard with the little steel ball you launched with a short, dry blow.

The catechism teacher spoke about the Jews. He was a nice old man who looked a bit like a Russian ogre, with short, thick eyebrows and drooping purple cheeks above a small puckered mouth which seemed very far away from his nose and blue-green, dismayed little eyes; over his cassock, he wore a jacket rather than a typical long black cloak. He had been on a pilgrimage to the Holy Land in his youth, and, to please him, we used to run over and ask him to "pray like a Jew, Father, pray like a Jew." He assumed a serious, inspired expression and breathed in deeply, filling his lungs, and then, staring straight ahead and opening his eyes wide, he would take one priestly shoe off and rest his foot on it, and beat a rhythm with his foot while pounding his chest, making it resonate like a drum. Then he would begin to recite the following Hebrew prayer: "Chinabì, chinabò, chinabì, chinabò, chinadan tan tan." These movements of his hands, feet, and eyes were a sincere attempt to give life to his memories of the bare feet of the Muslims, the pounding of the chest of the Catholic mea culpa, and a nursery rhyme from his now-distant childhood:

La spica l'è mica, lè pan pan pan, . . .
Chi n'à poc, chi n'à nen,
*Chi n'à tan tan tan.**

The poor, isolated, silly old priest was an endless source of entertainment for the students at the school.

%

Why did Roberto run away from school? Not because of the rations or the beatings but because he was constitutionally unable to accept false accusations. His archenemy was a cruel, foolish boy with double knees—one on the front and the other on the back of each leg—whose family name was Rude.[2] He was a giant, and his little Fascist cape did not reach fully over his shoulders; it looked like two grayish-green bat's wings. Only Roberto could have chosen to take

* "The wheat is a bread loaf, bread, bread, bread. Some have little, some have nothing, some have tons, tons, tons." Over the centuries, this chant had become a children's counting rhyme. Whoever the final *tan* landed on was "it" for that round.

on somebody with such a last name, but that's exactly what he did, and, in fact, in the end something good came out of that senseless violence, albeit after many trials.

Roberto merely punched this Rude character (who was perhaps the only truly nasty boy in the school) in the face. If you ask him about it today, Roberto will answer, as if it was yesterday, that anyone would have done the same thing, but the truth is that everyone else knew to stay well away from Rude. In any case, he punched him in the face, splitting his lip. This in itself was not an exceptional occurrence at the school, but Rude was a monster and could not accept that he had been beaten by this "puppy." (Roberto, because of his fan-shaped ears and delicate features, was often undervalued as a boxer and, in fact, had a mean left-hand punch.) He told the *Consigliere* and an assistant that Roberto had punched him while holding a piece of broken glass between his fingers.

"I've had it!" concluded Roberto, accused of this infamy and abandoned by the *Consigliere* and everyone else. He decided to run off and join *mamma* and *papà* in Cossato, where he thought they were staying. But they had given us a false address so that we could not be coerced into giving away their hiding place. This mentality of the hunted is what they had been reduced to, not without some obvious discomfort.

That afternoon, the priests began looking for him everywhere, and Monsignor Cavasin asked me how long it had been since I had seen my brother. In fact, I hadn't seen him for days, because I avoided his "circles," but I answered that I had seen him that morning. Monsignor Cavasin, who knew about the false address and was well aware of Rude's brutality and the *Consigliere*'s perfidy, understood immediately that Roberto had run away and went into red alert. The whole school was in danger, including priests, assistants, and children.

Monsignor Cavasin did not sleep at night because of a story he had heard about the SS coming into schools and asking the children to pull down their pants in order to reveal any circumcised students. Roberto was sure to end up in a police station somewhere within hours, perhaps even minutes. We had to find him immediately, wherever he was. All of the priests, except for the catechism teacher, who looked after the school in times of crisis, and the assistants, went out on bicycles—women's bicycles, with grilles over the rear wheels to keep their cassocks from becoming tangled in the spokes—and pedaled furiously under their skirts.

Roberto, meanwhile, had stopped at a dairy farm and told its inhabitants that his sick grandmother was sending him to Cossato to join his parents and that he had had nothing to eat or drink since leaving Turin. Who knows where he came up with the idea, perhaps from De Amicis's *The Heart of a Boy* (ed. Treves, 1935), but the farmers, with their love of children, swallowed his story whole. By all accounts, when the priest found him, he was sitting under a trellis in front of an abundantly laid-out table: he had already drunk one or two glasses of wine and was just starting on his second course of zucchini stuffed with meat, while the farmers, their cheeks resting on their large, callous hands and elbows on the table, listened to his stories about the long walk and his dying grandmother. The priest tried to pick him up by the neck like a chicken without even getting off of his bicycle, but the farmers, even after the truth had been revealed, demanded that Roberto be allowed at least to finish the zucchini. The story of the zucchini became a classic at the school; the boys told it over and over in their desperate attempts to calm their appetites. Monsignor Cavasin, who had finally understood that Roberto was a walking time bomb, gave the order that he should be treated well and left alone.

Writing the strange, absurd story of my brother's escape from the school has made me understand (only now!) that he was not living the same experience that I was, and so I have asked him, now that he is sixty years old, what he thought of me when I cried disconsolately on December first at the archbishop's and during those first terrible fifteen days at the school. He answered: "Well! I thought you were an unbearable jerk. When I saw you, it made me so mad, but I didn't say anything because otherwise it would have made matters worse. Why did you cry so much? All because you were being sent away to school along with me? *Mamma* had been threatening to send me away for years if I didn't behave. And now they were going to send you away as well, despite your hypocrisy, but you couldn't bear to accept your lot with dignity, you cried like a girl, and there was no stopping you. That's what I thought of you." Before we went to the mountains, he was a small boy who could only understand his own private dramas, not those of the entire world.

After the apparent return of *mamma* and *papà* in April 1944 and the escape into the rice fields and the passing of time, Roberto was softly deposited in a less unacceptable reality; in October 1944, he began to undertake acts which have become legends to this day. During the January 10th raid, a group of the German skiers in white outfits who had given me such a fright asked him where the partisans were hidden. As we know, they had not found them in town, so they tried to make up for failed strategy with ingenuity on the spot. The partisans had fled, but Roberto was still there, peeing in the snow. He finished peeing, and with the sleepy, idle air of one ignorant and indifferent to the troubles of the world—the result of absolute self-control—he sent them toward the sanatorium for consumptives and then ran off to hide at Nino's girlfriend's, who was not so appreciative of his great act of heroism.

Roberto adapted poorly to the school—in fact, he did not adapt to it at all, nor it to him—but he enjoyed those seven months in the mountains more than I, who was no great lover of nature, ever could. He became fast friends with the Dragos and the other children of Urì and even the Barca children, who didn't frighten him. He was strengthened by his surroundings, and he liked to catch small animals, especially—alas—frogs, and then release them. He walked through the snow from one valley to the next, free from scholastic duties. Finally, he had all the time he needed to dedicate himself to his one true passion: losing himself completely in the sea of his perceptions.

He loved the partisans because they had become a part of the vast natural world of the woods, which was his friend, and the partisans returned his affection. One morning there was a sudden, nearby shower of machine-gun fire, and *papà* went pale, as usual, because Roberto was outside. *Papà* ran out to look for him filled with fear and anger, which in those days were the only emotions he was capable of. A few minutes later, a young partisan only slightly older than the two of us came to our door, several times, laughing and turning away, stopping and repeating, "Come on, don't kid around, please give me back the weapon, *prufesur.*" *Papà,* indescribably angry, was holding the Parabellum machine gun by the barrel, and with the index finger of the other hand he pointed at an imaginary point next to his once-elegant shoes, now the worse for wear. "Come here and I'll give you your Parabellum, you'll see! I told you not to teach my boy to shoot that thing!" He had caught the two of them together: the partisan was standing and expounding on the use of the weapon while Roberto lay on the ground with a serious look on his little face as he machine-gunned a tree.

But my brother's legend—a legend which is now fading because the people we knew there are disappearing, replaced in the sixties by immigrants from the South, and now by people from outside of Italy—stems mostly from his abilities as an animal tamer. I only hope that the indescribable event of the San Nicolao frogs has been forgotten.

Near our houses there was a huge Bergamasco sheepdog which had been trained as a guard dog, against his sheepherding nature. The dog was overly ferocious and had to be kept on a chain. The terrible error in his training may have resulted in part from the fact that the facial expression of these dogs is masked by long fur; they appear friendly, even when they have decided to kill. The owners of the dog were forced to creep by, back against the wall, in order to get into their house, murmuring tremulously, "Good dog, good dog," their hands held out in front of them or at their hips, studying the dog's every move because even the smallest error could prove fatal. They had devised a system for feeding him: they threw food down from the first-story window, trying to hit him straight on while he was sleeping and dreaming his homicidal dreams, so that he could feed himself despite the short chain, licking his chops, barking and showing his teeth, his furious red eyes hidden by fur. He threatened passersby from his narrow passageway, everyone except for Roberto. When Roberto walked by, like a tiny Saint Francis, the dog would whine and hide his muzzle in his paws, raising his hindquarters and wagging his grayish, hairy tail.

One morning, the owners of the dog appeared at our house to warn us that Roberto had untied him and that they "did not take responsibility" for what might happen. That is how the friendship between Roberto and the dog began. They would run through the forests undisturbed because no one was brave enough to approach them, talking to each other and sharing observations, or at least so it seemed from a distance; they would stop and look at each other, exclaiming at the fascinating world that surrounded them. The owners gave up their guard dog, but he did not become wild or abandon them. He followed Roberto around during the day and circulated on his own at night, but at dusk he returned to the alpine hut to threaten his former owners with death, and they unhappily threw scraps from the window.

One Saturday evening, *papà* returned home in a terrible state. He had spilled the juniper soup and the *Podestà*'s *cotechino* broth all over himself, lost his bag in the snow, and hurt his wrist and ankle. While he was scrambling up the steep shortcut, he had seen the dog staring at him in the dark. At least, he thought that the dog had been staring at him. But the dog probably felt affection for him, having recognized him as the father of his only friend. In any case, *papà* had been startled, lost his balance, and fallen in the snow, twisting his wrist as he tried vainly to grab hold of an icicle. The dog came closer, probably out of curiosity and attracted by the smell of *cotechino,* causing my father to slip and tumble further down, producing even more damage.

I don't remember if the incident with the dog occurred before or after the infamous story of the San Nicolao frogs, but I think it was after, because I remember father saying that his miserable state might serve "once and for all" as a warning and a source of remorse to Roberto.

I would like to tell the story of the frogs and of what occurred in the false Neo-Gothic castle after the catastrophic events—the toads are still singing to this day—but I will desist, until that time, if it comes, when Roberto gives me permission to do so.

16 ✻ Nomads

In the multicolored and amorphous patchwork of memories of childhood and death that my brother and I sew and re-sew and embroider with the thread of suffering, each of us is indebted to the other for fragments, which, put together, make a single double-person living in a small town, wandering through the forests, observing the expressions of the partisans and of the birds, studying National Socialism in its bloody dusk and learning to milk cows, trying to comprehend the mystery of the Trinity and altering, for the love of frogs, the ecological balance. Roberto sews into his memory my memory of the green patches of the incipient spring of 1945, the forest-colored patches of the arrival of the woodcutters in our agricultural, pastoral valley which had reverted to subsistence in those times of war but continued to breathe in deeply its life before the collapse, the time of peace.

There were five or six families, maybe more, of woodcutters: men, women, and children, a caravan on mules which came from far away to cut trees on behalf of the landowners. The crew of mariners of the forest was armed with steel cables, giant hooks, boxes of grease, saws, axes, ropes, hawsers, brush hooks, muscles, rhythm, dedication, songs, and cries. They lived in the rooms above the local taverns and began work at dawn like spiders: a mule would move slowly up the mountain, with four or five men and women singing as they clambered up; the mule would fall behind, dragging an endless cable through the underbrush. Once they had reached one peak, they would pick the tallest tree and, with pure brute strength, yelling commands at the team down below in a rhythmic code filled with Magyar *e*'s and different accents and inflections, hoist up the steel cable, attach it to the tree—as the dissonant, Hungarian echoes continued—and continue their climb, laying a new span, and another, and another. The spider's web of steel cables, which were so thick that I could not even grasp them in my hand, became invisible in the vast valleys. These acrobats would slide down at an insane speed, attached to hooks along the cables, and slowly pull up the load of axes and four-handed saws. The forest seemed to collapse on itself as if by magic and descend through the valley along steel cables in huge bundles of trunks which ended their days bare and in bundles along the roadside.

The woodcutters were neither farmers nor shepherds nor manual laborers nor entrepreneurs but alien and sardonic wanderers, muscle-bound acrobats and clowns without ties or morals applicable outside of their small tribe. Their circus or giant sailboat was the mountains and the woods that they cut down on commission.

The robust, rough, and muscular women painted their faces like whores and at night made love with the peasants after winks, pats on the back, and smiles in ill-lighted Hogarthian taverns. At night, one lady woodcutter wore dove-colored, or rather purplish, jacket and trousers; she was bulging with muscles and prettified with heart-shaped lips and thin "ladies" cigarettes wrapped in colored paper and tipped with gold-colored filters. Despite her strange appearance, I would never have noticed on my own without the help of Dante Drago, my wicked, older friend: "That there is a man who thinks he's a woman and makes love with men. That one there."

The woodcutters were nomads who emerged in the present from a past of vast spaces and unlimited time, a different era with great expanses of woods crisscrossed by gypsies, brickmakers, diviners, friars, students, shepherds, actors, soldiers of fortune, and merchants.

After all, Jews too are nomads who at best crisscross from one dark age to the next, nomads in space but also, and especially, in time. Rapacious, clever gypsies who, after soldering pots and pans in a pitiful town fair, vanish into an uncertain future before the locals have time to discover the holes.

"Here is the miserable foreigner, he does not live in one place, his feet walk continually, he fights battles, is never vanquished, and never vanquishes."

This epigraph was considered by the Egyptians of the third millennium to be sufficiently true to be carved into granite for future generations. It is not clear to scholars whether it refers to Jews in particular or to some other race of vagabonds from the desert.

The *ebreu stermà* disappeared into the mountains that had protected and fed them, and no one saw them again. But where, where are they now? Will they ever return?

In the same way, the woodcutters disappeared one morning, in silence as they had come, without saying where they were going. Their carts rolled down toward Biella, weighed down with the savagely felled forest, transformed into wood for the entire winter of 1946.

Farewell

Basel, 7 February 1995

My dearest Mario Davide,

When you read this letter, many years will have passed from today, your fourth birthday, but already, now that I have finished this book I have written for you, the memories have begun to fade in clumps and strands. Telling one's own life is like lying down on the psychoanalyst's couch, as we all know, and it is because of you that in 1995 my psychic war against the Germany of the Third Reich, the Fifty Years' War, has come to an end, or so I hope. The score is even; I believe it is an armistice among ghosts.

You will already have heard about many of the events I speak of here because your mother, Lina, will have told you, as mine told me, about the highs and lows of the family history, even if she's not the type to tell the story of *The Raft of the Medusa* or the crossing of the Berezin or the earthquake of the Messina as if they were children's tales. Lina is like my mother, though to her good fortune she is more lovely; she resembles her but is not her, and times have changed beyond all imagining.

You will have heard many of these unhappy, joyful, or funny stories from a tender age, but only when you have grown up will you be able to fully understand the story of my childhood, which was not a childhood, and of these strange times in which I was a child, times which have now been forgotten and in many ways discredited.

You will be able to reconstruct the stories of your ancestors. I have not tried to overshadow the astonishing stories about your paternal grandfather, Mario,* in Spilamberto, Ferrara, and Kenya. Mario, the prophet of the Po, one of the few people living today who can speak in the arcane language of gestures, like my father.

We mainly speak to our parents once they are dead and only exchange a few words and games with our grandparents when we are small children, and that's it. This book is a heavy-handed attempt to slip myself into a future which is beyond my horizons.

* Mario Roffi. Mario was my father's name, and it is yours. In our family everyone is named Mario, including Uncle Roberto's son, so that now it is impossible to figure out which Mario we are talking about.

The impulse to write this book for you was brought on by the hope, perhaps naive, that your future might be sufficiently serene to make these tragedies from the thirties and forties—of "the last century"—seem even more extraordinary than they do today to the few people who remember or study them. Here I have told you my stories, which are anything but out of the ordinary.

Sometimes, in the chaotic traffic of Rome, I see a silver Aprilia, running on a mixture of alcohol and gas, zipping into a narrow alleyway. Who knows whether in thirty years it will still be roaming the streets of the city where you live—forbidding and fascinating? Yes, I think you shall see it, and when you do, follow it with your eyes, and your heart will be gladdened: the silver Aprilia is still among us, even during the long periods when we think it has been locked up in a garage or abandoned in a dump.

It has not been easy to describe our suffering; over time, it seems that only humor and religion survive, while memories fade with the life of the person who carried them.

I have already told you that times were different then, but if I had to describe in a few words where that difference lies, I would say that despite the massive connivance with Fascism and National Socialism, people then were less guilty than we are today. I don't mean to say that I regret those days, as one mustn't regret one's loss of virginity, but I believe that our age of innocence has passed. It has been replaced in recent times by belief in our own innocence and the consequent indignation and rage at the presumed guilt of others. I hope that once we have transcended this final problem, cruelty and madness will also disappear; these are the deadly parasites that destroyed innocence.

There once were innocents, blue-eyed and simple: the inhabitants of the Middle Ages, the farmers and nomads, the Jews and the anti-Fascists, scarce as they were, who fought for years and without hope, only because of their faith in principles and values to which people in Italy had not been particularly attached even before the rise of Fascism. And I, a young Jewish child, had the singular honor of being part of the powerful army of the last innocents who suffered and perhaps saved what was left of the world during the period between 1933 and 1945. A significant honor, if not an enviable one.

This book, which you call the book grandpa wrote for me, tells of how your great-grandparents Mario and Eugenia succeeded, after years of privations and humiliations, in saving their own lives and those of their children in the final few months of the war, a truly cruel period if one considers the statistics (calculated afterwards, but which we experienced directly at the time) that one out of three Italian Jews was killed. The Jews of Italy are considered among the most fortunate in Europe, after those of Denmark and Bulgaria. In the period of panic, from the end of September 1943 to mid-1944, in the few months during which most captures occurred, it seemed to those of us who were living those days moment by moment that there was no escape and that we would never see the "after" which we knew was there, waiting for us for seven long years . . . It was a terrible time, believe me.

We fled without much method or logic, pushed by a kind of automatic impulse: to defend the banner of life which has been victorious over thousands of years on this planet, despite the inarguable superiority of the forces of death.

Survival required intelligence, cunning, prudence, adaptability, calm, patience, and luck. But none of us would have lived to tell the tale if the small army of defenders of life—an army without uniforms or flags—had not shown up to help the dying and to rout the army of *The Time of Indifference* (Alberto Moravia, ed. Bompiani, 1929), which occupied Italy until 1943. I owe fifty not-altogether-useless years of my life to a handful of good, strange people to whom I pay homage in this book. I had the good fortune of seeing in my youth that there are people who help their brothers without even asking themselves why. This team of saviors had a paradoxical effect on me: that brief period of persecution, which occupies almost all of my sixty-year-old consciousness, is still the most terrible period of my life but has also become the best and the most yearned-for. And this strange turn in my consciousness has generated an even more worrisome effect: because of the people who saved us, I have acquired faith in my neighbor, a faith which has become faith in humanity, sustained by my Jewish heritage. I think these ideas of mine are no longer a secret . . .

This book has become like a novel, because at its heart it is a story, a story told many times to me about events which were real half a century ago but now exist only in a world of dreams. I have tried not to lie, but I suspect that some of the realities I describe have existed in my thoughts as a response to realities which I could not comprehend at the time. For this reason, I have never altered the concrete reality of memory, even when it contradicted a reality which I have since been able to ascertain. Where I became aware of a discrepancy, I have pointed it out, and in the cases where I haven't noticed, I console myself with the thought that this artifice is at the service of truth.

Another aside about my memories: in order to survive those dangerous times, it was necessary to bring together all of the necessary elements—luck, intelligence . . . ; it was not enough to have one or another. Our dead, who are scattered across the mud of Silesia, all made mistakes, whether it was one or many. And my family also made too many mistakes: your great-grandparents spent months and months in jail because of an insignificant mistake, an excess of faith; Roberto's escape from school could have meant, at the very least, his own death. But we were lucky. At times a tiny distraction could bring about the destruction of an entire family; and even small children had to exercise the utmost caution, as our mother illustrated every day with her terrifying stories.

There is the strange case of a cousin of your great-grandmother's who possessed every quality and took every precaution but was not blessed by luck. I don't even think he made any especially terrible mistakes, other than to consider life to be a kind of game of roulette. His name was Giacomo Tedeschi, but everyone called him Mino.* He owned a shop where he sold purses, suitcases, and wallets on Via Andrea Doria in Turin, on the corner of Via Lagrange. The shop is still there and has not changed much; one day I'll take you there, and you will be able to witness the fact that things last longer than people do and perhaps survive longer even than their memory. Thanks to chance or an act of God, that was not the case with the Caffè degli Specchi in Piazza Carlo Felice.

Mino Tedeschi was a small, ugly, rich, extremely clever womanizer. My father used to tell us with bright eyes about his assistants who were not just assistants, if you know what I mean: "One of them made the coffee, another one brought it over, and a third one poured the sugar and stirred!" When, overtaken by enthusiasm, he speculated about what might take place after the shop was closed, Mother would glare at him and hiss: "The children!" Mino the bon vivant was an "unrepentant bachelor," a *tombeur de femmes* from the cosmopolitan, uninhibited Turin of the twenties and thirties.

Mino has left a mark in my memory, and this despite the fact that I only saw him twice in his elegant ladies' shop. He

* Tedeschi, Giacomo (known as Mino). See L. Picciotto Fargion, *Il libro della memoria,* p. 580.

was a militant anti-Fascist who spoke only of politics, and as a child I found him a bit tiresome.

In October or November of 1943, he confided to us that he had sold his properties and acquired a rare, exceptionally valuable stamp which he kept hidden in his wallet. With this stamp in his trouser pocket, he was coldly calculating his escape to Switzerland, where the stamp would guarantee him an easy, comfortable life.

Mino showed it to me, child philatelist that I was, holding it up to the illuminated case: it was a rarity, a stamp from the Kingdom of Italy, from the nineteenth century.

Instead, he was captured with his minimalist baggage just as he was about to cross the border, and dragged off to Auschwitz.

I like to think that his Nazi killers did not discover his tiny treasure. When they worked over his dead body, the *Sonderkommando* extracted fillings, took his clothes and the contents of his wallet, but I doubt that those animals, destined for an early death, would have had the capacity or the time to estimate the value of the stamp! They were trained to look for gold, jewels, dollars, and pounds, which, accumulated by the greedy SS, filled Swiss bank accounts, defended in turn by the shadowy helmets on that bridge, which had so impressed me in Basel in 1939. And there they still lie, those that have not been collected by their "legitimate" predators. If, as is likely, the stamp was never discovered, a small group of stamp collectors is now in possession of specimens which have increased in value thanks to the disappearance of

Mino's stamp, which was one of three or four in the world. And the wheel turns.

But I am not writing to you from a happy period, and I confess that for some time I have again been feeling the chills of the forgotten past. Perhaps the winter is returning; my era is over, and a new one is beginning. This is not in itself a bad thing, but convulsive, confusing changes are taking place, not all of them positive, and violent events are occurring in the world that I try to believe are only temporary. It is almost as if civilization were only a flimsy screen under which the barbaric strata of the past continue to rage. Day after day, many hopes that we have grown accustomed to accepting as truths are blown out like candles.

But failures are the predecessors to new successes—though not always, I must admit. They open the way to new adventures, illusions, happy events that cannot be imagined in advance, and that, when you read this, you will already have experienced. My hopes are with you.

One day, eight days after your birth, four Februarys ago, you were brought to my house, where a rabbi and a doctor performed your circumcision. It is your lot to have been born Jewish, and circumcision—which is now a common practice in many cultures—is the sign of one of the covenants made long ago between God and humanity, at least according to believers.

It is your lot to have been born Jewish . . . But in your case this lot has been tempered by the love of the people around you and your innocence of the past. When I told my mother in 1960 that I was going to marry a non-Jew, she was upset, not for her own sake—she was agnostic and indifferent—but for my father's. He had been very stern on this point during his life, and after death, his position did not change.

My mother was comforted by the fact that Elena, my future wife, was an actress and a woman of the Left. But what truly convinced her—or so I believe—was the information that Elena's family, the Magoias, had been brickmakers for generations: nomads who went from one clay pit to the next. Brickmakers are like woodcutters, gypsies, and actors. And Elena was also an actress: finally, after years without the long notes of the Bach "aria," art was returning to our family.

When your mother, Lina, was born, I decided that she should be a Jew: to become one, she had to undergo a ritual, purifying bath because her mother, your grandmother, Elena, was a Gentile. My decision, determined more by feeling than by reason, was not made by me alone. Elena encouraged me to this sacerdotal act of welcoming our child into the headstrong people because of the love she felt for my mother. When I dipped our newborn child into the large bath of warm water in which I was also immersed—in my swimming trunks—and said the prayer, I unwittingly decided your destiny for you. For Jews, baptism is inherited, and Judaism is transmitted exclusively by the mother. So because of me, Mario Davide, you became Jewish thirty years before your time; and I didn't even know you.

In the first pact after the Great Flood, God promised never again to unleash the forces of nature and, in return, asked for obedience to a few rules of morality, or even common decency: not to kill one another or eat meat that is still alive. This pact is represented by the rainbow, which God uses after each storm to remind himself of his promise. The pious would like to believe that after each round of lightning, thunder, and rain, God is telling them, with his characteristic sense of humor: "Don't be afraid! Nature is not your enemy; I was just kidding around! You are masters of the Earth! Heh, heh, heh . . ." The floods of the Yellow River and the Blue River, the tidal waves of the Bay of Bengal, the earthquakes and volcanic eruptions that exterminate entire populations, seem to demonstrate that either God or man has not held up his side of the pact, and I leave it to you to decide who was the first to be derelict in his duties. Frankly, I can't figure this one out.

About the pact between God and the Jews—of which Abraham's circumcision, and your own, is a sign—my doubts are even more deep-seated, because though it is true that the Jews have not become a priestly people, as they promised He Of The Unpronounceable Name on Mount Sinai, it is even more true that God, if he ever existed, was not present at Auschwitz, and if he was, he died there.

And so you were circumcised for a complicated set of reasons that it is difficult and painful for me to work out. The feelings of your mother and father, mysterious and irrational, were important in the decision. But I am not innocent; in fact, I may be the principal responsible party in the shortening of your foreskin, because of an illness, a benign excrescence of my mind, that compels me to send out messages that sometimes become realities. It is useless for me to hide that at the moment of your circumcision, while you screamed and your mother cried, pale and faint like every Jewish mother at that moment, for generations, I was stolidly happy. But why? Mostly because I was and am convinced that with your circumcision, no matter whether it is sacred or futile, you did not inherit a curse, and that you will not experience a childhood like my own.

But that is not all. There is something else, which I confess only to you: as you may have already gathered, I am in general terms an atheist and not a practicing Jew, and I have lost faith in Zionism (though I hate anti-Zionism). But I subscribe to one unalterable Jewish superstition: I believe in the passage of time. In other words, I have faith in survival, I have hope in the future, and I fear the undecipherable present. Jews—black, white, yellow, or red—survive; they were there to see the tears of the fool Ramses II ("My armies, my horses, my chariots . . ."), and they lived to tell of the last days in the chancellor's bunker, when Hitler moved nonexistent armies across the map with trembling fingers. Irrationally, I connect this survival with circumcision, and I am convinced that despite all of their undeniable defects, the Jews, with their history, can bring solace to all those who have lost faith in the future.

The Waldenses considered the Jews to be living witnesses of the historical reality of Christ and, therefore, of the existence of God. In 1948, I went to a Jewish summer camp in Val Pellice in Piedmont, and one day a shy young Evangelist minister showed up there. He explained with a mournful expression—fearing rejection—that the oldest lady in the town had told him that the Jews had returned to the valley and the forests with tents—they were camping tents, but what difference; who knew where they had come from or where they were headed? She begged to be allowed to touch one of us, and no one could understand why. She was almost blind, and she wanted to meet a Jew before dying, in order to feel serene when her time came.

The minister, relieved that he had not been sent packing, accompanied me and Elena Ottolenghi (yes, the same one who had received the *Nuovissimo Melzi*), proudly dressed in our Scout uniforms—caps, whistles, and all—to the old lady's house. She hugged and kissed us in joy, because she had finally been able to "see" Jesus' folk. When she asked us to write something in the margin of her Bible, Elena (impeccable, as usual!) wrote: "Blessed is the match consumed in kindling flame," Hannah Szenes's words before parachuting down into the infernal night of the ghettos and the massacres to fight with the partisans in defense of human dignity. But things didn't go well for her.[1]

There is another pact, not part of Judaism but in some way connected to it: the Crucifixion. God sent his Son down to Earth (without a parachute) and promised eternal life for all, asking that in return for His suffering, men should love one another and God in His name. I am too brutish and superficial to pass judgment on this questionable deal, but I ask you to consider the question: Who fell out of love first?

But I must now confess to you that I do have a faith. I believe that the future must be better than the present, that it exists already but is also determined by our desires. I am convinced that there is no real contradiction between free will and predestination.

I hold firmly to my faith, even if I know that there is no proof of the existence of . . . progress—because that's what I'm speaking about. It is an irrational religion like any other, and one that has fallen out of vogue and is often, even generally, cruelly and brutally contradicted by real events and terrible disappointments. In 1945, I was convinced—and this is justified, because I was a child—that justice had returned to the world, announced by the two blinding flashes of Hiroshima and Nagasaki. But it wasn't so. And despite this disillusionment, despite everything—I know it's silly, but please, don't laugh—I still hope that one day it will happen. And I don't mind being ridiculous and contradictory with my old-fashioned dreams, though I hope never to fall into rhetoric and vain comforts. If I didn't fear ridicule, I would tell you that by progress I mean progress in every area: industrial, technological, scientific, moral, social, and civic. All of the positive ideals that began with the Industrial Revolution in the eighteenth century.

We are confused, afraid, disappointed, and uncertain, and perhaps this is a good thing, but as we flail around, confused by painful feelings and the sense of responsibility for our errors, we can sense a new revolution coming, like a "strange soldier, without crest or feathers in his helmet . . . ,"* destined to transform our very conception of the world.

Now that science has explained many, perhaps most, things about the way our world functions—but even Ptolemy believed he had done so—it is attempting to decipher the structure of human consciousness, including areas which were once the dominion of philosophy, already a major advance because before that, they were the dominion of religion, and before that, of myth, and before that, of superstition.

When you grow up, many of the mysteries of the mind will, I hope, have been solved. Cognitive science, which is now in its early stages, will help us understand "why" the stars exist, where today we know only "what" they are made of. Perhaps we will discover the meaning of the past, which hides behind our memories, and that of the future, which hides behind causality, chance, and will. Life will probably become more dangerous, more complex, and certainly more fascinating, full of potential futures (in plural) as never before. Our sense of uncertainty will increase, as will our right to satisfy our need for certainty. For some time, a dangerous

* From an old hymn of the Red Guard. Naively, I believe that it is highly unlikely that the new army in white lab coats will cover itself in grotesque medals, ranks, or other reddish, threatening symbols.

and mistaken idea has circulated: that industrial development, with its organization and bureaucratic anonymity, are the cause of terrible crimes, of Nazism and its future incarnations. I completely disagree with this superficial and clearly inconsistent hypothesis: the adventure of man has always been a risky one and has become more complex as thought has filtered down into the uncertain world of reality. We are all confronted daily with the objective reality of our dark side. What frightens people about industrial, technological, and scientific development could also have been said of the advent of agriculture, of sheep farming, of metalworking, of writing,* and of mercantilism. And, in fact, it has been said of the Greek civilization and of the Jewish culture, and it is a mistake. National Socialism is not a product of modernity, but its debris and its opposite. What threatened to destroy the world was not the *Banality of Evil* (Hannah Arendt, ed. Feltrinelli, 1964) but an infernal parody of "Love your neighbor as you love yourself" or "hate your neighbor . . ."

This terrible century (but not *all* terrible), in which man failed to create the Super-Man through blood and cruelty, has also failed in creating a "new man" made of illusions and dogmas. At the end of the century, we are left with un-

* The invention of writing implied the existence of the Bible, *Mein Kampf, Origin of Species, The Protocols of the Learned Elders of Zion,* the theory of relativity, and on and on, including anonymous letters, libelous articles in the press, obscene scrawls in the lavatory . . .

certainty and a promise: the return of Illuminism. This is not the Age of Reason but perhaps an age in which it is possible to discover what reason is, what its limits are, and how it can be used: in other words, its composition, properties, side effects, instructions, warning signs . . .

The mind lies in a fragile container, the brain, which possesses a large but not infinite number of physical connections. The use of language, however, to which we have been condemned, renders this container limitless. Syntax is the seat of free will, and with it man can explain every possibility. The fact that we know that the mind, unique and irreproducible, dies with the rest of the body, should increase our moral responsibility toward our fellow humans, differentiating us from our predecessors, who believed in ghosts that were either trapped in eternal prisons by their crimes or ecstatically hypnotized by the contemplation of eternity. Both of these visions are part of the dangerous life of the everyday that seems limited only to those who, lacking in imagination, prefer to add piquancy through senseless thoughts and actions, almost always of the worst variety.

You may ask how this story ends, but the fact is that it does not end, and this is why I am telling it to you.

I thought that the summer of 1945 had brought peace and that this peace, which I had never experienced, would stay with us forever. I was living the last luminous days of my adulthood, before a return to a belated childhood: days and hours that were neither numbered nor remembered, an abundance of time and scarcity of events, days to be lived in the assurance that there were more to come. Your days.

The blinding Turinese summer of 1945: this was the world that had been waiting for us for seven years on the other side of the Glockenspiel. Dancing in the park at night, red and tricolor flags, and girls dancing among themselves out of modesty:

Dove sta Zaza, o bellezza mia,
Dove sta Zaza, senza Isaia . . .[2]

Because I hadn't been to school much the previous year, in July I had to pass my exams to be allowed to enter the second year of middle school. There were special sessions for all of us, but I was nervous all the same. What would the test be like? What would they ask me? How would I answer, given that I didn't know anything?

Mamma decided that my condition as a child who had been condemned to death needed a visible manifestation, and so she bandaged my foot and told me to walk with a cane. "Don't worry, Aldino! You'll do fine!"

At the D'Azeglio School, behind a table in a large, empty classroom, sat the examination committee. It consisted of a male professor and a young female professor who smiled at me as I walked across the darkened room, still blinded by the sun outside, nervous and embarrassed by my uselessly bandaged foot. My mother had not wanted to make me appear injured but rather to bring out in me the humiliation of trying to pretend to be injured, thereby making manifest my real but invisible injury.

The man did not ask me any questions, and I think he may even have left the room. I was a pathetic sight, enough to weaken the tender of heart.

The woman was young, elegant, and fearless, and she smiled throughout the thirty, or perhaps fewer, seconds of the exam. She invited me to sit down and asked my name but did not ask any questions about my past or why I was taking the exam in the summer. She only asked me if I knew Latin declensions, and I answered yes, with conviction, because I did, in fact, know of their existence.

She breathed deeply and asked me to give her the declensions for *rosa-rosae,* and I answered, with complete aplomb: "Rosa." "Good, good. I think that will be enough. You can go," she concluded, looking over at the other professor, who had returned, relieved to have been spared the false testimony. I was admitted into the second year of middle school, maybe even with "good marks," but I would have to look back to be sure.

Outside in the light, the blinding light that was like a permanent bolt of lightning, I was dazed: I was a child again.

Love from your grandfather Aldo.

Translator's Notes

1 ⸭ The Glockenspiel

1. Where appropriate, I have given the English titles of books, while retaining the author's references to the Italian publishers.

2 ⸭ April

1. Colonna and Finzi were the names of two wealthy nineteenth-century Jewish families in Turin who bequeathed their estates for the founding of this Jewish elementary school. At the end of the nineteenth century, it was primarily a religious institution, but after the passage of the racial laws in 1938, it became the only school for Jewish children, even for the children of assimilated and non-observant Jewish families—who were by then no longer allowed to attend the public schools. It then became a mostly secular institution with a standard curriculum, including Fascist propaganda.

2. The owner of a charcuterie.

3 ✣ Bombardment

1. One of the first illustrated children's books published in Italy. The title can be translated as *Meo's Fists.*

2. The *Camicie Nere* (Black Shirts), *Avanguardisti* (Vangardists), *Giovani Italiane* (Young Italian Women), and *Gioventù Italiana del Littorio* (Italian Fascist Youth) were all Fascist groups.

3. Carducci (1835–1907), an Italian poet, won the Nobel Prize for Literature in 1906. He was made a senator for life in 1890 and was revered by the Italians as a national poet. The English translation is mine.

4 ✣ December First

1. The Kras is a mountain plateau north of Trieste which spans Italy and Yugoslavia, now part of Slovenia. During the First World War, the Italians fought the Austrians there in 1916 and 1917.

2. By the summer of 1943, the Fascist regime was collapsing. On July 24–25, the Fascist Grand Council met in Rome for the first time since the beginning of the war and passed a motion asking the king to resume his full constitutional powers, dismissing Mussolini. The army took over the key positions in Rome, *il Duce* was arrested, and the main Fascist institutions were dissolved. An armistice with the Allies was announced on September 8, 1943. The Germans immediately took over Rome; they had already, in the previous few weeks, taken over most of central and northern Italy. The Italian army, left without orders even to defend Rome, disintegrated. Italy became a war zone.

3. *Ente Italiano Audizioni Radiofoniche,* a state-owned radio station, predecessor of the RAI.

4. The Fascists organized activities for the working classes, including afterwork clubs, camping trips, tours, and cruises. On the "people's trains," blocks of discounted tickets were available for visits to the Italian cultural capitals such as Rome, Florence, and Venice on weekends.

5. *Havertà* means "housekeeper" in Turinese-Hebrew dialect. It is a term of endearment. The word probably derives from *haverah,* which can mean "companion" in Hebrew. The racial laws of 1938 had shrewdly cut off all ties between the Jews and the rest of the population, but after 1943 many *havertot* remembered their former employers and succored them in their hour of desperation.

6. *Società Nazionale Industrie Applicazioni Viscosa,* the largest producer of synthetic fiber in Italy. It was founded in 1917.

7. A large ironworks that specialized in the production of ball bearings. In 1930s Turin, it suggested power, modernity, and the promise of the future.

8. Motorbikes with flatbeds attached to them.

9. Officials of and adherents to the *Repubblica Sociale Italiana,* also known as the Republic of Salò, the puppet Fascist government set up in northern Italy by the Germans after the armistice (and headed, nominally, by Mussolini). They called themselves *"Repubblicani,"* after the Republic; *Repubblichini,* a joking diminutive, was a term meant to poke fun at their false power and the tiny size of their "republic."

10. A kind old witch who brings gifts on Twelfth Night.

5 ⸎ Bruegel

1. From Matt. 24:44. "Therefore be ye also ready: for in such an hour as ye think not the Son of man cometh."

2. A region north of Turin.

3. A small town near Vercelli, in Piedmont.

4. Peasants, farmers, or anyone who lives in the country.

5. A medieval crucifix depicting Christ dead on the cross.

6. A region around Vercelli, in Piedmont.

6 ⸎ Lina

1. The first "small" Lancia. It offered the luxury and comfort expected of a Lancia at a price that was affordable to the middle class.

2. Marcello Piacentini (1881–1960), a Roman architect and town planner. After the introduction of Fascism, he became Italy's leading exponent of Monumentalism.

3. A hill town above Turin.

4. A painter of idealized, pastoral landscapes.

5. Francesco Hayez (1791–1882), an Italian historical painter, born in Venice.

6. The pseudonym of Luigi Bertelli (1858–1920), a Florentine writer of children's literature.

7. Velvet slippers typical of Friuli, in the north of Italy.

8. Both are forms of the second person plural pronoun. The Fascists encouraged the use of the new and less formal "voi."

9. "Café of the mirrors."

10. The main street in Turin.

11. A carnival game, a kind of lottery with tickets drawn from a turning drum.

7 ⁂ The Colonna e Finzi School

1. A liberal-democratic/socialist, anti-Fascist organization of Italian emigrés.

2. A notorious Nazi propaganda melodrama centered on a conniving, ambitious Jewish businessman, Süß Oppenheimer.

3. Franti, the hero of this book, was a nasty child who took pleasure in others' pain.

4. A large dictionary.

5. A Fascist youth group, roughly equivalent to the Hitler Youth. Its members wore soldier-like uniforms.

6. The Israel Defense Forces *(Tzva Hagannah Leyisrael),* the army of the State of Israel.

7. In Roman dialect, an expression which one might use when speaking to a person of higher social standing.

8. Almirante was the leader of the Neo-Fascist Italian MSI party from 1969 until his death in 1987.

9. "See the little goat / My father bought me in the square / For two *levanim.*"

10. OVRA or *Operazione di Vigilanza per la Repressione dell'Antifacismo,* a secret police used to target, spy on, and imprison enemies of the Fascist state.

8 ⁂ Prison

1. Founder of the Salesian order.

2. *Unione Nazionale Protezione Antiaerea,* the National Union for Anti-aircraft Protection.

3. In 1944, Preziosi became Mussolini's Inspector General of Race, with the rank of Ambassador, and he argued that Italy was in the hands of Freemasons acting for the Jews. Preziosi asked Mussolini to appoint him head of what would have been an Italian Gestapo. In 1945, the Fas-

cist government of Italy was overthrown before it could act on this request.

4. Pavolini was a journalist who became Minister of Popular Culture in 1939. He was executed with Mussolini and hung up on Piazalle Loreto.

5. Henri Landru, an infamous French serial murderer. He was guillotined in 1922.

9 ※ The Salesians

1. Song of Sol. 6:13.
2. A clinic for the physically and mentally handicapped.

10 ※ Temple

1. An Italian-made luxury car.

2. One of the leaders of the Warsaw uprising. His *Notes From the Warsaw Ghetto* gave a detailed account of daily events and conditions in the ghetto. He was killed by the Gestapo in March 1944.

11 ※ Asti

1. *Polenta e osei,* or polenta served with small game birds, is a specialty of the Veneto-Friuli regions.

2. The National Fascist Party was subdivided into regional federations. The secretary of each federation was a *Segretario Federale,* or *Federale* for short.

12 ※ Tarcisio

1. In Italian prewar films, glamorous households always included a white telephone, which thus became a symbol for upper class society (and of a genre of films). Noris, Ferida, and Valli were contemporary film stars.

2. Francesco Crispi (1819–1901), premier of Italy, 1887–91 and 1893–96.

13 ✠ Bandenkrieg!

1. The beginning of the Battle of the Bulge.

2. A suburb of Alessandria in Piedmont where, it is said, the Arabs went after the fall of the fortress of Saint-Tropez.

3. Head magistrate under Fascism.

4. In Piedmontese dialect: "Holy Madonna of Oropa, what birds are these?"

14 ✠ Winter

1. *The Book of Knowledge.*

15 ✠ Roberto

1. In the early days of aviation, there was a kind of ongoing competition between the lighter-than-air zeppelin and the airplane. It seemed impossible to many people that the airplane could win, and a recurrent headline in the papers was: "If it's heavier than air, can it win?"

2. Which, in Italian as in English, means "ill-mannered, rough, crude."

Farewell

1. Szenes (1921–1944), a Hungarian Jew, was living in Palestine in 1943 when she joined the British Army and volunteered for a parachute unit that was to help downed Allied pilots, establish contact with resistance fighters, and aid beleaguered Jewish communities. With the goal of reaching her native Budapest, Szenes was parachuted into Yugoslavia in March 1944 and spent three months with Tito's partisans. On June 7, at the height of the deportation of Hungarian Jews, Szenes crossed the border into Hungary; she was arrested almost immediately, and five months later, she was executed by a firing squad.

2. The words to the song are: "Where is Zaza, my beauty? Where is Zaza, without Isaiah . . ."